BAPSI SIDHWA'S

Ice-Candy-Man

A READER'S COMPANION

BAPSI SIDHWA'S

Ice-Candy-Man

A READER'S COMPANION

edited by

RASHMI GAUR

abc

asia book club

Published by
ASIA BOOK CLUB
New Delhi 110 058
Ph. 9810943723

ISBN: 81-7851-11-1

Printed at Chaman Offset Press, New Delhi 110 002

Contents

Section I

Bapsi Sidhwa's *Ice-Candy-Man* An Introduction

Rashmi Gaur

II. Critical Perspectives

Comparative Studies

Author's Identity

Feminist Approach

Theme of Partition

Bapsi Sidhwa: Life and Works

RASHMI GAUR

Bapsi Sidhwa is now a significant voice in commonwealth fiction. A Pakistani Parsi woman novelist, now settled in the USA, Sidhwa is known for her keen perception, a sensitive portrayal of characters, diversity of themes, supple style, and above all, her punching sense of humour. She has published four novels so far—*The Crow-Eaters (*1978), *The Bride* (1983), *Ice-Candy-Man* (1988) and *An American Brat* (1994). Thematically Sidhwa's novels are rooted in the continent where she was born and brought up, yet they simultaneously possess a cosmopolitan appeal which readers can feel as a palpable presence beneath the characters and tales of a particular time and locale, and herein lies her charm.

Sidhwa was born in Karachi in undivided India in 1938 to Tehmina and Peshoton Bhandara. The Bhandaras were a prominent business family. She was brought up and educated in Lahore. She had polio as a child and spent a lot of time with the servants. The absence of an extended family made her a little isolated. She also read copiously to fill up her loneliness. She graduated from the Kinnaird College for Women, Lahore, in 1956. The very next year she fell in love with Gustad Kermani, a sophisticated Bombay businessman and married him. "Plucked out of childhood and thrust into big-city life and straight into adulthood," she felt traumatic in the beginning.[1] But she soon became enchanted with the open and fun loving Parsi community of Bombay. The marriage, though, did not last long. After living in Bombay for five years she got divorced and went back to Pakistan. She was allowed the custody of her daughter but was forced to part with her son who came to her at the age of sixteen after his father's death. She remarried Noshir Sidhwa, a Parsi businessman in Lahore and twelve years her senior. She spent her time as a housewife and had two daughters and a son. She herself has termed this span as a constricted sort of life. The vacancy of her life and a concern for others soon motivated her to take up social service. She took special interest in movements for women's rights. She was the secretary of Mother's and Children's House, a shelter for destitute women; President of International Women's Club, Lahore; Chairperson of social Welfare Committee, Punjab Club; and Pakistan's representative at the Asian Woman's Congress of 1975.[2] In 1991, she received Sitara-I-Imtiaz, the highest Pakistani award in the arts which can be bestowed on a citizen.

Sidhwa has won international acclaim for her work. Her works have been translated into French and German and are taught as part of academic curriculum in some American universities. Her *Cracking India* (The American title for *Ice-Candy-Man*) was named a Notable Book of 1991 by the *New York Times* and won the Literature Prize of the 1991 Frankfurt Book Fair. In 1993, she received an award of US$ 105,000 from the Lila Wallace Reader's Digest Fund. She has taught creative writing at Rice University in Texas and the University of Houston. She was a Bunting Fellow in 1986-87 at Radcliffe College, Harvard, where she also wrote her novel *Ice-Candy-Man* or *Cracking India.* She settled in Houston, USA in 1984 along with her husband and accepted the dual US citizenship.

While Sidhwa was living in Pakistan after her second marriage, she was troubled by a vague sense of vacancy despite her interest in social work. Her creative cravings were not fulfilled by her socialite life. In her interview to Julie Rajan she talks about the idleness of her iife in Lahore, "You play a lot of bridge, go to coffee breakfasts and do volunteer work. It was a mindless kind of life. Now, women are breaking out into many more fields of activity, but I did not have the educational background. I guess it just evolved automatically—writing took up the slack in my life."[3] Writing helped Sidhwa to fill up the intellectual vacancy of her life. It is interesting to note that Sidhwa had taken up writing only incidentally, as a result of a chance meeting with an Afghan woman on an aeroplane. In her interview with David Montenegro in March 1989, which was published in *Points of Departure: International Writers on Writing and Politics*, she remarks candidly that she used to treat authors as super human beings, "I am so fond of reading, and I used to think that a writer was some sort of a being who lives in another sphere. I never thought of the writer in human terms but almost as some disembodied power that automatically produced books. And suddenly by telling me that she [the Afghan woman] was a writer, she made me realize that writers are very fresh and blood persons. And that did make me want to write."[4]

Bapsi Sidhwa has published four novels so far. Her first novel *The Crow-Eaters* was issued in two imprints in Britain—Jonathan Cape in 1980 and St. Martin's Press in 1982. In India it was published by Sangam Books in 1980. The novel hilariously depicts the lives and fortunes of the Junglewallas, a Parsi family in British India. The novel was criticized by some critics and members of the Parsi community for presenting an unfair and rather a ribald picture of the community. In her preface to the novel Sidhwa has tried to explain her point of view. Expressing her admiration for her community she remarks, "Because of a deep-rooted admiration for my community—and an enormous affection for its few eccentricities—this work of satirical fiction has been a labour of love. The nature of satire being to exaggerate, the incidents in the book do not reflect at all upon the integrity of a community whose scrupulous honesty and sense of honour are renowned." The novel is humorous and also farcical at times, with occasional serious touches, accurately portraying the society it is set against. It has a "somewhat loose, episodic structure. Much of its comic energy and exuberance derive from a string of gags or comic episodes."[5] However, the novel has memorable characters, "individual but not atypical."[6] With its sprightly dialogue and ironical tone, the novel evocatively presents not only a particular time and locale, but also encompasses a people with deep historical consciousness. The novel ends with the threat of Partition looming large in the background.

The Bride, or *The Pakistani Bride*, as it is titled in India is Sidhwa's second novel which was published in 1983. It is a tragic story of the interaction of two different cultural paradigms—the patriarchal mountainous tribe and the westernized urban plain. Though *The Crow Eaters* is her first published novel, *The Bride* is the first novel which she had actually written. *The Crow-Eaters* was published first owing to certain political reasons. Sidhwa was apprehensive about the reactions to the novel as it is based on a true story which underscores the suppression of women in the traditional male-dominated society of Pakistan. While Sidhwa was camping in the remote regions of the Karakoram mountains, some army personnel told her the story of a girl who was taken from the plains by an old tribal to marry his nephew. Unable to put up with her harsh life she ran away and survived for fourteen days in the rugged mountains of Karakoram. Her husband and the tribesmen ultimately hunted her down and beheaded her. Sidhwa initially wanted to write a story on this incident which had deeply moved her, but it soon became an obsession, and was developed into a novel, giving an optimistic twist to the source episode. Dealing with individual stories, the novel lays bare the violence which the women have to face in a repressive society. The protagonist Zaitoon is pitted against a hostile environment and with sheer will power and grit is able to overcome obstacles strewn in her path. She is "ultimately protected and saved, which suggests that an awesome, ancient, natural order combined with a young girl's defiant spirit can overcome the oppressive shackles of a conspiracy of men."[7]

Sidhwa's third novel *Ice-Candy-Man* came out in 1991. In the United States of America, Sidhwa's publishers Milkweed Editions published it under the title of *Cracking India*. Using a child narrator, Sidhwa presents the kaleidoscopically changing socio-political realities of the Indian sub-continent just before the Partition. This extremely taut and highly sensitive story takes up the themes of communal tensions, using religion as a way to define individual identity, territorial cravings, political opportunism, power and love, and binds them together in a very readable narrative. The novel contains a rich undercurrent of legend and folklore and as Anatol Leven remarks in *The Literary Review*, her Rabelaisian language and humour impart a vivacious charm to it.[8] It presents the Parsi dilemma of retaining allegiance to political masters, as well as a Parsi Pakistani perspective of Partition. Without histrionics or preaching Sidhwa's novel communicates her desire that one should learn lessons from history. In her interview with Julie Rajan she comments, "If we are not going to learn lessons, we are doomed to repeat our evils. Historically people have gone on fighting each other for religion, for land, for women, for position, for greed—and those elements prevail still. Man's nature has not changed—but one can try, and hope it will."[9]

Ice-Candy-Man was filmed as a motion picture by Deepa Mehta with the title "Earth 1947." The movie does not include many incidents and characters of the novel, but Sidhwa feels that it has been successful in retaining the spirit of the novel and hopes that it would "widen the audience" and motivate them to approach the novel.[10]

An American Brat (1994) is Sidhwa's fourth novel. Set within familiar surroundings, her earlier novels portray different facets of human life in her home territory. In her latest novel the locale is shifted to the United States of America, yet the authorial concentration is still focused on problems related with individual and collective identities of her people. The novel narrates the experiences of Feroza Ginwalla, the rebellious daughter of Cyrus and Zareen Ginwalla, who is sent from Gulberg, Lahore to Denver, Colorado for some exposure to a liberal way of life. The young woman "journeys through three cultures—her own community's Parsi culture, her country Pakistan's Islamic culture and the Western culture of the United States of America."[11] Shy, traditional and conservative Feroza, who in her school days has objected to her mother's sleeve-less sari-blouse, quickly gains independence once she is in America. Her journey towards independence involves several choices, almost all of them forcing her to move away from the rigid, constricting mores of her childhood society. Her assertiveness is riddled with doubts and represents the confusion of her generations, which as a result of the burgeoning trends of globalization is forced to make many cultural adjustments. The protagonist partially reflects Sidhwa's appreciation of freedom she was able to find as a woman in America and maintains a light-hearted and entertaining tone even while discussing serious issues. Like most diasporic writing by authors from the Indian subcontinent, *An American Brat* also takes up the socio-political complexities of contemporary Asian people, weaving history and politics inseparably in its fictional narrative. The theme of migration and re-adjustment, which Sidhwa has taken up in her fourth novel, has been taken up by several contemporary novelists. Timothy Mo in *Sour Sweet* (1982), Bharati Mukherjee in *Jasmine* (1989), Jhumpa Lahiri in some of her short stories and Buchi Emecheta in several of her novels have taken up similar themes, yet Sidhwa has handled it with a lot of humour and a contemporary perspective, imparting a unique charm to her writing.

Sidhwa is a member of the Parsi Zoroastrian sect, a distinctive minority who, in the 7th century A.D. left Iran for South Asia in order to avoid religious persecution. Her novels present the vivid accounts of the Parsi mind, social behaviour, customs and value systems. She also possesses a fiercely individual voice which is never subjugated by the presence of a deep ethnic awareness. Despite including lengthy descriptions of Parsi rituals and gatherings, her novels never degenerate into bare sociological documentations. She describes socio-historical facts of the Parsi life, mixing them up with a satirical style and lampoon, aptly recreating the Parsi milieu. She chronicles the changing attitudes of the young, and the apprehensions of the elderly about the submersion of their identity with a humorous tone, though without ever diluting the gravity of these issues.

Like many people brought up in the sub-continent, Bapsi Sidhwa is fluent in several languages. She has complete command over English, Gujarati, Punjabi and Urdu. However she has always written in English. Terming herself as a "tail-end product of the Raj," she has commented in her interview with David Montenegro, that she feels comfortable in writing in English.[13] Her English though is punctuated with Parsi proverbs and

Gujarati and Urdu words, permitting her an elaborate word play and a racy flow of narrative. The verbal jugglery which she uses in her novels makes her style postmodernist. In her interview with David Montenegro she clarifies her views, "I think you just juggle for the best meaning, somehow. And certain words are so much more expressive in mother language. Something that is zestful comes out so much better said in Punjabi, or something that is emotional or romantic comes out better in Urdu. Or certain Gujarati words carry so much more meaning. And you just automatically adopt this mixture to be more expressive."[14]

Words of common parlance like *atash*, *Gathas*, *burqas*, *goondas*, *Arrey*; *janab*, *yaar* are frequently used in her novels to convey the local ambience. Words and phrases from regional languages give the reader a feel of the raw pulsating emotions, heightening their sense of appreciation of the narrative. When Feroza in *An American Brat* looks at the incredibly beautiful night-lights of Manhattan from a distance, she cries out in Punjabi: "*Vekh! Vekh! Sheher-di-batian*" (Look, look, the lights of the city). The Ice-Candy-Man recites verse after verse in Urdu to express his passion for Ayah, Jerbanoo in *The Crow Eaters* uses loose disjointed sentences to convey her meaning and vitality. The insertion of vernacular language into flawless English intoned sentences results in new language rhythms and intonations. The strain of extrovert ribaldry in her work has liberated the subcontinental English fiction from what Anatol Leven calls the prim and stilted norm. She has achieved what Khushwant Singh has crusaded for many years, greater freedom and less inhibition in the depiction of sexuality in English novels of the subcontinent. "Bapsi Sidhwa has been a trend-setter in this aspect. Namita Gokhale and the mellowed queen of smart, Shobha De are other modern Indian-English novelists to have followed this trend."[15] Normally she writes in a linear fashion—barring limited stylistic experimentation in *Ice-Candy-Man* and *An American Brat*, she adheres to the Dickensian method of a gripping story.

Sidhwa feels that in contemporary age, the author has a proselytizing role to play. Through her writings she wants to draw the readers' attention to various problems of the society—oppression of women, religious fundamentalism, unjust ppression of women, religious fundamentalism, unjust evaluation of historical events etc. are some of the maladies which are vociferously presented in her novels. She tells Montenegro: "But I do think that a writer can at least place facts so that people recognize themselves and stop taking themselves too seriously or start seeing themselves in a more realistic light. We all are so prone to see ourselves as a little better than the other person."[15]

Sidhwa's prowess over the genre is impressive. She is one of the most exciting commonwealth novelists writing at present. Her humorous tone, irreverence to established traditions, sense of fair play, subtle characterization and taut presentation of events impart a very specific charm to her novels. Bapsi Sidhwa holds a very special place among contemporary writers of English fiction in the sub-continent.

NOTES

1. http://www. monsoonmag.com/interviews/i3inter_sidhwa.html.
2. Makarand R. Paranjape, "The Novels of Bapsi Sidhwa," *Commonwealth Fiction*, ed. R.K. Dhawan (New Delhi: Classical, 1988), p. 80.
3. http://www.monsoonmag.com/interviews/i3inter_sidhwa.html.
4. David Montenegro, *Points of Departure: International Writers on Writing and Politics* (Michigan: Univ. of Michigan Press, 1991), p. 5.
5. Makarand R. Paranjape, "The Early Novels of Bapsi Sidhwa," *The Novels of Bapsi Sidhwa*, ed. R.K. Dhawan and Novy Kapadia (New Delhi: Prestige, 1996), p. 91.
6. Alamgir Hashmi, "*The Crow Eaters*: A Noteworthy Novel," *Ibid.*, p. 137.
7. Cynthia Abrioux, "A Study of the Step-father and the Stranger in the Pakistani Novel *The Bride* by Bapsi Sidhwa," *Commonwealth Essays and Studies*, 13, 1 Autumn 1990, p. 70.
8. http://members.aol.com/_ht_a/bsidhwa/crack_india_british.html?mtbrand=AOL-US.
9. http:/www.monsoon.mag.com/interviews/*i3inte_sidhwa.html.*
10. *Ibid.*

11. Indira Bhatt, "Journey towards Freedom: A Study of Bapsi Sidhwa's *An American Brat*," *Parsi Fiction*, ed. Novy Kapadia, Jaydipsinh Dodiya, R.K. Dhawan (New Delhi: Prestige, 2001), p. 93.
12. Letha Rengachari, "The Sub-continental Expatriate Woman's Novel as a Melting Pot for History and Politics: A Study of Bapsi Sidhwa's *An American Brat*," *Ibid.*, p. 70.
13. Introduction to *The Novels of Bapsi Sidhwa*, p. 12.
14. David Montenegro, p. 37.
15. *Ibid*, p. 51.
16. Introduction to *The Novels of Bapsi Sidhwa*, p. 25.

Ice-Candy-Man: The Text

Chapter 1

The chapter introduces the readers immediately to Lenny the raconteur, the narrator of the story, describing the physical boundaries within which the action shall gradually unfold. Lenny is an eight-year-old polio-stricken girl-child. Her imagination maps different landscapes, picking up points of reference which shall be repeatedly hinted at in different contexts in the narrative. The tone of the story is set when she brands her home on Warris Road as an abode of "perplexing unrealities." The precise location-description of her home imparts a perspective to the reader to assess the future happenings and imagine their cruelty with a better understanding. The reader also becomes acquainted with the constrictions of a child's viewpoint with which the novel has been presented, preparing him to accept the priorities from an un-adult vantagepoint. The reader is also introduced to Lenny's Ayah, a chocolate brown and short woman, everything about whom is "eighteen years old and round and plump." (3) The covetous glances she draws from all and sundry are intuitively understood by Lenny also, suggesting a keen dominant sensuality beneath the gullibility of a child. The complacent self-indulgence with which Lenny snubs the English gnome's advice regarding more physical exercise shows her inclination for easier options and also a proclivity towards fierce independence. Lenny's innocent coquettishness is evident in her description of the Godmother too.

Lenny has a deformity in her foot. Col. Bharucha had put a plaster cast over her leg to correct it. When he is taking away the cast Lenny is apprehensive that the fault might have been corrected. She is rather happy with her deformity as it imparts a special status to her. She does not like the probability of a shift to the ordinary life of a normal child. However as her foot is still deshaped, the doctor is forced to put a new cast over it. Lenny is shown as a child who is preoccupied with herself, treating her physical abnormality as a norm to gain favours, abhorring the competitive world of normal children. Despite it, she comes across as an astute observer of human behaviour with a keen insight into people's motives and their sharp understanding.

Chapter 2

The second chapter begins with a scene of close intimacy between Lenny's parents. Their happy married life and its palpable richness guarantees a life of comfort to Lenny. Looking at the intimate details of her parents' behaviour, Lenny matures quickly. Her desire to seek security in her physical deformity is presented again. It seems to give her a special status—protected, secluded and different, allowing her to indulge in her fancies and work out the whims. She feels reassured when Col. Bharucha instructs her to wear calipers for some more time. The traditional perception regarding gender-based roles is also evident in Col. Bharucha's attitude when he predicts a carefree and happy domestic life for Lenny.

The chapter also conveys the feeling of guilt which Lenny's parents possess on account of her disability, and their uncertainties about her future. The figure of Papoo is also introduced with the help of a brief interlude. The chapter also contains the first conscious statement of the Parsi attitude towards politics. Col. Bharucha, who is also the president of the Parsi community in Lahore, advises his people to hunt with the hounds and run with the hare to safeguard their interests. The readers also get first glimpses of the impending political turmoil in this chapter.

Chapter 3

The third chapter begins with a description of the Salvation Army march, which Lenny compares with a slick red and white caterpillar. Lenny is attracted towards this spectacle and links it with Ayah's burgeoning sexuality. Leaning against the gatepost, Ayah is compared with a magnet, who automatically draws the leering looks of all men. Her sexuality is again emphasized when

Lenny describes her evening outings. Lying on the grass, her head in Ayah's lap, she enjoys the attentions of Ayah's various suitors—the Masseur massages her feet, the Ice-Candy-Man recites stories to her. Lenny also enjoys the game of secret sensuality which Ayah and her admirers play. She becomes a silent partner in these games, covering up for their outings, and maintaining a canny silence about their doings. Lenny closely watches Ayah's escapades with the Masseur, the Fallettis Hotel cook, the Government House gardener, the Ice-Candy-Man, and records their attempts to be physically close to Ayah. She surreptitiously watches the scenes of physical intimacy and learns of "human needs, frailties, cruelties and joys." (20) She possesses a complacent understanding of her Ayah's flirtatious nature.

The chapter also records Lenny's encounters with her cousin, their sexual pranks and a fine sketch of the Electric-Aunt. Lenny also describes her recurrent nightmares in detail.

Chapter 4

The fourth chapter introduces us to the vivacious presence of Lenny's brother Adi. While Lenny suffers from physical constraints on account of her polio, the boy is healthy, beautiful and mercurial. He is absorbed in his games, swiftly moving from one activity to other. Lenny, though wants to play with him, also teases him in order to gain his attention. While she is kept busy by her sick person's routine, and is continuously haunted by her nightmares, Adi is superbly agile and as beautiful as an English baby—fair, chubby, naughty, and attends a regular school. Ayah encourages him to play with the English babies and feels happy with it.

The chapter also narrates the Ice-Candy-Man's alternate profession as a birdman during the bitterly severe winter season. He stuffs enormous cages with sparrows and common green parrots, displaying them at strategic points in the presence of white ladies. He pretends to slaughter them, to cut their throats, and moved to pity, women purchase birds from him and free them. But the business cannot always be good. Whenever he earns some profit, he treats the Ayah and the young kids to a dinner of pulao. Lenny is impressed with his understanding of the contemporary politics as he tells them about Subas Chandra Bose. He is so enamoured with Ayah that he keeps on prolonging his talks. When Ayah does not promise to meet him the next day he picks up Adi and threatens to drop him if she does not consent to meet him. Flabbergasted, Ayah promises and then chases him out of the bungalow.

Chapter 5

Lenny's family goes to Murree Hills at the foot of the Himalayas during the summer. During their stay, while Lenny is silently cursing her donkey, the news that the British have won the II World War comes. The electrified atmosphere is infectious, and even Lenny, who had subversively hoped that Bose and the Japanese army would win the war, feels elated. Their visit is cut short as the Parsis of Lahore decide to hold a Jashan prayer to celebrate the British victory.

Sidhwa intersperses the narrative with small and minute incidents which not only provide a peep into a slice of life, but also impart richness to the narrative by providing some glimpses into the mind-sets of the characters. When the tonga-horse carrying the family to the fire temple for worship falls down on the road, men—attracted by Ayah's sensuality—make mad sprints in the noon heat to help them. This minor incident highlights once more the impact of Ayah's sensuality on men. The minute details of the worship, the priests' dresses and rituals, the children's long wait, and the grown ups' lack of real interest, Lenny's mother's worry about her limp, and her nervous talk with Col. Bharucha are presented with a depth of understanding.

An ironical situation is presented during the thanksgiving itself. Col. Bharucha thanks God Almighty for defeating the Japanese and giving victory to the British, yet in the same speech he exhorts the people to use salt manufactured from the Indian ocean only. The gathering reacts in myriad ways—jest, anger, wisecracks are clearly audible in the gathering. But this incident underscores the worldly wisdom of the Parsi community. Col.

Bharucha, while happy for the British victory, also warns his community not to court arrest on any issue, as this short cut to fame and fortune is not meant for them. He warns the people that the struggle is not simply for autonomous self-rule, it is for power. He says that different communities are jockeying for power, and the Parsis shall be mangled into chutney if they jump into the foray. Dr. Mody questions this stand and says that it shall amount to betraying their neighbours. Dr. Bharucha rhetorically asks which neighbours—Hindu, Muslim or Sikh? He wants his people not to take any sides, and to reinforce his idea he quotes from their history. He reminds the gathering that when their forefathers were denied entry into the land of India, they had, by the symbolic gesture of stirring a teaspoon of sugar into the milk, suggested that they would harmoniously mingle with the people of India and sweeten their lives with their decency and industry. He wants that in the times of crisis the Parsis should opt for the same stand—they must abide by the rules of the land, whoever governs it. Undaunted by the sarcastic words of some, he asks the congregation to respect the customs of the rulers as they have always had without any attempt at proselytizing. Mr. Bankwalla also emphasizes this point and remarks that the Parsis should not try to exercise real power. The meeting ends in a mood of raucous merry-making.

Chapter 6

The sixth chapter begins with a description of an intimate domestic scene. Ayah is bathing Lenny and her mother is massaging her foot. It is followed by a description of the Sethis' tenants, the Shankaras, who are newly wed and "steamily in love." Lenny's latent sexuality is exhibited again in her description of the Shankars. The cooking smells of Gita's quarters are mixed up with the steam of their nightlong ecstasy. She loves to recite stories, and so does Ayah. When Ayah recounts the folk stories of Punjab, Lenny is drifted to its rural land, "to a breeze stirring in wheat stalks and yellow mustard fields. To village belles weaving through the fields to wells." (43) Ayah's large and eloquent eyes are soft with dreams when she shares these moments with Lenny. The charmed sensitivity of the scene is broken by the melee of servants trying humorously to undo the gardener's dhoti. It is a practised jest, a high spirited gambol and everybody knows that the gardener Hari would neither be hurt nor denuded. Lenny, as well as Papoo, the Sweeper's daughter, join in this good-natured romp. But suddenly Muccho, Papoo's mother, snatches her daughter from the crowd and starts beating her. Other servants try to save her but she is beaten mercilessly. She feigns unconsciousness, but breaks into nimble playfulness as soon as her mother shows some sympathy. All the servants criticize Muccho for her cruelty and enjoy her discomfort. Muccho is portrayed as an unjust mother who shows neither love nor tolerance for her daughter. This incident gives us an insight into the intricacies of mother-daughter relationship which is normally eulogized by writers. Bapsi Sidhwa has presented a facet of this relationship often left untouched by the majority of writers.

Chapter 7

The seventh chapter begins with the lecherous behaviour of Imam Din, the old cook, and gradually moves to record the growing religious divide of the pre-Partition era. Imam Din grabs the young children, as well as Ayah, when they enter kitchen, and rocks them gently on his lap. He calls it a little '*masti*'—a bit of naughtiness. Lenny dislikes it. As an old man he has been given a certain latitude. He is also respected for his wisdom by other servants, and also by his villagers. Lenny visits his village twice. Once Imam Din takes her to his grandson Dost Mohammad's village. Initially he refuses as the village is forty miles from Lahore, but Ayah's insistence ultimately wins and he takes Lenny on a bike ride to the village. They start early and "perambulate through the profusion of bared Lahori bottoms." The reader is introduced to an ironical description of the lurid ugliness of the morning scene, of people squatting along alleyways to defecate. Herein we also find the first mention of Sharbat Khan who later on sharpens knives in the Mozang Chowk bazaar. His particularly pale bottom arrests Imam Din's attention.

The skin is pink, still fresh and tingling from cold mountain winds. "'So, we have a new panther in town!' he muses aloud."

The ugliness of the scene is contrasted with the fresh and vivid beauty of the rural Punjab. Lenny and Imam Din are welcomed by Dost Mohammad. Lenny romps around in the fields while the children of the family look on in bewilderment. The girls, slightly older than Lenny, have the responsible air of much older women, affecting the tone and expression of their mothers and aunts. They are flabbergasted by the short dresses and equally short hair of Lenny. As in other chapters, the child's attraction towards the grotesque is presented in this chapter too. The inch-long portruding belly-button of Ranna, the young boy of the family, and Lenny's fascination with it are repeatedly mentioned.

The chapter ends with a discussion of the political problem, simmering subtly and spreading unobtrusively in the countryside. Imam Din cautions the villagers against it. The village chaudhry, the mullah, the granthi and other villagers strongly express their solidarity and vouch to protect each other, asserting that the city madness will not infect the villages.

Chapter 8

Sidhwa juxtaposes minor and major incidents to more significantly convey her ideas. In this chapter also a scene of bickering amongst children is juxtaposed with the more eloquent dinner scene which captures the intricacies of contemporary political situation. Mr. Singh and his American wife, Inspector General of Police and Mrs. Rogers are the guests for dinner. Lenny and Adi slip unobserved under the table. Mr. Singh is an uncouth Jat who loudly converses in vituperative Punjabi, while Mrs. Singh is placid and other-worldly. The Inspector General of Police does not welcome the jokes of Lenny's father and soon has a heated discussion with Mr. Singh. The Inspector General calmly puts forward his opinion that the Congress has blown the last chance for an undivided India by rejecting Lord Wavell's suggestion and claims that the Akalis are a "bloody bunch of murdering fanatics." Mr. Singh, who was already vociferously refuting these ideas, loses his patience and grabs Mr. Rogers, trying to attack him with a fork. Soon however the commotion subsides. Mr. Rogers is made to apologize and the dinner continues in a strained silence till the children are discovered and sent back to bed.

A good-humoured sketch of the Sethis' second hand Morris Minor and the struggle to push-start it and turning its cranks is given soon after the dinner incident, followed by an equally light-hearted narration of Lenny's parents' mock-fight over money. They squabble in low voices, conscious of the servants, and Lenny also joins them. A rare scene of Lenny's closeness with her parents is given towards the end of the chapter.

Chapter 9

Once more Bapsi Sidhwa juxtaposes the insignificant playful antics of children against the more serious talk of the grown-ups, which later on shall assume a menacing tone. Rosy is hurt when Adi shoves her roughly and Lenny accompanies her with a hypocritical protectiveness. Lenny's temptation for Rosy's miniature glass jars is presented with an awareness that one's desire for things gives people power over him.

The second part of the chapter introduces us to Ayah's two new admirers—a Chinaman and a Pathan. In his excessive attraction towards the Ayah the Chinaman can be compared with her other suitors whom she tackles frivolously and keeps under control with gestures of limited coquettishness. The Chinaman is "dapper, thin, brusque and rude" (73) and visits them twice a week. Lenny's mother soon loses her patience with him, but Ayah is snared by the shimmering colours of smooth silk. He gifts small items to Ayah and the children's room soon blossoms with embroidered bosky-silk doilies. In contrast with the Chinaman, the Pathan admirer, whom Lenny soon recognizes as Sharbat Khan, whose pink and tingly bottom she had witnessed while cycling to Imam Din's village, possesses a seductive hold over Ayah. He is a knife-sharpener, pushing a pedal on his machine and turning the large slender wheel dizzily he roams around the markets. He is a tall and imposing man. He brings the news of the market to Ayah. He also helps her in carrying out money transactions by loaning her money to others and thereby bringing her small profits. He tells her about the market stabbings and killings, warning her about the rising communal tension.

Sharbat Khan's presence radiates a warmth in Ayah, which is different from the dark heat generated by Masseur's fingers and the lightning-strikes of Ice-Candy-Man's toes. Ayah is nervous and shy in his presence. He tells her tales of the mountain and promises to bring nuts to her. Even Lenny can recognize the intensity of their passion for each other. The chapter ends with the narration of an intimate family scene which describes how young girls are encouraged to learn the art of maneuvers and small talks to please their men-folk.

Chapter 10

In this chapter we learn about Mr. and Mrs. Pen. Since Lenny cannot attend a regular school, she is sent to Mrs. Pen to study. Mrs. Pen is English—fair, soft and plump, while Mr. Pen is an Anglo-Indian. Lenny compares Mrs. Pen with Ayah, and is conscious of her aged body—its whiff reminding her of spent passion and lingering yearnings. She feels sorry for her.

Lenny also steals the three toy glass jars from Rosy. In order to escape suspicion she hides them at Godmother's house. Her act of thievery is found out when the Slave sister rummages through boxes to find out an old Japanese kimono. Lenny tries to defend herself by saying that Rosy had gifted them to her, but Godmother immediately senses her ruse. She tells Lenny that the life of crime is not for her as her voice and face give her away. Lenny feels that she has been condemned to a life of honesty.

History intrudes in the person of Gandhiji. During his visit to Lahore, Lenny and her mother go to visit him. Gandhiji is shown as sitting cross-legged on the marble floor of a palatial verandah, surrounded by women and knitting. Lenny is puzzled when he talks about bowel movements and enema. Only when their eyes meet she realizes that he fuses everything that is feminine, funny, gentle and loving. She also comments that it was after many years that she was able to understand his hidden strength.

Chapter 11

The readers are made aware of the changing communal pattern of the society. The subtle changes which suddenly become significant are described through the gatherings at the Queen's Park. Surrounded by Ayah's admirers, Lenny listens to their arguments and unmalicious jokes. The Government house gardener comments that Lord Wavell was removed as he could not suppress the Muslim League in the Punjab elections. He draws fierce retorts from the Masseur and the Ice-Candy-Man. Jokes developed to ridicule other religions suddenly become favourite and people strangely are made conscious of their own religious practices. Ayah is also carried away by a devotional fervour and offers joss sticks and flowers to gods in the temples. Imam Din and Yousaf also turn into religious zealots, taking Friday afternoons off for the Jumha prayers. Lenny realizes that instead of mixing freely people prefer to stay separate and form groups based on the similarity of religion. Crammed into narrow religious slots, they are diminished and dehumanized.

The chapter also includes a little information about Papoo, who is still cruelly treated by her mother and forced to spend her time finishing off household chores. We are told that her mother is planning her marriage. There is another episode about the Ice-Candy-Man, who poses himself as a Sufi, telephoning Allah and earning money with the help of such antics. This description highlights his chameleon-like qualities.

Chapter 12

The chapter begins with the frolicking activities of children who suddenly discover the presence of a strange black box in the bathroom. The mystery remains unsolved. The box disappears as suddenly as it had appeared and soon we are transported to the rural Punjab. Imam Din, accompanied by Lenny, visits Ranna's village. They also visit the Baisakhi fare in Dera Tek Singh, a neighbouring Sikh village. Stuffing herself on sweets and enjoying herself on the creaking ferris-wheel, Lenny suddenly senses a change in the atmosphere. She notices Ranna's fear, his sudden strident laughter and strained smile, and feels nervous. Villagers also notice the presence of grim strangers and visit the granthi to find out its reason. The villagers are told that the city Akalis have come to drive the Muslims out of East Punjab. The granthi is sad and resigned, and cautions the peasants to reach their homes before it gets dark. Back in Pir Pindo, the villagers listen to the radio broadcasts of Congress and Muslim League spokesmen and feel reassured.

Reality seeps through a fortnight later when an army truck disgorges a family of villagers, distant kins of Imam Din from Pir Pindo, outside the gates of Lenny's bungalow. They have been evacuated by Army. The prosperous land owners and the rich Muslims had refused to leave their land, but hired hands left the village to reach the safety of Pakistan, a new state about the existence of which they are not very sure.

Chapter 13

The chapter begins with a verse from Iqbal, summing up the mood of the rest of the narration. The cold weather has gripped the land and has also percolated to the hearts of the people. With minor incidents the distancing between people is beautifully suggested throughout the chapter.

Lenny feels unnerved when the Slave sister tells her about the murder of Mr. Rogers, the Inspector General of Police. To soothe her the Godmother starts a discussion about the Tower of Silence. The bickering of the two sisters allays Lenny's fears and she becomes her old playful self once again, asking Yousaf to go through the Lawrence Gardens. Her vague fears about the torn Punjab and the jagged cracks of its rivers surface again when a Brahmin Pandit throws away his eatables as he feels that they have been corrupted by their shadow. She realizes that one man's religion can be another man's poison. These fears take a concrete shape when the playful pickings at the gardener's dhoti turn into ugly violent movements and he is suddenly denuded. Like her Ayah Lenny is also afraid and chilled, but feels secure by the sudden appearance of the Ice-Candy-Man.

Chapter 14

The fourteenth chapter describes the growing intimacy between Ayah and the Masseur. Lenny accompanies them on their long tours to isolated spots and is a witness to their passion. Lenny also senses the mute and invisible presence of the Ice-Candy-Man, constantly chasing the Masseur and the Ayah on their wanderings. He chases them throughout the day and comes back in the evening with his inexhaustible fund of gossip. He boasts of his helpful nature and the strength of his friendship in his evening chats, but does not desist from his chase. His cycle remains unobtrusively parked outside the gate when the Masseur visits the Oldhusband every Thursday, and is watched by Ayah in a spellbound manner. Lenny's cousin tells her about it, but its significance is soon lost in the verbose narration of the man's exploits. When he tells Ayah and Lenny about Bhagwandas the tailor, his bitter voice betrays his acrimony towards the Masseur. It changes the complexion of their talk. Ayah and Lenny become restive. The Ice-Candy-Man soon regains his composure and controls his mood, but a shadow has already been cast.

Chapter 15

Like most of the previous chapters, this chapter also begins with the descriptions of the children's game, which soon develops into a parody of the contemporary times. As the British prepare to leave, the park is abandoned by the people. Ayah and the group of her admirers assemble at the Wrestler's restaurant now. The free friendly atmosphere of previous gatherings is however missing—even Lenny is perturbed by the constant quarrels and arguments among friends. Religion has become more important than the individual. Lenny closes her eyes in the hope that they will open on a "suddenly changed world" (129), but the arguments about the division of the land continue in a vociferous manner. The Sikhs, the Hindus and the Muslims look at the issue from different angles. The Ice-Candy-Man castigates Nehru as being the sly one, stating that he would walk off with the lion's share. During these heated conversations Lenny suddenly realizes that they were thirteen, sitting and debating in the Wrestler's restaurant. Quoting the last supper and the story of Judas's betrayal, Godmother explains to her that thirteen is an unlucky number. Lenny has a disturbed sleep, full of fearful dreams and an awareness of the distant, pulsating sound of slogan chanting.

Chapter 16

Lenny goes to attend the lecture of Master Tara Singh along with Ayah. The Fallettis Hotel cook had secured a place for them over the hotel's roof so that they could have a clear view. Wielding long, curved sword in each hand, Master Tara Singh declares that the Sikhs would not allow the creation of Pakistan. His words are soon nullified as soon after this event the Ice-Candy-Man takes them to show the burning markets of Shalmi. He is frank about his fanaticism and hatred for other communities. Safe and sheltered in their place, they watch the cruel drama unfold suddenly before their eyes.

Mesmerized by naked terror Ayah and Lenny look at the processions carrying a nabbed child twitching on a spear blade, at the mob tying the legs of men to jeeps being driven in two opposite directions and spraying petrol on burning buildings. Lenny is horrified while people assembled on the hotel roof laugh and hug one another. She is aware of the evil paralyzing spell of the mob terror. Back at home she wants to re-enact the scene with her dolls. She asks her brother Adi to pull a leg of a life-like doll while she is holding the other. The cloth skin of the doll is ripped right up to its armpits spilling chunks of grayish cotton in the room. Only then she internalizes the extent of the horror she had witnessed and collapses. Their Hindu neighbours have already fled. In the abandoned house of Daulatrams they still go to play and see the Mozang Chowk burn. The city burns and its memory is etched out on Lenny's conscience—the fire itself could not burn for months, but in her memory it is "branded over an inordinate length of time." (139)

Chapter 17

The chapter records the birth of a new nation. Lenny remarks, "I am Pakistani. In a snap. Just like that." (140) Lenny is disappointed when her birthday fails to arouse any enthusiasm in her parents. Dulled by their lack of interest she goes to Godmother's and is offended that they are preparing sweets not to celebrate her birthday but to welcome Dr. Manek Modi, their middle sister's husband. The routine parrying of words between Godmother and Slave sister is also silenced. Lenny's spirits are restored when her cousin happily greets her and valiantly offers to arrange a party for her at his place. Munching her cake, she listens to Jinnah's inaugural speech at the constituent assembly session guaranteeing religious freedom to all the citizens of Pakistan.

Chapter 18

Mr. Singh comes to meet Lenny's family along with his American wife and two children. He is dishevelled and nervous. He tells Lenny's mother that all the Hindu families have already left Warris Road, and the two Sikh families which are still left will soon leave. He wants Lenny's father to store a few things for them in the hope that things would subside.

Ayah's admirers have also been affected by these goings on. She does not move out of the residence, her suitors come and sit with her on the Shankars' neglected verandah. Masseur, Hari, Sher Singh and Gardener are discussing Gurdaspur's assimilation into India, when suddenly the Ice-Candy-Man appears—dried up and shrivelled, looking breathless and frantic, he tells them of the train from Gurdaspur which is loaded only with dead bodies. All through his dialogue, his eyes are riveted to the face of the young Sardar Sher Singh. Sharbat Khan has also returned from the mountains and now has a roaring business of sharpening knives. In the tense communal situation people want their tools and weapons sharpened. Lenny feels a perceptible change in Ayah's attitude towards the Pathan. She has lost her awe and excitement in his presence and acts calmly. Masseur and Pathan appraise each other with cautious suspicion. The secret communication of intimacy between Ayah and the Masseur is not wasted on Sharbat Khan. Conceding the round with quiet dignity he goes away without a single word.

Chapter 19

The chapter begins with the playful activity of bathing a buffalo, as if such peacetime pleasures shall shut out the violence and eccentricity of the times. Adi discovers the presence of the gun hidden in the black box placed inside the bathroom. Adi and Lenny play guards with the double barrel gun while the disturbances of the city occupy the background—the slogan shouting of the Muslim and Sikh goondas, occasional tongas and cycles, a policeman marching along the prisoners. When their father returns in the afternoon and finds Adi standing as sentry on the gate with the gun, he is left speechless and snatches it from him.

Ice-Candy-Man visits them after a long gap. Lenny notices the changes in him—he has acquired an unpleasant swagger and a strange way of looking at Hari and Moti. He tells them stories of plunder and murder. He tells them how the house of Kirpa Ram, the moneylender, was looted. He offers a gold coin to Ayah, but she refuses to accept it. Instead she inquires about Sher Singh, the zoo attendant. The Ice-Candy-Man tells them how his Muslim tenants whom earlier he had got rid of, exposed themselves before his family women, insulting his sister and killing his brother-in-law. When the Government House Gardener questions him about his complicity in the incident, he flares up and comments in bitter wrath that the mutilated bodies on the train from Gurdaspur have changed him and now he feels no hesitation in killing even those people whom he has known all his life. The Hindus listening to him are restless. The Gardener talks about joining his family in Delhi as evil will only spawn evil. Moti and Papoo discuss the possibility of converting to Christianity. The Ice-Candy-Man advises him to change his name also. Lenny is startled and terrified by these changes.

After everybody has left, the Masseur reassures Ayah assuring her of his love and asking her to marry him. Ayah submissively admits her love towards him. Lenny protests and cries out that she will never allow another Ayah to touch her.

Chapter 20

The chapter begins with a sordid account of the devastation unleashed by Partition. The children's games are forgotten. Refugees flood newly created states, within three months seven million Muslims and five million Hindus and Sikhs are uprooted in a terrible population exchange. Lenny comments on the changing politics of the British too. Once the objective to divide India is achieved, the British start doling out favours to Indian political leadership represented by Nehru. Nehru is young and charming, close to the Mountbattens while in contrast Jinnah is austere and deathly ill, past the prime of his elegant manhood, he is sallow, whip thin and uncompromising.

Lenny is shown a photograph of Jinnah's wife, a Parsi woman, by her mother. She is told about her beauty, grandeur and boldness, and also about her untimely death. Lenny feels that her daring was fruitless and her defiance had been humbled, but she also feels that Jinnah perhaps also died of a broken heart. She also sympathizes with the fact that Jinnah who was once hailed as an ambassador of Hindu-Muslim unity was later on caricatured as a monster by British and Indian scholars.

Chapter 21

The beginning of the chapter firmly replaces the children's play with the dark foreboding incidents of the aftermath of Partition. Hari converts into a Muslim and his circumcision generates a curious sexual game between Lenny and her cousin. The sexual awareness of a young girl is underscored again and again by Bapsi Sidhwa through the portrayal of Lenny. Her innocent games, earlier with Ranna, and now with her cousin, are laced with this curiosity, and are abetted by the fact that she is often a witness to the physical games Ayah indulges in.

The chapter is mainly devoted to the description of how Lenny spent the night after her birthday at Godmother's. In her room, resembling the barracks' dormitory, five cots are laid out at different angles, leaving hardly any space to walk. Dr. Manek Mody is visiting them and he presents a burlesque dialogue almost intimidating Lenny with his graphic descriptions of how he would like to pounce on her Roda Aunty and eat her up, "Roast leg of Aunty or barbecued ribs? Of course! I'll make a nice jelly from her trotters! Seasoned with cinnamon and orange juice—slurp-slurp! Just like Imam Din's jelly." (163) The mood is immediately taken up by the sisters and they fight themselves off to sleep. Their verbal duel continues in the morning also and their bickering over delay in preparing breakfast is given in detail. This episode does not seem to be linked with the main plot, till the reader suddenly finds the shadow of Partition corrupting Godmother's party of four students from the King Edward Medical College. Two of them, a Sikh and a Hindu, have moved to safer places. Soon Dr. Mody starts his comic act once again, catching a fly and slaughtering it with a loud clap. His testy outbursts are however confounded by the Oldhusband, remarking churlishly about the nonsensical fuss over "this business about eyes." (170)

Chapter 22

The chapter begins with the bewilderment of children at the sudden busy air of secrecy and preoccupation their elders have taken up. Their mother and Electric-Aunt shoot off in the Morris after their father's routine departure for office. Ayah prompts them to get a look in the car's dicky, telling them that it is full of petrol cans. Children know that it is an offence to store petrol as it is rationed. Forced by her imagination Lenny concludes that her mother and aunt are arsonists. Terrified by the image of her handcuffed mother she covers her head and prays to God. Her concern is shared by Adi and her cousin.

Hari, alias Himat-Ali, is accompanying Lenny to Mrs. Pen, when troubled by a steely reek they find the Masseur's body in a gunnysack. The incident is reported in an objective manner. Shorn of any display of sentiments, it highlights the macabre morbidity of the scene.

Chapter 23

The chapter opens up with a scene of Lahore which is emptied of Sikhs and Hindus. Lenny notes that the colourful turbans and caste marks of Sikhs and Hindus are no longer visible in the markets. The city is now populated with hordes of Muslim refugees, who salvage every bit of scrap from the gutted shops and tenements of Shalmi and Gowalmandi and loot the palatial bungalows vacated by Hindus in affluent neighbourhoods. The Singh's annexe is abandoned but their main bungalow and the Hindu doctor's abandoned house behind the Sethis show surreptitious signs of occupation. The vacant houses decay quickly. With cracks in cement and patches of damp on walls they look haunted—like Ayah's eyes are by memories of Masseur. She silently mourns his death. She still walks with Lenny in the marble terraces of the Shalimar Gardens and climbs the slender minarets of Jehangir's tomb. But her eyes have lost their lustre and she is inconsolable in her empty ache for the dead Masseur. Wherever they go, they are still followed by the Ice-Candy-Man.

The processions of looters and violent mob are still heard in various directions, but Lenny feels that they have lost their urgency. Their street has also been bypassed for some time when suddenly the rumble of carts and the roar of men shouting slogans can be heard just in front of their house. Lenny immediately senses danger. Children, their mother, Ayah, and other inhabitants of the servants' quarters assemble on the verandah. Ayah disappears as the roaring crowd nears. The crowd rides into the house opposite theirs, and then charges up their drive. The portico and the drive are soon filled with men whose "ideals and passions have cooled to ice." (179) Men in front are quiet, like merchants going about their business, while the rest of the crowd chants perfunctorily. Imam Din emerges from the kitchen, still beating the eggs in an aluminium bowl, and angrily challenges them. The crowd inquires about the Shankars and then asks for the gardener. When Imam Din tells them that Hari has now converted to Islam, they tease him and ask him to recite the kalma. They also inquire about Moti, the sweeper and joke about his conversion to Christianity. Suddenly somebody inquires about Ayah. After a split second's silence Imam Din calmly says that she has already left Lahore a day before. When the crowd pesters on, he swears by God, and the crowd is silenced. Suddenly the Ice-Candy-Man—his hypnotic, reassuring face transforms into a saviour's, blotting out the ugly frightening crowd. Putting his arms around Lenny and putting on a charming face he asks about the Ayah. She unwittingly blurts out a fragment of an overheard conversation "on the roof—or in one of the go-downs." (182) The Ice-Candy-Man's face undergoes a sudden change and then only Lenny realizes that she has betrayed her Ayah. Men shove part them and drag Ayah out in grotesque strides and push her on to the cart with triumphant grimaces.

Chapter 24

The chapter heightens the grimness of the previous chapter. The previous chapter had presented the cruelty and treacherousness of an age, while the present chapter presents an unusually cruel facet of mother-daughter relationship.

While Lenny tries to punish herself for blurting out the truth, preparations are on for Papoo's marriage. Huddled in bunches, families come for the occasion and cajole Papoo into a docile silence. Whenever Papoo gains some courage, particularly during Lenny's presence, her eyes regain their roguish sparkle and she flings herself on the floor in protest.

The day of marriage arrives, the courtyard is filled with women in bright satin and the air is permeated by the aroma of spicy food. Bedecked in finery Papoo, huddled in a corner, is fast asleep. When Lenny shakes her she opens up her eyes drowsily, as if she is drunk. Lenny runs out of the room to receive the baraat, and judges the bridegroom, on the basis of his height, to be a young boy of eleven or twelve. When the sehra swings out she is shocked to see the pockmark-pitted face of a dark, middle aged man. He is a dwarf and the smirk lurking about his thin, dry lips give him "an impression of cruelty." (187) Lenny is shocked at the grotesque possibilities awaiting Papoo. She is further mystified by the contented smile on Maccho's face—her smug and vindicated smile suggests that she still had the upper hand! Lenny belatedly realizes that Papoo had been doped deliberately so that the marriage ceremonies can go on peacefully.

Chapter 25

The servants' quarters behind the Hindu doctor's residence now house some women. A tall and burly Sikh guards them. Unable to get any answer from the servants, the children sneak up the stairs and peep into the enclosed courtyard. They are able to make out dark shapes of several women lurking between cots. They are the women who were abducted during the riots, have now been rescued, but their families have refused to accept them. Children though are ignorant of this detail.

A woman presents herself before Lenny's mother for the ayah's job. Lenny recognizes immediately her desolate and pallid face as belonging to the women's jail, but decides to keep quiet. Lenny addresses her as Hamida as she cannot bring herself to call her Ayah. She also comes to know that all the grown-ups are looking for Ayah. Her parents and aunts, as well as Sharbat Khan and other servants, go around with urgency for searching her. Meanwhile Hamida is being trained for daily household chores. She is unable to do even the simplest task. During these days Imam Din's relatives from Pir Pindo take shelter in his quarters. Among them is Ranna, the young boy with whom Lenny had spent some happy days. Lenny is horrified to look at him now, his skeletal figure is covered with welts and there is an "improbable wound" on the back of his shaved head. Bit by bit Lenny reconstructs his plight, which is a testimony to the brutalities unleashed during the Partition days.

The majority of Muslim villagers in Pir Pindo had refused to move away. Some of them had gone to Pakistan, disguising themselves as Sikhs or Hindus. But despite Jagjeet Singh's advice most of the villagers stayed back, discrediting the danger, and making half-hearted preparations to ward off the possible attack. Villagers are soon startled by the wails and the hoarse voices of shouting coming from nearby villages. They gather in the mosque and wait for Dost Mohammad and his party who had been sent out to find out the reason of disturbance. When the scouts return they tell the villagers that the marauding bands of thousands of Sikhs are destroying villages, killing all Muslims, setting fires, raping and mutilating women. Villagers review their preparations—girls and women will burn themselves, young men will engage the marauders in fight and young boys will be locked in secluded back rooms. But the plans go haywire. The attack comes at dawn and the villagers are mowed down. Ranna hides in a room with some other people. He witnesses the slaughter of his father and brothers and loses consciousness when struck with sword on the back of his neck. He regains his senses in a devastated village and taking shelter of shadows cautiously moves towards his aunt's village. Hiding in fields and burrowing like a small animal through crop he makes it to his aunt's village and finds that it is being vacated by army. He faints as soon as he reaches his uncle's house. They think that he would die in a few moments and go away with the army, leaving him alone. When the mob attacks the empty village Ranna hides in a barn and is miraculously saved. Gradually he moves to Amritsar, where many similarly abandoned children were scavenging in the looted houses. Ranna also stole chapaties and grains from houses strewn with dead bodies. He per chance stumbles on to the station cordoned off by barbed wire and recognizes a huddle of Muslim refugees. A kindly soldier allows him to join them and along with other refugees he is herded into a camp for two months till the fate unites him with his Noni Chachi and Iqbal Chacha.

Chapter 26

Cousin's cook passes on a hint about the where-abouts of Ayah, but does not reveal any vital clue. Lenny spends a week with her Godmother during the summer vacation. Godmother has an immense "network of espionage" (210), of which she herself is unaware. She always wanted to know things and thus gained access to many ears. She arranges a seat in the Convent of Jesus and Mary for Ranna. Ranna soon acclimatizes himself with the new environment. Lenny also senses that Godmother is eager to find out Ayah, though she is not told anything explicitly. She also witnesses her parents' fights and is still intrigued by the women in the neighbouring courtyard. Lenny tells Hamida that she had seen her there and wants to find out more about these women. Hamida tells her that it is a camp for fallen women. Lenny is unable to understand it. She asks Godmother the meaning of the phrase. She is palmed off by changing the course of conversation to her marriage. She claims that the cousin wants to marry her, but her claim is discredited by Mini Aunty. She talks to cousin to assure herself of his intentions remaining the same. Cousin is also disturbed as Lenny does not allow any intimacy to him. He asks her to tell him about all the people she finds more attractive than him. His ironical tone is lost on her and she takes him literally, later on pointing, as Cousin terms it, "roughly ten per cent of the male population in Lahore." (220)

Chapter 27

Lenny keeps a watch on the quarters of the "fallen women" in the hope that one day she will be able to find her Ayah there. She asks Hamida whether she does not miss her children. Hamida outlines her constraints stating that even if she tries to stealthily meet her children, her husband shall torment them. When Lenny is not convinced, she tries to explain her point with the tale of a prince who was eaten by a tiger. The story underlines the fatalistic acceptance of whatever life has to offer without struggling against it. Lenny begins to show her disagreement when suddenly they are disturbed by an uproarious din coming from the kitchen. Imam Din has trapped a huge black and battle-scarred cat in a screen door and is trying to chastise it. Mother returns in her Morris and when she finds Imam Din tormenting the cat, swats him with a fly swat. Imam Din is hurt and bewildered and complains to Father. Still shouting goodnaturedly, Mother manages to pacify the cook. Lenny enjoys these moments when her parents talk to each other directly commenting that such moments are becoming rare. She also realizes somehow that the hunt for Ayah is off and feels troubled by it.

Chapter 28

This brief chapter tells us about a new facet of Lenny and her cousin's relationship. Cousin ignores her constantly. When Lenny imposes her presence on him, he prefers to talk to Adi, responding to her in monosyllables. His aloofness makes Lenny restless and she chases him relentlessly, doing small jobs for him. She ignores Ranna in the process whose visits become less and less frequent. One day Cousin suddenly announces that he has seen Ayah going away in a taxi at Charing Cross, made up like a film actress. During this conversation Lenny also realizes that his aloofness was merely a pose to lure her towards him. Their goodnatured fight is taken to Godmother for solution, with whose help they reach a compromise—Lenny promises to keep an open mind and let bygones be bygones, and Cousin agrees to stop wooing her vigorously for a couple of years.

Chapter 29

Lenny sees Ayah going away in a taxi at Mozang Chowk, exaggeratedly made up and flanked by two thin poets. She and Adi go to Godmother's to spend a night with her and to meet Dr. Manek Mody who is visiting her. Godmother and Slave sister keep on their incessant bickering and Dr. Mody offers to exorcise the demon which Godmother had said has taken a lodging in her sister. This comic relief is followed by Lenny's discovery that the Queen's statue is missing from the garden. She tells Godmother about having seen Ayah. She tries to avoid her questions and tells her that her mother had arranged for Ayah to be sent to her relatives. Lenny is shocked and fearful. Godmother also comments that they haven't seen the Ice-Candy-Man for a long time. Cousin tells her that Ayah has become a dancing girl and is residing in the Hira Mandi. With this knowledge she confronts her mother. But she can only bring herself to ask about the petrol cans in the car's dicky. Her mother tells her that they smuggle rationed petrol to help their Hindu and Sikh friends to run away. Lenny complains that she could have also trusted her, but loathes herself for having broken Ayah's trust.

Godmother informs Lenny that Ayah is in Lahore, has married, and her husband shall come to meet them that very day. Lenny finds out that the bridegroom is none else but the Ice-Candy-Man. He has become thinner, softer, droopier, his brash talk has been replaced by a canny silence. When Godmother criticizes him for living in the Hira Mandi, he loses some of his assurance and tells her that he himself is a bastard, a product of the Kotha. He also tells them that his family women cultivate singing and dancing skills and that his wife has now been accepted by his family. Godmother furiously scolds him for lifting the Ayah, for allowing her to be raped by butchers and drunks, for compelling her to behave like a performing monkey before other men. Ice-Candy-Man is shaken but Godmother is relentless in her attack. She points out that Ayah was lifted in February but the marriage took place in May, only when Lenny's mother had arranged to have her sent to Amritsar. Ice-Candy-Man is devastated; repentance, grief and shock are compressed into his face. The protected world of Lenny suddenly shatters and the emotional storm raging round her exposes her to the "demands of gratification—and the unscrupulous nature of desire." (252)

Chapter 30

Godmother plans to meet Ayah. Lenny wants to accompany her but she is evasive, saying that the children should not visit such places. Lenny insists that she wants to tell her Ayah that she is still a friend and does not think her bad just because she had been kidnapped. Egged on by Mini Aunty's protest, Godmother agrees to take Lenny with her. The silent alleys, closed shops, heavily made up girls with cropped and frizzed hair using the broad and comfortable gestures of men leave a strange oppressive impression on Lenny. The Ice-Candy-Man welcomes them in his home and fetches Ayah, whose name has now been changed to Mumtaz.

Ayah is bedecked in bridal finery—silk and gold has made her appearance charming but her eyes are so vacant that Lenny feels the soul has been extracted from her living body. Expressing her hatred for staying with the Ice-Candy-Man, Ayah tells

Godmother that, she wants to go to her family. Godmother tries to reason with her, asking her to bury the debris of the past, accept her marriage with the Ice-Candy-Man, and go on with the business of living. But Ayah reiterates that she wants to go to her family, even if they may not accept her. Ice-Candy-Man senses her resolve and pleads with Godmother to assure Ayah of her future happiness. Godmother is cold and unresponsive towards him. Lenny feels that if Ayah is haunted by her past and cannot forgive the monster who has killed her spirit, the Ice-Candy-Man is haunted by his macabre future which seems to be already stamped on his personality. Lenny tells her cousin about her visit to Ayah who disapproves it.

Chapter 31

This chapter introduces us to a new character Dr. Selzer, a German medical practitioner who has taken up the rooms vacated by the Shankars. Lenny's mother has taken the responsibility of promoting his medical practice. Over evening tea he is introduced to Mr. and Mrs. Phailbus, while a sudden commotion in the compound of "fallen women's jail" disturbs them. The Sikh guard is fiercely beating somebody. A crowd has gathered there, the servants also try to intervene and when the fighters are pulled away Lenny recognizes the frantic amber eyes of the Ice-Candy-Man. Beaten and crushed he skips away with his cronies. Lenny's mother is also outraged and furiously scolds the skipping men.

Ayah has been rescued from Hira Mandi with the help of Godmother. With her influence she was able to overcome the bureaucratic delay and rescue her with police help. The Ice-Candy-Man and his friends, despite following her in three galloping carts, could do nothing.

Chapter 32

After Ayah is kept in the rescued women's home, Ice-Candy-Man constantly patrols that road. All the residents including the Sikh guard become used to his presence and to his couplets. He has acquired the air of a fakir who has renounced the world for his beloved. He peacefully chases Ayah whenever, accompanied by the guard, she goes to Mr. Phailbus for homeopathic treatment. Each morning Lenny awakens to the fragrance of flowers flung over their garden wall at dawn by Ice-Candy-Man. The courtyard of the recovered women's camp is also strewn with petals and sometimes with cheap candy wrapped in cellophane. One morning Lenny misses the fragrance in the air. In consternation she rushes to the kitchen only to find out that Ayah has gone to her family in Amritsar, and the Ice-Candy-Man too has disappeared across the Wagah border into India.

Treatment of Partition in *Ice-Candy-Man*

RASHMI GAUR

Ice-Candy-Man describes the harrowing tale of Partition days when the lofty ideal of nationalism was suddenly bartered for communal thinking, resulting in unprecedented devastation, political absurdities and deranged social sensibilities. Sidhwa has sensitively portrayed the political anxiety and social insecurity which was shared by all the divided people during the Partition days. The days preceding the largest forced migration of population in human history, and the demographic dislocation it entailed, had their own complexities. People who have survived this holocaust, or witnessed it from a distance try to exorcise this past through memories. Imaginative and literary recreation helps people to recover "some of the lost density of life."[1] Perhaps this is the reason that prominent literary figures in India and Pakistan have constantly taken up themes related with Partition and try to replicate their memories in all details. Chaman Nahal's *Azadi*, Khushwant Singh's *Train to Pakistan*, Manohar Malgonkar's *A Bend in the Ganges*, B. Rajan's *The Dark Dancer*, Salman Rushdie's *Midnight Children* and Amitav Ghosh's *The Shadow Lines* are expressions of different sensitivities about Partition. However, *Ice-Candy-Man* is different from these works as it presents the turbulent upheaval of Partition from the viewpoint of a handicapped Parsi girl child. Stressing the vulnerability of human lives, and maintaining a fine balance between laughter and despair, Sidhwa presents various nuances and complexities related with a decision of political pragmatism through Lenny, a child narrator and chronicler. Lenny looks at characters belonging to different communities through the prism of her own Parsi sensitivity. Shorn of biases the child's narration also imparts an authentic credibility to the novel. Like most of the other novels, *Ice-Candy-Man* also presents the horrifying details of cruelty, human loss and dislocation, but it does so with a subtle irony, witty banter and parody, forcing the readers to desist from maudlinly sensitive reactions, and to concentrate more on the inscrutability of human behaviour. It also describes a society which has lost its courage, and therefore only crumbles away. It not only presents the barbaric details of atrocities perpetrated by one community over other, but also delineates various manifestations of pettiness and degenerated values which, like termite, had hollowed the inner structural strength of the society. *Ice-Candy-Man* narrates a society which has deflated chivalrous attitudes, encourages petty self-serving tendencies and indifferent tolerance of pogroms so long the self stays alive with a whole skin; a society which was given what it deserved—a sanguine and blood-curdling mindset, which made Partition of India a grim reality. The characters and events of the novel suggest that "vanity, hypocrisy and self-deception . . . somehow constitute a truer reality than altruism, self-sacrifice and heroism, even when these are known to have existed."[2] This reinterpretation, Andrew Rutherford argues, of historical and psychological reality by art involves an opposition not only between high and lower mimetic modes, but between the low mimetic and the ironic, highlighting what he terms as "a disbelief in the psychological probability of the ideal."[3]

Khushwant Singh in his review in *The Tribune* has commented that *Ice-Candy-Man* deserves to be ranked as amongst the most authentic and best on the Partition of India.[4] Githa Hariharan also comments in *Economic Times* that Sidhwa has captured "the turmoil of the times, with a brilliant combination of individual growing up pains and the collective anguish of a newly independent but divided country."[5] Seen through the prism of a marginalised minority girl-child, it focuses on the deteriorating communal climate in pre-Partition days. "Lenny's naivete, her privileged position, and her religious background lend her version of Partition a quality that other novels about this tempestuous period in Indo-Pakistani history lack."[6] Protected by her religious background and her parents' status, Lenny is not directly affected by the contumelious situation of Partition days, but she keenly observes and comments on the events happening around her. The tone of a reporter which she adopts for recording the events or commenting on them enhances the poignancy of the emotions which are linguistically underplayed. The hilarious tone of the Parsi's Jashan prayer, organized to celebrate the British victory in the Second World War is soon replaced first by the acrimonious bickering between Mr. Rogers and Mr. Singh, then by the vague fears and apprehensions unsettling Lenny's group, and later on by the details of murderous mob fury unleashing death and destruction over whoever comes across them. Lenny learns that India is going to be broken, and has many unanswered queries, "Can one break a country? And what happens if they break it where our house is? Or crack it further up on Warris Road? How will I ever get to Godmother's then?" (92) Ayah ventures that perhaps a canal will be dug to crack India (93). Though Lenny is baffled by such questions, she simultaneously becomes aware of religious differences. She worriedly remarks, "It is sudden. One day everybody is themselves—and the next day they are Hindu, Muslim, Sikh, Christian. People shrink, dwindling into symbols." (93) In a changed world which responds not to individuals but religious identities Lenny feels that the Parsis have been reduced to "irrelevant nomenclatures." (94) Her perception of people also changes and she becomes aware of religious symbols acting in, and moulding the individual lives—the tuft of bodhi hair rising like a tail from Hari's shaven head, Cousin's fresh crop of Sikh jokes, the subtle changes in the Queen's Garden, are presented with increasing regularity. Lenny's parents also acquire a strange black box containing, as we are told later, a gun. Their neighbours leave for safer places. Hari, the gardener, is circumcised and converted to Islam for protection, Moti, the sweeper, opts for Christianity, the masseur is killed grotesquely, the markets burn and living beings are torn asunder. The insensitivity of the social climate is highlighted and individual deeds of kindness and support eclipse out. The massacre of Pir Pindo narrated in the words of a young boy Ranna presents perhaps the vilest side of adult nature which continuously haunts the reader. Lenny senses the changing situation and is perturbed. Listening to the verbal parrying of Ayah's admirers she closes her eyes in frustration, "I close my eyes. I can't bear to open them, they will open on a suddenly changed world. I try to shut out the voices." (129)

The brutal realities of the Partition depicted in *Ice-Candy-Man* with a candour, do not overshadow the resilience of spirit exhibited by several characters in the novel. Rodabai, the God-mother arranges free education for Ranna, Lenny's mother and Electric-Aunt store petrol in order to facilitate the escape of their friends, Hamida is rehabilitated. Dormant possibilities of the re-surgence of human spirit can also be sensed in Ayah as, taking a bold decision, she determines to go back to her family. She rejects the constricting present and decisively wants to face future in all its tentative probabilities. The resilience of women characters saves the novel from being a heart-rending depressing rendition of journalistic reporting.

Ice-Candy-Man also includes several comments on contemporary political figures. Sidhwa has presented the Pakistani perspective regarding these figures and almost all the major contemporary Indian political figures are either caricatured or presented in an unfavourable manner. During her interview with David Montenegro, Sidhwa comments:

> The main motivation grew out of my reading of a good deal of literature on the Partition of India and Pakistan. . . . What has been written has been written by the British and the Indians. Naturally they reflect their bias. And they have, I felt after I'd researched the book, been unfair to the Pakistanis. As a writer, as a human being, one just does not tolerate injustice. I felt whatever little I could do to correct an injustice I would like to do, I have just let facts speak for themselves, and through my research I found out what the facts were.[7]

Gandhi's visit to Lahore is presented in such light as makes him "an improbable mixture of a demon and a clown." (87) Lenny recalls how he interminably talks about enema, personal hygiene and sluggish stomachs. Sidhwa portrays him as a politician, changing his stances to suit his needs. During the heated discussions among Ayah's admirers the butcher snortingly terms him as "That non-violent violence-monger—your precious Gandhi-jee." (91) In an attempt to soothe him the masseur says, "He's a politician yaar. It's his business to suit his tongue to the moment." (91) Lenny remembers him as a small, dark and shrivelled old man very much like their gardener Hari. (86) Sidhwa also criticizes the British designs, commenting that after obtaining their objective to divide India, they favoured Hindus over Muslims: "they [the British] favour Nehru over Jinnah, Nehru is Kashmiri, they grant him Kashmir. Spurning logic, defying rationale, ignoring the consequences of bequeathing a Muslim state to the Hindus." (159) She further says in derogatory terms, "Nehru wears red carnations in the button holes of his ivory jackets. He bandies words with Lady Mountbatten and is presumed to be her lover. . . . He is in the prime of his Brahmin manhood." (159) Similarly the Akalis, led by Master Tara Singh, are termed as "a bloody bunch of murdering fanatics." (63)

Sidhwa has also tried to redefine Jinnah's role in history. She feels that most of the Indian and British writers have dehumanized him, holding him responsible for the Partition.[8] While Nehru has been portrayed as a "sly one," Jinnah is lauded for his intellectual capabilities. The off duty sepoy remarks during one of the discussions held regularly at Queens Gardens, "Don't underestimate Jinnah. He will stick within his rights, no matter whom Nehru feeds! He's a first-rate lawyer and he knows how to attack the British with their own laws!" (131) Jinnah is portrayed with a sympathy not showed for any other political leader. He is depicted as "austere, driven, pukka-sahib accented, deathly ill, incapable of check kissing" (159), past the prime of his manhood, he is "sallow, whip-thin, sharp-tongued and uncompromising." (160) Sidhwa also quotes Sarojini Naidu to substantiate her portrayal of Jinnah. As the story unfolds, we are introduced not only to Jinnah, the political leader, but also to Jinnah, the lover of an eighteen year old, breathtakingly beautiful Parsi girl, who had braved the censure of her wealthy knighted father to marry a Muslim. Lenny feels sad on learning her premature death, but her sympathies clearly lie with Jinnah:

> But didn't Jinnah too, die of a broken heart? And today, forty years later, in films of Gandhi's and Mountbatten's lives, in books by British and Indian scholars, Jinnah, who for a decade was known as 'Ambassador of Hindu-Muslim Unity', is caricatured, and portrayed as a monster. (160)

The analysis of the political leadership during the Partition days by Sidhwa is subjective and at times seems even prejudiced. Despite it, the final message of the novel is clear and unambiguous. It rejects the two nation theory and suggests that religious, social and cultural differences are artificially created and exploited by unscrupulous people. She also suggests that power should be used for the good of the people and to suppress the evil. In her interview with Julie Rajan, she comments on the main theme of *Ice-Candy-Man:*

> I was just attempting to write the story of what religious hatred and violence can do to people and how close evil is to the nature of man. Under normal circumstances people can be quite ordinary and harmless; but once the mob mentality takes over, evil surfaces. Evil is very close to the surface of man.[9]

Ice-Candy-Man is criticized by some critics for misrepresenting historical facts. Sidhwa's description of Gandhiji's visit to Lahore can be quoted as an example. There is no historical record of Gandhi's visit to Lahore during the pre-Partition days. Similarly, the reference to the famous Dandi March by Col. Bharucha dates it in 1944, whereas it had actually taken place in the early months of 1930. The vivid description of the Sikh attack on the Muslim village of Pir Pindo is also historically inaccurate. Such inaccuracies are however fictionally justified as these events are imaginatively used to impart an easy continuity and flow to the narrative and communicate the author's point of view successfully.

The theme of horror accompanying the transfer of population in 1947 has been delineated by several authors in Indo-English fiction. In his essay "The Partition in Indo-English Fiction" Saros Cowasjee has commented on the characteristics of the Partition novels.[10] He says that most of the Partition novels written by Sikh authors portray a romance between a Sikh boy and a Muslim girl, strive for historical accuracy loading their fiction with documentary evidence gleaned from newspapers, government reports and G.D. Khosla's *Stern Reckoning: A Survey of the Events Leading upto and Following the Partition of India* (1949) and suggest that Sikh atrocities against the Muslims had taken place only in retaliation. Cowasjee has based his argument on a study of Raj Gill's *The Rape* (1974), H.S. Gill's *Ashes and Petals* (1978), Kartar Singh Duggal's *Twice Born Twice Dead* (1979) and Khushwant Singh's *Train to Pakistan* (1956). Manohar Malgonkar's *A Bend in the Ganges*, selected by E.M. Forster as the best novel of 1964, probes the Gandhian ideology of non-violence in relation to man's hidden capacity for violence. Chaman Nahal's *Azadi* (1975) propagates the theme of human kindness. Attia Hosain's *Sunlight on a Broken Column* (1961) has the distinction of being the only novel on Partition by a Muslim woman. It tells us of the effects of Partition not on those who were forced out of their homes, but on the members of a Muslim family who, far from the scene of action, struggle to keep their family from splitting up and argue over the priorities of different loyalties. Balchandra Rajan's *The Dark Dancer* is saturated with idealism and hope and concentrates on the basic nobility of human nature. In Hindi, Urdu and Bengali too, there are some brilliant novels on this theme—*Jhutha Sach* of Yashpal, *Tamas* of Bhisham Sahani, *Adha Gaon* of Rahi Masoom Raza, and *Epar Ganga, Opar Ganga* by Jyotirmoyee Devi, *The Skeleton* (1987) by Amrita Pritam can be mentioned as examples. *The Shadow Lines* by Amitav Ghosh and *What the Body Remembers* (1999) by Shauna Singh Baldwin are more recent attempts to grapple with the memories of Partition which, as Krishna Sobti has remarked, is difficult to forget but dangerous to remember.[11] Ghosh's novel traces the sources of communal violence. Ghosh effectively uses political allegory to stress the need for a syncretic civilization to avoid a communal holocaust. His novel is against artificial divisions and violence and is an affirmation of unity and enrichment of life.[12] Baldwin traces the oppression of men which the female body remembers with contrasting and constantly shifting viewpoints in her novel.[13]

Ice-Candy-Man stands apart in its rendering of the theme of Partition. Lenny reveals the trauma of Partition through her memories with a sprinkling of humour, parody and allegory, describing how friends and neighbours become helpless and ineffective while faced with the mob frenzy. Sidhwa also describes how political leaders manipulate the ideals and generate feelings of suspicion and distrust in the psyche of the common man. Once communal and obscurantist passions are aroused, the social fabric is torn asunder, leading to wanton and reckless destruction. Sidhwa has also commented on the historical inevitability of social process, suggesting that people who do not learn from history are condemned to repeat it. The tragic events combine with the witty freshness characterizing the narrator's attitude of a distanced watcher. The novel poignantly describes the mindless Partition violence and focuses on its socio-historical consequences to women. Moreover, "the craft of describing violent and humorous scenes alternatively and of freely mixing historical tragedy with witty comedy is not the result of a compromise but it rather displays a lively authenticity which very few novels can be credited with."[14] *Ice-Candy-Man* enables the readers to understand the extent of the trauma of Partition and review it in its historical context, and thus suggestively delineates the fruitlessness of violence in individual and collective lives.

NOTES

1. M. Asaduddin, "Against Forgetting: Memory as Metaphor in 'Dream Images'," *Translating Partition*, ed. Ravikant and Tarun K. Saint (New Delhi: Katha, 2001), p. 124.
2. Andrew Rutherford, *The Literature of War: Fine Studies in Heroic Virtue* (Hong Kong: Macmillan, 1978), p. 3.
3. *Ibid*, pp. 3-4.
4. http:// Members.aol.com/_ht_a/bsidhwa/crack_india_indian. Html? Mtbrand= AOL_US.
5. *Ibid.*

6. Robert L. Ross, "Cracking India: A Feminine View of Partition," *The Novels of Bapsi Sidhwa*, ed. R.K. Dhawan and Novy Kapadia (New Delhi: Prestige, 1996), p. 183.
7. David Montenegro, *Points of Departure—International Writers on Writing and Politics*, 1989, p.36.
8. *Ibid*, p. 50.
9. http:// member.aol.com
10. Saros Cowasjee, "The Partition in Indo-English Fiction," *Explorations in Modern Indo-English Fiction*, ed. R.K. Dhawan (New Delhi: Bahri, 1982), pp.18-29.
11. Urvashi Butalia, *The Other Side of Silence: Voices from the Partition of India* (New Delhi; Penguin, 1998), p. 357.
12. O.P. Mathur, "The Indian Ambience of Amitav Ghosh's *The Shadow Lines*," *Points of View*, Vol. VII, no. 1, Summer 2000, p. 55.
13. Mary Conde, "A Feminist View of Partition, Shauna Singh Baldwin's *What the Body Remembers*," *Atlantic Literary Review*, Vol. 2, no. 1, p. 62.
14. Pier Paolo Piciucco, "The Hidden Strength of Women: A Key to the Reading of Bapsi Sidhwa's *Ice-Candy-Man*, *Atlantic Literary Review*, Vol. 1, no. 1, p. 215.

Women Characters and the Feminist Perspective in *Ice-Candy-Man*

RASHMI GAUR

Ice-Candy-Man has strong women characters who want to forge their independent identity. In a patriarchal set-up which is essentially discriminatory against women and emphasizes on conditioning them for life-long and willing subjugation to men, the women of *Ice-Candy-Man* are not only conscious of their desires, but also eagerly assertive about their independent handling of situations. The male characters, despite the fact that they initiate almost all events of the novel, remain peripheral and apathetic, lacking the will to change and transcend their circumstances. The women characters "subtly but effectively subvert the ingrained elements of patriarchy, privileging female will, choice, strength along with the feminine qualities of compassion and motherhood."[1] *Ice-Candy-man* can undoubtedly be termed as a feminist novel—the traditional novel eulogizes the heroic qualities of men only, while in feminist narratives women acquire such attributes by their active involvement in and control of situational contexts. Lenny, the narrator in *Ice-Candy-Man* is also the centre of the novel, retaining her independent identity in diverse situations. Her attitude towards her nameless cousin significantly portrays the feminist need for assertive equality. At this point it shall be interesting to note that all women's writing may not be necessarily feminist. A piece of writing which justifies, propagates or perpetuates discrimination against women cannot be termed as feminist. Only that artistic work which sensitizes its readers to the practices of subjugation and opposes them can be treated as being feminist in nature. *Ice-Candy-Man* not only sketches and critically reviews the dehumanizing patriarchal norms engendering a discriminatory social climate, but also portrays the struggle against them, as well as the desire to manifest an assertive self-will on the part of its women characters.

Lenny, the child narrator of the novel, witnesses the barbaric cruelties of the Partition days, including the inhuman commodification of women. Yet what emerges as the dominant note/thematic motif in the novel is not the victimization of women, but their will and sustained effort to fight against it and overcome it. Most of the other Partition novels in English, as well as in other languages, have concentrated largely on the helplessness of women pitched against oppressive male forces. Chaman Nahal's *Azadi*, Khushwant Singh's *Train to Pakistan*, Manohar Malgonkar's *A Bend in the Ganges* in English, Jyotirmoyee Devi's *Epar Ganga, Opar Ganga* in Bangla, Yashpal's *Jhootha Sach* in Hindi, and the short stories of Saadat Hasan Manto and Kishan Chander in Urdu highlight the trauma women had to undergo during the catatonic times of Partition. Even the more contemporary authors have not been able to escape it. Amitav Ghosh in *The Shadow Lines* has talked about the national trauma of Partition using the device of the child narrator and taking the linear time narration. Shauna Singh Baldwin in *What the Body Remembers* talks about the mutilation of woman's body and its impact on the collective gender memory. Sidhwa on the other hand treats the theme of Partition with a clever juxtaposition of images and an underlying ironical humour without compromising with the innate independence of women.

Lenny is a handicapped girl representing a miniscule minority. She is also free from the effect of social conditioning most of the Indian girls have to undergo. She is a young, curious and vivacious child, eager to know what is happening around her and participating in it vigorously. The socio-religious divide creates in her an awareness of her own identity, but even prior to that she had become conscious of the creation of the gender, the socially accepted role of women and girls, and also of her burgeoning sexuality. She is aware that her "world is compressed." (1) This awareness is intensified when Col. Bharucha prophesies her future, "She'll marry, have children—lead a carefree, happy life. No need to strain her with studies and exams." (15) Lenny observes the gender-based relationship in the society and accepts it as a peripheral part of her experiences, without allowing it to colour her own individuality. She notices how in Col. Bharucha's clinic a woman has to discuss her child's health through her husband. (12) During her visit to Pir Pindo she notices how Khatija and Parveen, the adolescent sisters of Ranna, like the other girls in the village, already wear the responsible expressions of much older women "affecting the mannerisms of their mothers and aunts." (54) They are perplexed by Lenny's cropped hair and short dresses. These early impressions of Lenny, presented with multiple strains of irony, humour and wit exhibit her awareness of gender stereotypes. She perceives many differences in the personality traits and interests of men and women. However Lenny is neither influenced nor conditioned by her perception of gender based social stereotypes—that she assertively retains her interests is evident in her attitude towards her Ayah, Hamida and her cousin. When Godmother arranges a meeting with Ayah, Lenny insists on accompanying her. She feels that Ayah has been wronged and ashamed by her friends and she shares her humiliation. She wants to "comfort and kiss her ugly experiences away." (254) She does not think that sexual exploitation should remain a stigma for any woman, "I don't want her to think she's bad just because she's been kidnapped." (254) She also keeps Hamida's past a secret under the impression that if revealed her mother may sack her. Her sympathy bonds her to all the women characters in the novel.

Very early in the novel the reader notices Lenny's consciousness of her own burgeoning sexuality. Her open background and liberal upbringing make her receptive to her early sexual stirrings. She enjoys the admiring covetous glances Ayah receives from her admirers and displays traditional feminine smugness and coquetry. She vividly portrays Ice-Candy-Man's toes, Ayah's furtive glances towards Sharbat Khan and the Masseur's intimacy with Ayah. Her relationship with her cousin, allowing clandestine forages into physical intimacies, shows her mental independence. During their walks to the bazaars and gardens she irreverently points out boys and men to her cousin whom she finds attractive. She sums up her attitude neatly when she says, "Maybe I don't need to attract you. You're already attracted." (220) Cousin angrily complains to Godmother, "She loves approximately half of Lahore . . . why can't she love me?" (232)

Despite the pressures of socially constructed gender-roles and expectations the awakening of an individuality which is pulsatingly present in Lenny can be felt in other women characters too. Lenny's mother belongs to the privileged economic strata of the society. She can engage several servants to look after the children and other daily chores. She is kept busy with her social obligations—entertaining guests and partying exhaust her time. Lenny's physical handicap has generated a sense of guilt in her which often surfaces in her conversations. She says to Col. Bharucha, "It's my fault, I neglected her—left her to the care of Ayah." (16) Lenny admires her delicate beauty, but resents her "all-encompassing" motherliness. She is initially possessive about her mother but soon learns to cope with it. Her mother's voluptuous appeal generates a subtle jealousy too in her psyche:

> The motherliness of Mother. . . . How can I describe it? While it is there it is all-encompassing, voluptuous. Hurt, heartache and fear vanish. . . . The world is wonderful, wondrous—and I perfectly fit in it. But it switches off, this motherliness. . . .
>
> Mother's motherliness has a universal reach. Like her involuntary female magnetism it cannot be harnessed. . . . I resent this largess. As father does her unconscious and indiscriminate sex appeal. It is a prostitution of my concept of childhood rights and parental loyalties. She is my mother—flesh of my flesh—and Adi's. She must love only us! (42)

Lenny is given ample personal space by her mother. Though decisively controlling and channelizing her children's lives, she allows them to frolic around and view life from their own standpoints. Lenny is permitted to accompany Imam Din twice to a village Pir Pindo, her visits to parks and restaurants with Ayah are also unchecked. She is also able to effortlessly control the entourage of servants and run her household effortlessly. Despite her liberated handling of children and a modern life-style, she is very much a traditional wife, humouring constantly the wishes of her husband. She is almost servile in her attitude towards her husband, coquettishly appeasing him and trying to create an atmosphere of pleasant mirth around him. Lenny sceptically looks on when her mother chatters in saccharinely sweet tones to fill up the "infernal time of Father's mute meals." (80) Though Lenny is not able to decipher it, her remarks hint at the presence of an inner void in her mother's personality. Most of the women writers have hinted at the presence of an inner hollowness in the lives of women, which is often shielded by the deceptively beautiful screen of their social graces and obligations. For women like Mrs. Sethi, social elegance is not simply a pleasure, it is also a bondage, because herein they are forced to accept their role as female. The conversation during the party the Sethis organize for the Rogers and the Singhs explicitly suggests that it is a woman's erotic capacities, not her intellectual calibre, which is integrated with the life of society. Her driving sprees along with the Electric-Aunt to smuggle petrol in order to help their stranded Hindu and Sikh friends, and the rehabilitation of Hamida shows her humanitarian understanding of the situation, and also a desire to do something meaningful.

A major part of the novel's discussion is centred on Lenny's Ayah Shanta. She is a Hindu girl of eighteen and everything about her is also eighteen years old (3). Though she is employed with considerate masters, her condition is that of an unprotected girl whom everybody treats only as a sex object. Looking at Ayah, Lenny also becomes conscious of her sexuality:

> The covetous glances Ayah draws educate me. Up and down, they look at her. Stub ended twisted beggars and dusty old beggars on crutches drop their poses and stare at her with hard, alert eyes. Holy men, marked in piety, shove aside their pretences to ogle her with lust. Hawkers, cart-drivers, cooks, coolies and cyclists turn their heads as she passes, pushing my pram with the unconcern of the Hindu goddess she worships. (3)

While the sexuality of Lenny's mother lies beneath the veneer of sophistication and unfulfilled longings, Ayah's is transparent and self-serving. She is fully aware of her sexual charm and uses it without any inhibition to fulfill her desires. She has accumulated a good number of admirers who regularly assemble in the Victoria Garden—the Ice-Candy-Man, the Masseur, the Government House gardener, the restaurant owner, the zoo-attendant, and a knife-sharpening Pathan are her regular admirers. Lenny also learns to identify "human needs, frailties, cruelties and joys," (20) looking at these people during her outings:

> I learn also to detect the subtle exchange of signals and some of the complex rites by which Ayah's admirers co-exist. Dusting the grass from their clothes they slip away before dark, leaving the one luck, or the lady, favours. . . . I escape into daydreams in which my father turns loquacious and my mother playful. (19)

Ayah uses her charm to obtain easy gains—cheap doilies, cashew nuts, extra serving of food etc. She successfully uses her charm as a strategy of survival and manipulation till the violence of Partition destroys her familiar world. Her portrayal also represents the male exploitation of female sexuality. Ice-Candy-Man manages to kidnap her with the help of some hooligans and forces her into prostitution. Despite her conviction that she is now an impure person, she retains her will to go back to her family and face life anew. Her refusal to admit defeat despite physical and emotional mutilation and her determination to probe into future alternatives imparts a moral courage to her.

Godmother and Slave sister—Rodabai and Mini Aunty—are other major female characters in the novel who are presented with a sense of glee. The one-and-a-half-room abode of her godmother is termed as her haven by Lenny, her "refuge from the perplexing unrealities of my home on Warris Road." (1) She is also a surrogate mother for Lenny in a mutually fulfilling relationship. Her portrayal is presented to us by Lenny in a fascinated manner, as if she is an idolized entity. She is presented as an old lady, plainly attired in Khaddar sarees, covering herself from head to foot, possessing a penchant for sharp wit, accurate repartee and a profound understanding of human psyche.

She makes it her business to know everything about everybody (239), and tries to help people whenever she can. She donates blood, seeks admission to a boarding school for Ranna, traces the Ayah in Hira Mandi and manages to send her back to her people. She is a formidable person too and scolds the Ice-Candy-Man for disgracing the Ayah, "Oh? What kind of man? A royal pimp? What kind of man would allow his wife to dance like a performing monkey before other men? You're not a man, you're a low-born, two-bit evil little mouse!" (248) Despite Slavesister's protest she permits Lenny to accompany her to Ayah's place. She is also a sensitive person. When she realizes that Ayah, despite her marriage with Ice-Candy-Man, does not want to live with him, decisively sets about to rescue her. Pier Paolo Piciucco comments that the plot of the novel comes to a head because of the Godmother. Her visit to the Ayah has the trappings of a trial: she sits and acts as a judge[2]. Unlike other female figures of the novel Godmother has transcended her sexuality and emerges as an authoritative presence, able to achieve her desires. She incarnates the ideal of strength in female characters.

Godmother's attitude towards Mini Aunty, whom Sidhwa has very aptly termed as the Slave sister, draws the reader's attention for its incongruous eccentricity. In her dealing with people outside her immediate family circle she displays compassion and understanding, but her attitude towards her husband and her sister is shorn of such sentiments. She fully dominates her household in which her husband is only a peripheral presence. She is insensitive, churlish and cruel to her sister and constantly bosses over her. Her sister does all the household chores, while she only criticizes her nastily:

> If you think you have too much to cope with you can live someplace else. (244)
>
> Don't think I've not been observing your tongue of late! If you're not careful, I'll snip it off. . . . God knows, you've grown older—and fatter—but not up! This child here has more sense than you. (164)

Lenny adores her godmother as she fights her battles for her, though it cannot justify the Slave sister's exploitation.

Muccho, the sweepress, and her daughter Papoo are other female characters who can be mentioned here. Muccho takes Papoo as her rival and saddles her with all the household chores, beating and abusing her on slightest pretexts. Ayah and other servants constantly try to save the young child from this abuse but often their efforts are fruitless. Once she had to be admitted to hospital for two weeks as she had concussion as a result of her mother's severe beating. But despite this senseless maltreatment, Papoo cannot be browbeaten into submission. She is strong and high-spirited, but as Sidhwa suggests very early in the story, "There are subtler ways of breaking people." (47) Muccho arranges her marriage with a middle aged dwarf whose countenance betrays cruelty. Papoo is drugged with opium at the time of ceremony to suppress her revolt. Lenny curiously studies Muccho's face during the wedding ceremony and is startled to find a contented smile on her lips—"smug and vindicated." (188) The sketch of Muccho suggests that women themselves are unconsciously bound by their conditioning and saddle their daughters with a repetitive fate, treating marriage as a panacea of all ills.

The women characters of *Ice-Candy-Man* draw our attention to the facts of victimization of women and their compulsions to define their lives according to the pre-fixed gender roles. They also expose the patriarchal biases present in the archetypal social perceptions. Lenny, the child protagonist, recognizes these social patterns and exhibits the vivacity to transcend them. She also records the multi-faceted trauma women had faced during the unsettling and devastating days of Partition. The narration of the story by a girl-child ensures that the surrounding world would be seen through a feminine eye. The novel presents women as a "twice oppressed category on stage: firstly, as human beings suffocated by violence and secondly, as women burdened by the bond and impositions of a patriarchal society."[3]

NOTES

1. Subhash Chandra, "*Ice-Candy-Man:* A Feminist Perspective," *The Novels of Bapsi Sidhwa*, ed. R.K. Dhawan and Novy Kapadia (New Delhi: Prestige, 1996), p. 177.
2. Pier Paolo Piciucco, "The Hidden Strength of Women: A Key to the Reading of Bapsi Sidhwa's *Ice-Candy-Man*," *The Atlantic Literary Review*, Vol. 1, no. 1, p. 214.
3. *Ibid*, pp. 208-09.

Parsi Perspective in *Ice-Candy-Man*

RASHMI GAUR

In the novels of Bapsi Sidhwa the Parsi community is a constantly living presence, treated as a source of deep pleasure and linked with her protagonists' desire to live through their life and experience it fully. The relationship of her characters with their community is complex and continuous, moulding their perceptions and holding a peculiar value in their lives. The presentation and analysis of this relationship imparts an evocative sensitivity and a definite pattern to Sidhwa's novels. Community as an identity is centrally focused in the narratives of many immigrant writers and writers from minority communities. Authors like Firdaus Kaŋga in *Trying to Grow* (1990), Farrukh Dhondy in *Bombay Duck* (1990), and Rohinton Mistry in *Tales from Ferozeshah Baug* and *Such a Long Journey* (1991) have presented different shades of Parsi patois, exhibiting "consciousness of their community in such a way that the community emerges as a protagonist from their works, though on the surface these works deal with their human protagonists. By centralizing their community in their narratives they centralize and preserve and protect themselves, and thus use it as a psychological crutch."[1]

The Parsi people are said to be the descendants of the Aryan tribes which migrated from the Pamirs of Central Turkistan to West Asia, particularly Iran. The word Parsi is an ethnic term, which means a native of Fars, an ancient Persian province, now in Southern Iran. The religion they follow is known as Zoroastrianism which was founded around 2000 B.C. Their religion is based on the teachings of Zoroaster. Their religious texts are collectively known as the *Avesta.* Their religion is quintessentially preserved in five *gathas* or divine songs, which are basically the dialogues of Zarathushtra, the Prophet, with God and reveal the essentially ethical nature of his gospel. The Parsis were forced to leave their homeland about 1,200 years ago to save their religion from being Islamized by the invading Arabs.

To understand the paradoxes and identity crises of the Parsi community, which have been so aptly reflected in Sidhwa's novels, an acquaintance with the history of this community is essential. Hunted out of their homeland in eighth century A.D., the Parsis first arrived at the port of Din. After their stay here for about 19 years, they set sail towards the South and landed at the port of Sanjan in Gujarat around 785 A.D. which was then ruled by King Jadhav Rana, a liberal monarch. He gave them refuge with certain stipulations, enjoining on them the adoption of Gujarati language, veneration of cow and forbidding any attempt at conversions to their religion. These stipulations were always respected by Parsis, reflecting their characteristic spirit of adaptability which enabled them to prosper in a country of diverse religious practices.

Ironically these very conditions which encouraged resilience and adaptability in the Parsi community, also generated a sense of alienation and ambivalence in the Parsi youth in the beginning of the twentieth century. The Parsis had prudently decided to follow the rules and customs of the ruling classes of the country in order to avoid the possibility of any controversy. They were the first people to encourage English language and English ways under the British Raj and became the most westernized Indian community. They were baffled and flabbergasted when the Raj started to disintegrate. In India and Pakistan they had to cope with the hegemonic forces of the dominant community and feared that as a community they may lose significance after Independence. Such fears, coupled with the difficult choice between retaining loyalty to the British and pragmatic demands of aligning with the freedom movement, created a feeling of deep-rooted insecurity among them. *Ice-Candy-Man* delineates this dilemma with sensitivity, irony, and witticism.

Sidhwa has captured the turmoil of the Partition days from a Parsi perspective in *Ice-Candy-Man*. Much has been written on this theme by British, Indian and Pakistani authors, who were seldom able to transcend the subjectivity associated with their experiences. Sidhwa narrates the story through Lenny, an eight year old Polio struck Parsi child. A child possesses no biases at all. Lenny is young enough to retain her perceptual independence and pass on events to the readers without looking at them through any religious prism. Without siding with any warring community she expresses the paradoxical Parsi situation during the pre-Partition days. The first glimpses of the Parsi insecurity can be found in the Jashan prayer which is held at Lahore to celebrate the British victory in the Second World War. Sidhwa turns Parsi history into art by her clever use of irony. The Parsis were never a power factor in the subcontinent and realized that they can practice their religion and prosper only when they remain loyal to the ruling people. This basic attitude has been carefully explored by Sidhwa in almost all her novels. In *The Crow Eaters* sycophancy is shown as a need to exist. In *An American Brat* the dissatisfaction against the constricting social changes is discussed in hushed-up tones within the family only. In *Ice-Candy-Man* the Sethis, Lenny's parents, regularly hold parties for the British Superintendent of Police. The peaceful routine of maintaining pleasant terms with the rulers is jeopardized with the beginning of the Nationalist movement. The Parsis are confused as to which side shall ultimately emerge as the ruler. Col. Bharucha, the domineering President of the 'Parsee Anjuman' and a medical practitioner, hopes that "no Lahore Parsee will be stupid enough to court trouble." (36-37) Silencing the acrimonious debate he rhetorically remarks, "No one knows which way the wind will blow. . . . There may be not one but two—or even three—new nations! And the Parsees might find themselves championing the wrong side if they don't look before they leap!" (37) People are doubtful as they do not trust other religious communities. A person impatiently asks: "Does it matter where they look or where they leap? . . . If we're stuck with the Hindus they'll swipe our businesses from under our noses and sell our grandfathers in the bargain: if we're stuck with the Muslims they'll convert us by the sword! And God help us if we're stuck with the Sikhs!" (37) Col. Bharucha reminds them that their community has never fought back. Referring to the original migration he advises his people to remain neutral, "Let whoever wishes rule! Hindu, Muslim, Sikh, Christian! We will abide by the rules of their land." (39) Col. Bharucha feels that the movement for Home Rule is a power struggle in which the majority communities shall be the gainers. He thinks that the agitators are opportunists who are sure of the resultant political glory (36). He advises maintenance of status quo and perpetuation of the old attitudes. The neutral narrative voice of Lenny represents the collective sub-conscious of the Parsi people and is rooted in the racial psychology of her people.[2]

Beneath the gloss of good-natured repartee, raucous laughter and humorous banter of *Ice-Candy-Man* readers can feel the pulsating presence of fearful apprehensions about future, and a sense of foreboding. Sidhwa's treatment of the collective sense of insecurity in her community during the Partition days can be compared to Laura Roychowdhury's depiction of the plight of the Anglo-Indians in *The Jadu House* (2000). Laura depicts the distrust the Anglo-Indians possess about the prevalent system and depicts their desperate search for self-identity. Mr. Vanjo and his daughters Maris and Marice, Carol, Gary and many others are forced to spend their lives in a society to which they do not belong—forced by circumstances they have become prisoners of a land they are unable to escape. The Parsis living in Lahore during pre-Partition days similarly feel that escape is impossible and they are captives of the time.

The patterns of communal amity which have always been present in the Indian social fabric were torn asunder in the holocaust of Partition. As communal tensions increase Parsis become more conscious not only of their identity, but also of their neutrality. This change is conveyed to the reader through Lenny's narrative. She feels that the verbal skirmishes among the Ayah's admirers gradually take up communal overtones. As the British prepare to leave, they change their habitual meeting place—instead of assembling near the Queen's statue in the park they now assemble at the wrestler's restaurant. Being a Hindu the Government house gardener insists that Lahore will stay in India as it has too much Hindu money, while the Masseur and the Butcher coarsely insist that owing to a Muslim majority it shall go to Pakistan. The Sikh zoo attendant Sher Singh also argues the case of the Sikh peasants. Troubled at this change Lenny remarks, "I close my eyes. I can't bear to open them: they will open on a suddenly changed world. I try to shut out the voices." (129) The wrestler's predictions of a bloody aftermath massacre of people startle not only Lenny, but all others too in an uneasy silence. His comments that history will repeat itself and once the line of division is drawn in the Punjab, all Muslims to the east of it will have their balls cut off (130) have the impact of an explosion, they are shocked into a silence "as in the aftermath of a blast, the silence excludes all extraneous sound." (130) The Masseur tries to smooth out the differences, but acrimony remains. The Ayah comments that the Britishers shall "crack India with a long, long canal (93), but the common masses are unable to foresee the extent of devastating havoc to be unleashed by the Partition of the Indian sub-continent. She was a common passion among men belonging to different communities, but as the history relentlessly rolls ahead, she also becomes a representative of her religion. Lenny remarks:

> It is sudden, one day everybody is themselves—and the next day they are Hindu, Muslim, Sikh, Christian. People shrink, dwindling into symbols. Ayah is no longer just my all-encompassing Ayah—she is also a token. A Hindu, carried away by a renewed devotional fervour she expends a small fortune in joss-sticks, flowers and sweets on the gods and goddesses in the temples. (93)

Imam Din and Yousaf also turn into religious zealots, taking Friday afternoons off for the Jumha prayers. Lenny sees through the hearts and minds of the people, "but their exteriors superimpose a new set of distracting impressions." (94) The names of Gandhi, Jinnah, Nehru, Iqbal, Tara Singh, Mountbatten do not simply remain names for Lenny, they become representative symbols of various sects. People are defined by the narrow religious slots they have been rammed into. Lenny is perceptive enough to feel that people do not mix-up freely anymore in public, they hold subdued hushed up discussions in groups. The aloofness of the Parsis is indicated by the ridiculing tone Sidhwa has introduced in her narrative. Lenny's bantering tone and light-hearted responses to the increasing communal rift represent her understanding of the marginalized status of the Parsis. She remembers how her cousin erupts with a horde of Sikh jokes and wonders whether there are "Hindu, Muslim, Parsee, and Christian jokes." (95) In these times of religious identities the Parsis are reduced into "irrelevant nomenclatures." (94) Sidhwa also suggests that the political leadership was also responsible for fomenting communal distrust. The Inspector General Rogers feels so when he mildly chastises Mr. Singh about his advocacy of the Home Rule during the dinner party, "you think you'll be up to it." (61) Later on he accuses Congress leaders for blowing away the chances of undivided India by rejecting Lord Wavell's suggestions. This concern is shared by Sharbat Khan also. When Ayah casually remarks that leaders like Jinnah, Nehru and Patel are not fighting the common man's fight he thoughtfully says, "but they are stirring up trouble for us all." (76)

The divide between the majority communities can be clearly discerned in Lenny's visits to Pir Pindo, a Muslim village thirty miles east of Lahore. During her first visit, the Sikhs and the Muslims pledge their lives for each other and convey their pride over their unity. Muslims of Pir Pindo and Sikhs from Dera Tek Singh, a neighbouring village, sit together to discuss the violence pervading in the cities, but feel that it shall not affect the villages. The Sikh priest, Jagjeet Singh, who is highly respected by all the villagers, says, "Brother, our villages come from the same racial stock. Muslim or Sikh, we are basically Jats. We are brothers. How can we fight each other?" (56) However during her second visit to Pir Pindo Lenny feels that the communal tensions have destroyed the normalcy of life. The presence of the blue tubaned Akalis can be felt as signals of the impending disaster. Lenny accompanies members of Imam Din's family to the Baisakhi fare being held in Dera Tek Singh. Amidst the gaiety of the festival even Ranna, a child roughly of Lenny's age, becomes conscious of an oppressive suspicion and fear:

> And despite the gaiety and distractions, Ranna senses the chill spread by the presence of strangers: their unexpected faces harsh and cold. A Sikh youth whom Ranna has met a few times, and who has always been kind, pretends not to notice Ranna. Other men, who would normally smile at Ranna, slide their eyes past. Little by little, without his being aware of it, his smile becomes strained and his laughter, strident. "What's the matter? I ask him, "Nothing," he says, surprised. (106)

When the grown up people approach Jagjeet Singh, the Sikh priest, he admits his helplessness and warns them to be on their guard as the Akalis are planning to drive the Muslims out of East Punjab (107). Mutual friendship and harmony between communities has been replaced by fear, doubts and suspicions.

These changes also affect the Parsi neutrality. The worsening situation and rising communal discord forces them to shun passive neutrality and work actively, though surreptitiously, to help their friends and acquaintances. The compromises with their neutral stand are solely guided by humane considerations. Lenny's mother and Electric-Aunt smuggle the rationed petrol to help their Hindu and Sikh friends to run away, and also for the convoys to send kidnapped women to their families across the border (242). Lenny's mother also employs Hamida, a woman who had been kidnapped, rescued and later on spurned by her family, as Lenny's new Ayah to rehabilitate her. Lenny's Godmother Rodabai, who has "access to many ears," also arranges Ranna's education in a boarding house after he had been orphaned (211). The social commitment and willingness to help the needy is best perceived in Godmother's rescue of Ayah. Ayah was kidnapped by some rogues led by Ice-Candy-Man. She is forced to become a dancing girl. Later on Ice-Candy-Man marries her, converting her to Islam and re-christening her as Mumtaz. Godmother traces Ice-Candy-Man and in her cold rage reduces him to a state of bafflement, calling him a "shameless badmash! Nimakharam! Faithless" and the "son of pigs and pimps." (248-49) When she finds out that Ayah does not want to stay with the Ice-Candy-Man, she rescues her, sends her to the Recovered Women's Camp and then helps her to return to her relatives in Amritsar. Godmother's deft handling of the situation is an example of the humane acts performed by Parsis during the stormy days of Partition. It also shows that the Parsis, though not directly targeted at by any fanatic group, could not remain passive spectators of the rampant violence and chaotic mayhem surrounding them and thus chose an active neutral role for themselves, helping the needy and the destitute, without compromising their situation.

Thus we see that *Ice-Candy-Man* aptly projects the Parsi perception of reality during the troubled times of the pre-Partition days. The threats and insecurities which forced the Parsis to opt for neutrality and the historical background of this choice are very vividly presented in the novel. The factors which later on compelled this community to provide humanitarian relief to the suffering people are also sensitively delineated. The novel beautifully chronicles the changing attitude of the Parsi community during Partition.

NOTES

1. Avadhesh Kumar Singh, "The Sense of Community in the Parsi Novels," *Literary Criterion*, Vol. 32, No. 3, 1996, pp. 28-29.
2. Jagdev Singh, "*Ice-Candy-Man*: A Parsi Perception on the Partition of India," *The Novels of Bapsi Sidhwa*.

The Child Narrator in *Ice-Candy Man*

RASHMI GAUR

Ice-Candy-Man is Sidhwa's most famous and serious novel till now, possessing several layers of connotative and enigmatic interpretations. Critics have vociferously commented on the political, allegorical, social and feminist interpretations of the narrative. The novel was published as *Cracking India* by Sidhwa's American publishers Milkweed Editions in 1991, though there were no textual changes. The changed title suggests a different perspective to the reader about the dominant theme of the novel. It focuses on the collective political reality of the Partition of Indian sub-continent, while the earlier title *Ice-Candy-Man*, which has been retained for Indian editions, suggests a metonymic or even character-oriented interpretation. *Ice-Candy-Man*, the third novel of Bapsi Sidhwa, is the only novel in which she has used a child narrator. Whatever perspective is suggested initially to the reader by the title, the poignancy of emotional trauma and the sense of entrapment in the current situation is enhanced by the fact that the narrative is presented by a child. Negation of fruition to individual lives gains a suggestive urgency when it is reported by a child.

The figure of a child again simultaneously represents several marginalised identities generating a suggestive ambivalence. Lenny, the eight-year-old narrator of the novel is a polio-stricken girl belonging to a miniscule Parsi community. Lenny narrates the incidents and the characters of the novel to the readers, commenting and ruminating on various issues, also deftly camouflaging the writer's omnipresence. Anita Desai has compared Lenny with Oscar of Gunter Grass's *Tin Drum*.[1] The physical disability of both these characters isolates them and gives an obliquity to their perspective which gradually develops into a criticism of the supposedly rational maturity of the adult world, exposing the abnormality of its behavioural norms. Lenny's keen observation presents the traumatic upheavals of a world in which the older values are suddenly crumbling and the new ethos is yet to take a final shape. The simplicity and straightforwardness of Lenny's perception at moments reminds us of Nellie, the child-heroine of Dostoevsky's *The Insulted and the Humiliated*, on account of her sensitive understanding of human emotions and motives. As in Dostoevsky, the monstrosities of the adult world become transparent to the reader in their horrifying details in Sidhwa's novel also when contrasted with Lenny's naïve logic.

Several books have been written about the growing up process of boys. Twain's twin novels *The Adventures of Tom Sawyer* and *Huckleberry Finn* are perhaps the best examples of this genre in which the young protagonists gradually come to an understanding of themselves and their country. R.K. Narayan's *Swami and Friends* is another example in which a boy gradually develops an understanding of the self within a wider socio-political context. The use of a girl-child as a narrator of a story to understand and capture the horrifying details of a turbulent history is unique in itself. Told in the present tense and first person through an eight year old girl, the novel beautifully captures the human struggle of the Partition days, though simultaneously the device seems to put some constraints on the novelist. Lenny tells us in the very beginning of the novel: "My world is compressed." This self-imposed and culturally constructed limitation is successfully overcome by Lenny as she naively presents her comments on human relationships and their inscrutability against the backdrop of an unfolding history. With a child's wonder she observes social and demagogic changes, and interesting side-lights, occasionally indulging in judgement making. Her childish innocence enhances the sharpness of the irony and lays bare the devastating cruelty of a patriarchal order. Keeping a balance between despair and laughter, Sidhwa is also able to present the tragic holocaust of Partition without criticism, morbidity or pedantic preaching, with the help of the device of the child narrator. *Ice-Candy-Man* has a beautifully combined gripping Dickensian story with a postmodernist narrative experimentation. "Like Rudyard Kipling's Kim or the fourteen-year old narrator in Doris Lessing's story "The Old Chief Mshlanga," Lenny's growing up is marked as much by a loss of political and racial egalitarianism as by her developing sexuality."[2] Lenny is also compared to the persona that Chaucer adopts in his Prologue to *The Canterbury Tales*, rendering credibility by being almost a part of the reader's consciousness.[3]

Ice-Candy-Man is often termed as a bildungsroman. The term means a novel which follows the development of the protagonist from childhood or adolescence into adulthood through a troubled quest for identity. Lenny's quest is also autobiographical as there are many palpable commonalities she shares with the author. In her interview with Julie Rajan, Sidhwa admits that her life as a child in Pakistan was very much like Lenny's life in *Ice-Candy-Man*.[4] Like Lenny she also had polio and spent a lot of time with servants. She also had a number of operations, and wasn't sent to school. She read voraciously to engage herself. When she was growing up in Lahore it was a city of five million with only 200 Parsis. The Parsis easily adopted the mores of the dominant society which made Sidhwa comfortable—like Lenny—with a whole medley of identities. The persona of a child enables Sidhwa to narrate her impressions freely, ask questions which grown up people avoid, and also to exercise a close watch over the narration itself. Since many details of the novel match the details of Sidhwa's life, it was easier for her to present her general convictions about individuals and their various relationships through the child narrator, and still control the narrative somehow, retaining thick encrustations of interpretation.

Lenny does not simply "inform" the reader of happenings. She questions happenings, people, motives and emotions in order to grasp their fullest interpretation. The naivete of the child permits her to look at things from unconventional angles. She lacks prejudices—the hatred and biases one learns as one grows up. Her innocence gives her the strength to raise doubts and ask questions which cannot be comfortably answered by any grown-up, and also to reach at conclusions intuitively. "What's a fallen woman," she asks her godmother. She also tells her godmother that her Ayah has "nothing to be ashamed of." (253) Rather it is her friends who have irrevocably shamed her and she cannot be "bad" just because she's been kidnapped (253-54). Troubled by the surrounding communal frenzy she sometimes lapses into rhetoric postures also, asking in a grown up voice, "What is God?" (94) Such postures convince us that the narrator's voice is controlled and guided by the author.

Through Lenny's narrative Sidhwa has raised some gender related issues too. Her impressionable young mind receives several images of man-woman relationships which lead her to question status quo. She notices how in Col. Bharucha's clinic a woman has to discuss her child's illness through her husband, as any direct conversation between genders was looked down upon by the society. During visits to Pir Pindo she meets young girls of roughly her age who have already unquestioningly accepted their socially designated gender roles. Ranna's sisters Khatija and Parveen wear the responsible expressions of much older women and affect the mannerisms of their mother and aunts. (54) Being a young child she herself is not influenced by such stereotypes, but her neutral reporting sensitizes the reader to the extent to which they have seeped into the collective social thinking. Ayah's raw sexuality, her manipulation of it for small gains, and ultimately its destruction by force, awaken profound responses in Lenny and she lays bare the gender-based structure of contemporary India. Lenny also records how her mother, despite her modern life-style, is very much a traditional wife, almost servile in her desires to please her husband. Lenny also becomes a party to her games of coquettishly creating an atmosphere of pleasant mirth whenever her father is at home. However, the victimization of girls/women is not limited to man-woman relationship only. The novel also exposes the extent of gender conditioning through the description of Papoos', the Sweeper's daughter's, marriage to a middle-aged dwarf. Her mother Muccho, not only passes on several of her household chores to her, but also maltreats her, sometimes even inflicting serious injuries to her. Her marriage to a leering middle-aged dwarf and Muccho's smug satisfaction underscore "grotesque possibilities awaiting Papoo," (187) which had been perpetrated by her own mother. Lenny's shock at Papoo's marriage is an oblique though profound criticism of the prevalent gender bias. It also suggests that women themselves unconsciously perpetuate victimization of their own daughters, saddling them with a repetitive fate and treating marriage as a panacea of all ills.

The child's voice also generates a tone of authentic documentation of the Partition horrors. The innocence of her childhood days is suddenly snatched from her when she witnesses the fissiparous tendencies on the rise, the growing communal hatred and open gestures of arson and violence. Her familiar compressed surroundings suddenly distort into a topsy-turvy world in which values and allegiances shift suddenly. Lenny listens to the warnings of Sharbat Khan (76), watches an emaciated person being torn into two pieces by jeeps (135) looks on as the Shalmi market burns (137), notes Hari's conversion to Islam, his adopting a new name and a new dress code (162), and listens in snatches to the harrowing experiences of Ranna (195-208). She is also a witness to the betrayal of Ice-Candy-Man. These experiences compel her to define her own position in the society, forcing her to recognize and adapt to her own marginality. She becomes aware of her religious and gender related identities—her consciousness of these multiple layers of existence becomes her initiation into maturity.

The narrative technique in *Ice-Candy-Man* also helps us to understand the political irony of the situation. Like a wide-eyed child Lenny comes to know about the statements of various political leaders. The Government House Gardener and Ice-Candy-Man jibe about Nehru, Gandhi, Jinnah and Tara Singh. Their opinions and repartee enable Lenny to grasp the remoteness of political issues from the lives of common people. She concurs with Ayah's statement that the political leaders do not fight for masses, "What's it to us if Jinnah, Nehru and Patel fight? They are not fighting our fight." (75) When the butcher contemptuously slanders Gandhi as "that non-violent violence monger—your precious Gandhijee," (91) the Masseur tries to placate him, ur precious Gandhijee," (91) the Masseur tries to placate him, commenting that "he's a politician, yaar." (91) Lenny also notices the changing nature of jokes and is startled to find that suddenly there are "Hindu, Muslim, Parsee, and Christian jokes." (95) The stirrings of vague fears and apprehensions which Lenny feels at such moments convey the political reality of contemporary India.

Protected by her religious background and her family status, Lenny is not directly affected by the growing cruelty of these times. She remains on the periphery, watching the events unfold and commenting on them in a reporter's tone. Coupled with the innocence of a child's viewpoint, her detached tone enhances the poignancy of the emotions which are linguistically underplayed. Like any other child she is also flabbergasted at many details, "Can one break a country? And what happens if they break it where our house is? Or crack it further upon on Warris Road? How will I ever get to Godmother's then?" (92) The device of the child narrator enables Sidhwa to reveal the trauma of Partition, with a sprinkling of humour and allegory, and without any histrionics.

Thus the device of the child narrator has been very successfully used by Sidhwa in *Ice-Candy-Man*. The use of a girl-child as a narrator in the novel enables her to simultaneously present a critique of several issues from multiple angles. Lenny's narrative voice is not unidirectional, the very ambivalence of her narration enriches the readers' understanding of the presence of multilayered meanings in the text.

NOTES

1. Introduction to *The Novels of Bapsi Sidhwa*, ed. R.K. Dhawan and Novy Kapadia (New Delhi: Prestige, 1996), p. 19.
2. *Ibid.*, p. 20.
3. *Loc. cit.*
4. http://www.monsoonmag. com/interviews/ i3inter_sidhwa.html.

Communal Frenzy and Partition: Bapsi Sidhwa, Attia Hosain and Amitav Ghosh

NOVY KAPADIA

The article discusses the fictional representation of Partition as depicted in the works of three major novelists—Bapsi Sidhwa, Attia Hosain and Amitav Ghosh. Kapadia's exploration of the theme shows how these novelists deal with the horrors of Partition, aroused by suspicions, distrust and rumour. He also underscores how by using humour, parody, allegory and other stylistic devices, they are able to focus on how the dangers of compromising with religious obscurantism affect the historical processes, and how the communal frenzy is invariably contemporaneous despite being located in different time-zones.

Editor

Throughout history, fanatics as well as ideologues, pushed to the emotional brink of daring their lives, have taken the plunge, which has triggered off a chain reaction of rigid mental fixations and attitudes. Bapsi Sidhwa's novel *Ice-Candy-Man* examines the inexorable logic of Partition as an offshoot of fundamentalism sparked by hardening communal attitudes. First published in 1988 in London, this novel is set in pre-Partition India in Lahore. It belongs to the genre of the Partition novel like Manohar Malgonkar's *A Bend in the Ganges* (1964), Chaman Nahal's *Azadi* (1975), and Khushwant Singh's *Train to Pakistan* (1956). However in Indian-English fiction it is the second novel on Partition by a woman author. The other novel is *Sunlight on a Broken Column* (1961) by Attia Hosain. Both these sensitive women writers share similar perspectives on the calamities of Partition. The denouement of both novels is quite similar. Both stress a similar vulnerability of human understanding and life, caused by the throes of Partition which relentlessly divided friends, families, lovers and neighbours.

Ice-Candy-Man is a novel of upheaval which includes a cast of characters from all communities. There are Hindus, Muslims, Christians, Sikhs and Parsis, so a multiple perspective of Partition emerges as viewed by all the affected communities. Bapsi Sidhwa uses a narrator to tell the tale. A precocious Parsi girl, eight years old with a handicapped foot, narrates the story of her changing world with sophistication and wonder. Lenny is like the persona that Chaucer adopts in his Prologue to *The Canterbury Tales*, rendering credibility by being almost a part of the reader's consciousness. With the wonder of a child, she observes social change and human behaviour, noting interesting sidelights, seeking and listening to opinions and occasionally making judgements. Her childish innocence is like the seeming naive display of Chaucer's persona, a source of sharp irony. The device of the child narrator enables Bapsi Sidhwa treat a historical moment as horrifying as Partition without morbidity, pedanticism or censure. The highlight of the novel is that the author throughout maintains a masterful balance between laughter and despair. The subtle irony and deft usage of language creates humour which does not shroud but raucously highlights the traumas of Partition. Sensitively the author shows the human toll of Partition, when a concerned Lenny asks: "Can one break a country? And what happens if they break it where our house is?" (92)

The Parsi paradox of whether to support "Swaraj" or to maintain their loyalty to the British Raj is also humorously delineated. A piquant touch is given to this dilemma. With the impending news of Independence, the paranoid feelings of the Parsis, a minuscule minority, get accentuated. The Parsis in Lahore at a special meeting at their temple hall in Warris Road, have an acrimonious debate on the political situation. The meeting is interesting as it expresses the insecurity of the Parsis not because of communal antagonism, but the apprehension of their status at the departure of the British. Already the unstinted loyalty to the colonial power is declining. Col. Bharucha and Lenny's father blame the British for bringing polio to India. So at the meeting, India's smallest minority tries to redefine their strategy which

Col. Bharucha claims as "We must hunt with the hounds and run with the hare." (16)

The ambivalent attitude of the Parsis towards Partition and Independence emerged at the main-hall meeting at the Fire-Temple. Col. Bharucha, the President of the community in Lahore, advocates status quo. He warns fellow-Parsis to shun the anti-colonial movement and nationalist agitation spearheaded by Mahatma Gandhi. His reasoning is based on expediency. If there is "Home Rule," political glory, fame and fortune will be acquired by the two major communities, Hindus and Muslims. He considers Home Rule as a power struggle, saying "Hindus, Muslims and even the Sikhs are going to jockey for power and if you jokers jump into the middle you'll be mangled into chutney!" (36) He also advocates caution, because of the Parsis's long-standing attitudes of loyalty to the British. This attitude stemmed from the Zoroastrian religious belief of loyalty to a ruler and a close relationship between state and community. The other cause for loyalty to the British was purely economic. The Parsis primarily traced their secured status as a prosperous minority to British rule, identified as the "good government" of the African prayer. So loyalty was a self-evident precept to the Parsis. Thus Col. Bharucha does not want any Parsi of Lahore to offend British sensibilities by espousing nationalist causes. In a tone of admonition he says, "I hope no Lahore Parsi will be stupid enough to court trouble—I strongly advise all of you to stay at home—and out of trouble." (37)[2]

In her first novel *The Crow Eaters* (1978), Bapsi Sidhwa portrayed the dying businessman Faredoon Junglewalla vehemently protesting against the nationalist movement and exhorting his offspring to remain loyal to the British Empire. Col. Bharucha has a somewhat similar attitude. However with Independence imminent and Partition inevitable, there is a subtle change in the attitude of the Parsis of Lahore. The patriarchal advice of Col. Bharucha is opposed. Dr. Mody promptly poses a plea for involvement in the freedom struggle. He says, "our neighbours will think we are betraying them and siding with the English." (37) The banker Mr. Toddywalla says that the Parsis should support the Indian community which appears to be in a dominant position or will acquire political power after Independence. So he asks the assembled congregation to formulate attitudes and actions on Independence based on self-interest. Finally the assembled Parsis resolve to remain in Lahore and abide by the rules of the land. Wafting in self-esteem they agree to Col. Bharucha's suggestion, "Let whoever wishes rule! Hindu, Muslim, Sikh, Christian. We will abide by the rules of the land." (39)

Some Parsis in the congregation express apprehension about remaining in Lahore after Independence and wish to migrate either to London or Bombay (where majority of their co-religionists lives). However such fears get over-ruled and the herd mentality desire of staying only in Bombay is also rejected. The final resolution is one of adaptability and compromise. The President of the Lahore Parsis Col. Bharucha says, "As long as we conduct our lives quietly; as long as we present no threat to anybody; we will prosper right here." (40) Through this animated conversation, Bapsi Sidhwa reveals the implicit, lurking fear of the Parsis, a vulnerable minority losing their identity and getting swamped by the majority communities—either Hindus in India or Muslims in Pakistan. So even amongst the Parsis the smallest minority in undivided India, the Partition sparked off an impulse for migration from their homelands. Bombay was opted for, primarily due to safety in numbers rather than the safeguards of democratic India. Historically however the movement to Bombay, as the novelist also indicates, was minimal. The Parsis remained in urban areas of India and Pakistan, trying to preserve their identity by not meddling in political matters. The advice of Mr. Toddywalla is followed, "But don't try to prosper immoderately. And remember don't ever try to exercise real power." (40)

Amidst banter, repartee and humour Bapsi Sidhwa subtly portrays the underlying fears of the Parsis about Partition and Independence. The depiction of their mental turmoil can be compared to John Masters's depiction of the plight of the Eurasians commonly called Anglo-Indians before the British left the subcontinent. In his novel, *Bhowani Junction* (1954), John Masters aptly depicts the identity crises of the Anglo-Indians. For instance, the loud-mouthed and arrogant Peter Taylor had talked of going "Home" to England (which he has never seen) and wore his solar hat all day to be recognized as an Englishman. Even the anglicized Peter Taylor has a foreboding of impending Independence. He asks Victoria in sheer frustration, "What are we going to do." (42)[3] Knowing that they could become neither English nor Indian, Taylor's conclusion is "we could only stay where we were and be what we were." (21) This shows how Taylor and the Anglo-Indian community have become total prisoners of circumstances. Bapsi Sidhwa shows how the Parsis are similar captives of circumstances in the upheaval of Partition.

Adaptability being part of their social code, the Parsis of Lahore adjust to the changing circumstances after Partition. In *The Crow Eaters,* Bapsi Sidhwa had only hinted at the necessity of changing allegiances after Independence but in *Ice-Candy-Man,* the change in attitudes is depicted. Col. Bharucha and Lenny's father curse the British for bringing polio to India. Lenny suffers from polio and the disease is considered as another example of British treachery. Later in the novel, Lenny's mother, Mrs. Sethi and other Parsi women help Hindu and Sikh families escape in safe convoys to India and assist in rehabilitation of destitute and kidnapped women. Lenny's Godmother rescues the Hindu Ayah forcibly married to her former Muslim friend, the seller of ice-candies. The Godmother helps Ayah return to Amritsar, under police escort. There is already a sense of involvement, with the new reality as Lenny's parents, Godmother and Parsi friends try to bring some semblance of sanity in frenzied Lahore.[4]

With witty remarks and subtle usage of language, Bapsi Sidhwa presents the impact of Independence and Partition in vivid images. The altered social reality becomes even more striking, as narrated by the innocent eight-year-old Lenny. Independence becomes evident to Lenny when she visits the Queen's Garden: "I cannot believe my eyes. The queen has gone! The space between the marble canopy and the marble platform is empty. A group of children playing knuckles, squat where the gunmetal queen sat enthroned." (236) So within her restricted space, Lenny aptly reveals the fading away of an Empire and its value systems. The theme of separation caused by Partition is also revealed in a simple but vividly poignant observation by Lenny. During her romp at the Queen's Garden, she notices the absence of the cosmopolitan gathering:

> The garden scene has depressingly altered. Muslim families who added colour when scattered among the Hindus and Sikhs now monopolize the garden, depriving it of colour. The absence of the brown skin that showed through the fine veils of Hindu and Sikh women, and beneath the dhoties and shorts of the men, has changed the complexion of the queenless garden. (236)

Through the wondering eyes of the precocious Lenny, the novelist shows the disruption of a settled order and traumatic separations of friends, the legacy of Partition.

The impact of Partition is psychologically understood and narrated through the feelings of a child, who is a member of a minuscule minority. The sense of loss is aptly demonstrated as Lenny and her brother Adi wandering through the garden observe, "Adi and I wander from group to group peering into faces beneath white skull-caps and above ascetic beards. I feel uneasy. Like Hamida I do not fit. I know we will not find familiar faces here." (237) The uprootedness of Partition is revealed as Lenny drifts through the Queen's Garden searching in vain for familiar faces and acquaintances. Even in the child there is a feeling of insecurity. She clings to the hands of her Ayah and cajoles her not to marry the Masseur. A Muslim, the Masseur is one of Ayah's numerous admirers and promises to marry and protect her during the throes of Partition. Overhearing this, Lenny desperately urges Ayah not to get married, as it would mean separation. Later when Ayah is abducted it is Lenny who urges her family to search for her. Lenny's responses show the dislocation of life during Partition. The Partition novels of Manohar Malgonkar, Khushwant Singh and Chaman Nahal focus on Punjab and the dislocation of life and human feelings in that region. So Bapsi Sidhwa's novel is similar to the novels in this genre. The only difference is that the pointless brutality of communal frenzy is parodied as it is unfurled and narrated by the child-narrator

Lenny. She and her younger brother Adi watch "the skyline of the old walled city ablaze and people spattering each other with blood." (134) Fire destroys Hindu, Muslim and Sikh houses and shops at Shalmi. "*The* entire Shalmi, an area covering about four square miles, flashes in explosions." (137) Fire knows no religion. The shrieks and shouts of "Pakistan Murdabad! Death to Pakistan! Sat Sri Akaal; Bolay so nihaal!" of the Sikh mobs when listening to Master Tara Singh at Queen's Garden and "Allah-O-Akbar! Yaaa Ali! and Pakistan Zindabad!" of the rampaging Muslim mobs gives Lenny as many nightmares as when she recollects the roaring of the lions in the zoo. With such subtle comparisons and ironic exposures, Bapsi Sidhwa shows the brutalization which communal frenzy causes. Even lovers turn hostile. Ice-Candy-Man, the Muslim lover of the Hindu Ayah, watches Shalmi and Mozang Chowk burn with "the muscles in his face tight with a strange exhilaration I never want to see." The transformation of a fun-loving man who frolicked and acted the buffoon in the park into an ogre due to communal frenzy is aptly revealed by Lenny's horror at the sadism in his face. A vivid image which is a stark reminder of the brutality of the times. This is the way Bapsi Sidhwa handles the delicate theme of Partition, through subtle insinuations, images and gestures. So the stark horror of loss, bloodshed and separation is portrayed without verbosity, sensationalism, lurid details and maudlin sentimentality. The sensitive portrayal of the horrors of Partition enhances the poignancy and cruelty of the event without the author ever appearing pedantic or pretentious.

Allegory is another literary device used by Bapsi Sidhwa to depict the trauma of Partition. The child-narrator Lenny is also affected by the violence at Lahore: "The whole world is burning. The air on my face is so hot I think my flesh and clothes will catch fire. I start screaming: hysterically sobbing." (137) The scenes of violence and arson and above all the venomous hatred of friends who had months earlier rationalized about the impossibility of violence, have a frightening impact on the young Parsi girl Lenny. Violence breeds violence and Lenny is also a victim. Her rage is directed at her collection of dolls. In a frenzy she acts: "I pick out a big, bloated celluloid doll. I turn it upside down and pull its legs apart. The elastic that holds them together stretches easily. I let one leg go and it snaps back, attaching itself to the brittle torso." (138) The destructive urge overcomes Lenny and she is not satisfied till assisted by her brother Adi she wrenches out the legs of the doll and examines the spilled insides. This violent act by Lenny is an apt allegory on the mindless violence of Partition. With a morbid sense of humour, Bapsi Sidhwa reveals how the violence of Partition has serrated the roots of people of different communities, irrespective of ideology, friendship and rational ideas. In such a depiction, Bapsi Sidhwa resembles the horror portrayed by William Golding in *The Lord of the Files* (1954). Golding indicated that there is a thin line between good and evil in human beings and it is only the structures of civilizations which prevent the lurking evil from being rampant. At the end of *The Lord of the Flies,* boys of Jack's tribe like barbarians got a sadistic delight in hunting Ralph. The situation is saved as a Naval officer reaches the island and by his presence curbs the pointless brutality of the abandoned boys. Golding had written this novel after World War II and the allegorical meaning was evident. In the world of fiction, a grown-up stepped in to curb the atrocities and brutality of the boys, but when countries commit atrocities there is no restraining power. Lenny's destruction of the doll also has allegorical significance. It shows how even a young girl is powerless to stem the tide of surging violence within, thereby implying that grown up fanatics enmeshed in communal frenzy are similarly trapped into brutal violence. Lenny breaks down and cries at her pointless brutality, a sombre message by the novelist that unless there is re-thinking, brutality and insensitivity becomes a way of life, such is the conditioning of communalism.

Another Partition novel, Attia Hosain's *Sunlight on a Broken Column* (1961), also uses a narrator-heroine to similar effect. Attia Hosain's narrator-heroine Laila reveals the trauma of Partition through her memories and insights of her Taluqdar family disintegrating. Like in the *Ice-Candy-Man,* the enigma of Partition is sensitively shown. When Zebra, her cousin married in

Pakistan, returns to Hasanpur, she quarrels with Laila about protection of Muslim culture and language. The disagreements were no longer youthful verbal quarrels but echoed bigger divisions. Laila surmises the cruelest aspect of Partition when she says, "In the end, inevitably we quarrelled, and though we made up before we parted I realized that the ties which had kept families together for centuries had been loosened beyond repair." (303) Like Lenny, the grown-up Laila is also both nostalgic and restless. Laila ruminates and wanders in her disbanded ancestral home Ashiana after Partition. Memories come flooding back. However her nostalgia is controlled. Whilst walking through the rooms of Ashiana, she remembers the past, but does not wish for the old order to return. Her new-found identity and struggle to be Ameer's lover and wife, curbs any desire for a return to the cloistered feudal order. Instead it broadens her horizons of life. She comes to detest dogmatism, either in the name of religion or radicalism. Her views and perspective of life developed after intense personal struggle enable Laila to tackle the loss of her husband Ameer and the trauma of Partition. So both narrator-heroines, Lenny and Laila, react against communal responses and the horrors of violence. The mature Laila rationalizes against communal tension whereas the young Lenny instinctively reacts against the horrors of communal violence.

There are other similarities between the two novelists, Bapsi Sidhwa and Attia Hosain. Both realize there are no easy solutions to communal holocausts except intense struggle against dogmatism. Laila's concerted attempts at breaking from traditional customs, the negation of despair and recognition of struggle are upheld by Attia Hosain. Her narrator-heroine does not lapse into a glorification of the past or take refuge in mysticism, epicureanism or jingoism. Similarly Bapsi Sidhwa shows there are no winners in the communal holocausts of Partition. This is revealed by clever juxtapositioning of images. Gramophones and speakers mounted on tongas and lorries pour out the melody of Nur Jehan's popular film song,

> Mere bachpan ke sathi mujhe bhool na jana—Dekho, dekho hanse na zamana, hanse na zamana. (159)

Ironically the sentiments of the song are not followed and instead there is turbulence and violence. At the festival of Holi, instead of splattering friends with bright colours, people are splattering each other with blood. Bapsi Sidhwa shows the human loss in Partition:

> Instead, wave upon scruffy wave of Muslim refugees flood Lahore—and the Punjab west of Lahore. Within three months seven million Muslims and five million Hindus and Sikhs are uprooted in the largest and most terrible exchange of population known to history. The Punjab has been divided. (159)

Bare facts present the horror of the greatest communal divide in history. Bapsi Sidhwa aptly shows the inexorable logic of Partition which moves on relentlessly leaving even sane people and friends helpless and ineffective. Jagjeet Singh with a furtive group of Sikhs visited a Muslim village Pir Pindo under cover of darkness to warn them of an impending Akali attack. Pir Pindo is attacked at dawn and swamped by Sikhs. Men, women and children are killed. Similarly Sikh families are attacked in Lahore. The neighbour of the Sethis, Mr. and Mrs. Singh leave with their two children and a few belongings. Other goods are left behind with Lenny's parents. Sher Singh the zoo attendant flees from Lahore, due to insecurity, after his brother-in-law is killed. Similarly the student fraternity of King Edward's Medical College is disrupted. Prakash and his family migrate to Delhi and Rahool Singh and his pretty sisters are escorted to a convoy to Amritsar. In Lenny's household the gardener Hari is circumcised and becomes Himat Ali, and Moti becomes David Masih, the politics of compromise and survival. Ayah's lover the Masseur's mutilated dead body is found in a gunnysack. The moneylender Kirpa Ram flees leaving guineas and money behind. Even middle-class families like the Shankers flee in haste. Partition is shown as a series of images and events depicting human loss and agony. The dislocation of settled life is aptly revealed by Lenny's understanding of the demographic change in Lahore. In awe she observes, "Lahore is suddenly emptied of yet another hoary dimension: there are no Brahmins with caste-marks—or Hindus in dhoties with bodhis. Only hordes of Muslim refugees." (175) Lahore is no more-cosmopolitan. Even the Sikhs have fled. The child-narrator senses the difference and pain caused by the huge exchange of populations.

Bapsi Sidhwa also subtly delineates the psychological impact of the horrors of Partition on the lives of people. The communal frenzy has a distorting effect on people—and leads to feelings of suspicion, distrust and susceptibility to rumours. Even the children, Lenny, Adi and their cousin are intrigued and suspicious of any minor deviations from normal behaviour. Mrs. Sethi and Aunt Minnie travel all over Lahore in the car but do not take the children with them. Deprived of long drives, Lenny and her cousin are intrigued at the movements of their mothers. Ayah enhances the sense of mystery when she states that the dicky of the car is full of cans of petrol. The author shows that in a highly surcharged atmosphere, suspicion and distrust become inevitable. The Ayah is also suspicious about the movements of cans of petrol by the two Parsi ladies. If she suspects they are distributing petrol to the arsonists she does not state so. The three children are stupefied by this revelation and let their imagination run wild. Finally they come to the same conclusion. "We know who the arsonists are. Our mothers are setting fire to Lahore!—My heart pounds at the damnation that awaits their souls. My knees quake at the horror of their imminent arrest." (173)

Bapsi Sidhwa cleverly parodies the feelings of suspicion and distrust of the children for their mothers. The imaginary fears of Lenny, Adi and their cousin are a source of humour but also a grim reminder of how rumour becomes institutionalized in a highly surcharged atmosphere. The children only fantasize about their mother's dangerous acts but the author shows how rumour preys upon the frenzied minds of men vitiated by communal hatred. On the radio there is news of trouble at Gurdaspur, which the Ice-Candy-Man and his friends at once interpret as "there is uncontrollable butchering going on in Gurdaspur." (148) There are further rumours of a train full of dead bodies coming to Lahore from Gurdaspur. The Ice-Candy-Man returns panting after a frantic cycle ride and adds to the horror, by describing atrocities on women and stating that the dead are all Muslims. The acquaintances of Queen's Garden believe this rumour and harbour revenge against Sikhs. They now look with hatred on long-standing friend Sher Singh, compelling the latter to flee from Lahore.[6]

In the vitiated communal atmosphere, insanity prevails as ordinary men lose their rationality. Such a degradation is best exemplified in the rage of Ice-Candy-Man who says: "I'll tell you to your face—I lose my senses when I think of the mutilated bodies on that train from Gurdaspur . . . that night I went mad, I tell you, I lobbed grenades through the windows of Hindus and Sikhs I'd known all my life! I hated their guts." (156)

Revenge becomes the major motivation for the Ice-Candy-Man and his friends. The role of rumour and the consequent pattern of violence as depicted by Bapsi Sidhwa is compact and realistic. It is also very contemporary as similar patterns of violence are depicted by Amitav Ghosh in his novel *The Shadow Lines* (1988).[7] Using the narrative technique of unfurling events, by reading old newspaper reports, Amitav Ghosh shows how communal violence spread in Calcutta and cities of erstwhile East Pakistan in 1964. As he stresses, rumour took over. The poisoning of water, the trains of dead bodies, all incredible rumours, further vitiated the communal frenzy and increased the violence. Amitav Ghosh's novel is very contemporary and relevant as it shows how communal fanatics thrived on the spread of rumours which intensified feelings of anger and triggered off violence. The bland newspaper reports and memory technique of Amitav Ghosh remove the impact of time. It is implied that the riots are contemporaneous. The 1964 Calcutta riots could be the 1984 Delhi riots, the 1987 Meerut riots or in recent times the 1989 Bhagalpur killings. They all follow a similar pattern, suspicion, distrust and rumour activating conditioned minds, all sources of terrifying communal violence.

Very perceptively Amitav Ghosh shows how different cultures and communities are becoming antagonistic to a point of no return. Hence in *The Shadow Lines* he effectively uses political allegory to stress the need for a syncretic civilization to avoid a communal holocaust. Bapsi Sidhwa's concerns are also similar. The message in Bhisham Sahni's novel *Tamas,* that "those who forget history are condemned to repeat it," is applicable to *Ice-Candy-Man* also. Sidhwa's novel written at a period of history when communal and ethnic violence threaten disintegration of the subcontinent, is an apt warning of the dangers of communal frenzy. Bapsi Sidhwa shows that during communal strife, sanity, human feelings and past friendships are forgotten. At the Queens Park in Lahore, friends and colleagues had argued endlessly about the impossibility of violence against each other and of fleeing from their homeland. Yet ironically, whilst the elders—Masseur, Butcher, Ice-Candy-Man, Sher Singh and Ayah—gossip about national politics the child-narrator senses the change in the days before Partition: "I can't put my finger on it—but there is a subtle change in the Queen's Garden." (96) The admirers of Ayah, in the pursuit of love temporarily sidetrack communal feelings and "Hindu, Muslim, Sikh, Parsi are as always, unified around her." (97) The others without such motivations are deliberately sitting with members of their own community, huddled together preserving cultural and religious identities. The Brahmins form their own circle of exclusivity. Burkha-clad Muslim women and children have their own group. The saddest fact as observed by Lenny is that even the children do not mix whilst playing.

Lenny attempts social interaction with a group of Sikh children but Masseur tries to pull her away. Sikh women ask her name and the name of her religion. When the child states that she is a Parsi, the Sikh women express amazement at the discovery of a new religion. It is then that Lenny instinctively realizes the social divide between communities. Rationalizing her feelings she says, "That's when I realize what has changed. The Sikhs, only their rowdy little boys running about hair piled in topknots, are keeping mostly to themselves." (96) The author implies that the events at Queen's Garden are a reflection of a crystallization of feelings at a larger scale in Lahore and other cities of India.

Cultural and religious exclusivity leads initially to indifference and later to contempt which becomes the breeding ground for communal violence and bigotry. With a subtle parody, Bapsi Sidhwa conveys the dangers of social exclusivity. The Ice-Candy-Man, in striking attire, enters the Queen's Garden, "Thumping a five-foot iron trident with bells tied near its base." (97) He is in the guise of a holy man and chants "Ya Allah!" With his ash-smeared face and eccentric manner, he pretends to be Allah's telephone. The author implies that in an atmosphere which encourages religious bigotry, even charlatans emerge as holy and godmen. The difference between appearance and reality is slim. The Ice-Candy-Man pretends to talk to God on telephone. The scene is ludicrous and a source of rich humour. However amidst laughter the real meaning of such clowning emerges. The Ice-Candy-Man's antics provoke amusement but it is a pointer to the duplicity of people in the name of religion. Their sheer gullibility is exposed in a scene vividly described:

> Suddenly he springs up. Thumping his noisy trident on the ground, performing a curious jumping dance, he shouts: Wah Allah! Wah Allah! so loudly that several people who have been watching the goings-on from afar, hastily get up and scamper over. Sikhs, Hindus, Muslims form a thick circle round us. I can tell from the reverent faces around me that they believe they are in the presence of a holyman crazed by his love of God. And the madder the mystic, the greater his power. (99)

The message is clear. If charlatans can arouse such fervour, then obscurantism needs little prodding to slide into bigotry.

The secular group, Ayah's admirers maintain a facade of unity by cracking ribald jokes on community characteristics. However they also become vicious—and prey to communal frenzy in the near future. The Ice-Candy-Man is part of the frenzied mob which abdicates Ayah and keeps her in the brothels of Hira Mandi. So even the passion of love is powerless against religious bigotry. Later in the novel, the Ice-Candy-Man attempts to make amends. He forcibly marries Ayah, changes her name to Mumtaz, and recites love poetry to her. But even here love is shown as powerless. Ayah has revulsion for her newly acquired

Muslim identity. With the help of Lenny's Godmother she is taken to a Recovered Women's Camp and then sent to her family in Amritsar. The Ice-Candy-Man, now a "deflated poet, a collapsed pedlar" follows her to Amritsar in vain. Their relationship is serrated forever, one more victim of communal frenzy and Partition. Love does not conquer all, when communal and obscurantist passions are aroused.

With a sprinkling of humour, parody and allegory Bapsi Sidhwa conveys a sinister warning of the dangers of compromising with religious obscurantism and fundamentalism of all categories. Otherwise a certain historical inevitability marks this historical process. Though her novel is about the traumas of Partition, Bapsi Sidhwa like Amitav Ghosh reveals that communal riots are contemporaneous and that those who do not learn from history are condemned to repeat it.

NOTES

1. Bapsi Sidhwa, *Ice-Candy-Man* (London: William Heinemann, 1988).
2. The sentiments and ideas of Col. Bharucha represent a prominent social code of behaviour amongst the Parsis. They have always venerated loyalty. Dr. Homi B. Dhalla in his essay, "The Zoroastrian Moral Imperative: Its Relevance in the Late 19th and Early 20th Centuries" published in the Delhi Parsi Anjuman's *Dar-E--Meher* (fire-temple) silver jubilee celebrations souvenir (1986) gives instances of loyalty. He states: "Large gatherings of Parsis have over the years, assembled for public acts of worship or thanksgiving (jashan). To cite a few: on July 16, 1854, a jashan was performed where about 6,000 Zoroastrians offered prayers for Britain during its war with Russia. As a mark of celebration, a mammoth jashan was organized on Queen Victoria's Golden Jubilee on Feb. 16, 1887 and again on June 20, 1897 to commemorate her Diamond Jubilee." Also cited in James Boyd and Firoze Kotwal, "Warship in a Zoroastrian Fire Temple," *Indo-Iranian Journal,* 26, 1983, pp. 308-10. Col. Bharucha was thus just following a Parsi moral imperative.
3. John Masters, *Bhowani Junction* (New York: The Viking Press, 1954), p. 42.

4. Charity and social usefulness is a Parsi moral code, based on the teachings of the prophet Zarathushtra. This is amply revealed in Eckehard Kulke's scholarly book, *The Parsis in India: A Minority as Agent of Social Change* (Delhi: Bell Books, 1978). Kulke states that Parsi charities are cosmopolitan and communal as the ancient scriptures and daily prayers extolled philanthropy. Kulke states "This charity system was made possible and furthered by the basic attitude of the Parsis, motivated by their religion, that wealth is fundamentally positive, that it brings, however certain social obligations along with it." So charity is part of the Parsi ethos.
5. Attia Hosain, *Sunlight on a Broken Column* (Delhi: Arnold Heinemann, 1979).
6. The role of rumour in both the nationalist movement led by Mahatma Gandhi and the traumas of Partition is best explained in Sumit Sarkar's book *Modern India 1885-1947* (Madras: Macmillan India, 1983). In his chapter "The Role of Rumour," Sumit Sarkar shows how peasants and workers responded to institutionalized rumours.
7. Amitav Ghosh, *The Shadow Lines* (Delhi: Ravi Dayal Publisher, 1988).

Bapsi Sidhwa: "I am Pakistani"

NIAZ ZAMAN

The article beautifully traces Sidhwa's compulsions to retain her ethnic identity—writing in a literary vacuum, she had to establish her political credentials and proclaim her cultural allegiance vociferously. Illustrating from Sidhwa's earlier novels, though focusing on Ice-Candy-Man, *it shows how the author has picked up some historical personalities and events to depict the unfair treatment meted out to the Pakistani people and history. Seeking refuge behind the persona of a child-narrator, Sidhwa presents the Pakistani side of the Partition of the Indian subcontinent, even though she possesses the sensitivity to reject the two-nation theory.*

Editor

In Bapsi Sidhwa's *Ice-Candy-Man,* the narrator, Lenny, muses about the absurdity of the Partition of the Indian subcontinent: "I am Pakistani. In a snap. Just like that."[1] Nevertheless, despite her narrator's musing over the absurdity of Partition, Sidhwa's Pakistani perspective is evident in her writings. Sidhwa is perhaps the first Pakistani writer to receive international recognition—apart from Zulfikar Ghose, who seemed to have cut himself off from his Pakistani roots after *The Murder of Aziz Khan.* As a Pakistani writer, Sidhwa feels it incumbent upon her to explain her Pakistani background to those unfamiliar with her milieu. Because she is also a Parsi, she attempts to explain this heritage as well.

Sidhwa is not alone in her need to explain her heritage, but shares with other Third-World writers, particularly those writing in a non-native language, the compulsion to explain her culture to an audience unfamiliar with that culture. Thus *The Crow Eaters*[2] as well as *The Bride*[3] and *Ice-Candy-Man* are firmly rooted in a historical-political consciousness and concern directly or indirectly, the Partition of the Indian subcontinent and the creation of the newly-independent states of India and Pakistan. *The Bride,* her first written novel, though published after the success of *The Crow Eaters,* begins some years before Partition and, for the earlier part of the novel, describes the communal tension during Partition, a train massacre, and the displacement consequent upon Partition. It is only after describing the turmoil of Partition and its aftermath, that the story of Zaitoon and her adopted father, the hill-man Qasim, is developed. *The Crow Eaters* ends just before Partition, with Faredoon Junglewalla, the protagonist of the novel, pronouncing, in his inimitable fashion, upon the bickering politicians who are going to cut up the country. *Ice-Candy-Man,* tighter in focus than the other two novels, concerns wholly the turbulent events of Partition as they affect the lives of a Parsi family and the people who come into their lives. When *Ice-Candy-Man* was published in the United States in 1991 the title was changed to *Cracking India,* focussing on the Partition rather than on the eponymous character.

The Crow Eaters traces the fortunes of Faredoon Junglewalla, Freddie for short, who leaves his home in India some time at the end of the nineteenth century for the fertile plains of Punjab, settling down in Lahore. *The Crow Eaters* might easily pass off as an Indian rather than a Pakistani novel. While much of the story is situated in Lahore, the story takes place before Partition, and the Junglewallas seek a bride from Bombay for Billy. Furthermore, Sidhwa herself seemed to see the book as Indian, by explaining that the title is taken from an idiom belonging to the Indian sub-continent: "The title is borrowed from an idiom which belongs to the sub-continent. Anyone who talks too much is said to have eaten crows." Early critics too saw the book as Indian. Judy Cooke, for example, in the *New Statesman* says, "Bapsi Sidhwa's *The Crow Eaters* is an excellent novel, her first, a book about India." Similarly, Frank Rudman in the *Spectator* notes that "*The Crow Eaters* is a wholly charming passage to India." That critics should have seen *The Crow Eaters* as an Indian book rather than a Pakistani one is not surprising: pre-Partition Lahore may be Indian or Pakistani—or even Anglo Indian. Thus, no one would call Ved Mehta a Pakistani writer because he writes about Lahore, or Kipling either. But with Sidhwa's international recognition came the need for ethnic identity, and Sidhwa—and her publishers—latched on to her Pakistani nationality. The Fontana/Collins edition, for example, made a point of stressing that *The Crow Eaters* is Pakistani by noting on the cover that it is "A Novel of Pakistan." However, neither *The Bride* nor *Ice-Candy-Man* need to be similarly identified. They are clearly Pakistani in setting and sensibility. Nevertheless, to prevent any possible confusion, the 1990 Penguin India edition of *The Bride* is renamed *The Pakistani Bride.*

Unlike the Indian writer of today who has a long literary heritage and does not have to make new beginnings, Sidhwa was writing in what was essentially a vacuum. Hence it was necessary for her to establish her political credentials, proclaim her cultural allegiance. Salman Rushdie too seemed to be doing much the same by beginning *Midnight's Children* on August 15, thus establishing his Indianness. At the same time, by exploiting his Indian-Muslim heritage, he revealed his difference from Hindu India. His increasing need to draw upon his own heritage led to *The Satanic Verses* and the unfortunate fall-out. Some of this need to establish her own identity also inspired Sidhwa and caused similar—if not as grave—consternation among her Parsi community. Sidhwa makes it clear that, while she is Parsi, her political identity is with the people west of the Indo-Pakistan border.

Sidhwa establishes her political identity in two significant ways: first, by focusing on the worst Indian atrocities committed in the Punjab, and secondly, by reappraising the character of Jinnah and attempting to improve this image by suggesting that the British were less than fair to both Pakistan and Jinnah. Sidhwa's political stance is clearly depicted through her treatment of Partition—which it may be noted, is a focal point in each of her books. Even *The Crow Eaters* which ends before Partition, refers to it. *Ice-Candy-Man* narrates what takes place in Lahore during the traumatic events that accompanied the division of the Indian sub-continent. And Sidhwa's first book, though inspired by the murder of a tribal woman, begins with the gruesome account of a train massacre during Partition. In *The Bride*, Sidhwa combines her feminist concerns with a compulsion to explain the culture of Pakistan to audiences unfamiliar with that culture. It is this combination that gives the novel its structural weakness but also its perceptive insights.

Thus, Sidhwa uses the train massacre to explain how the hillman Qasim comes upon a little girl whose parents are both killed. The detailed and vivid description of the massacre allows Sidhwa's audience to experience the horror of Partition.

> Only now does the engine driver realize there is something further down the track. A roar rises from the mass of jolted refugees. The train's single headlight flashes on. It spotlights the barricade of logs and some unaligned rails. White shingles flicker in and out of the glare. The train brakes heavily and the engine crashes into the logs. People are flung from their scant hold on the footboards, roof and buffer. Women and children pour from the crammed compartments.
>
> Now the mob runs toward the train with lighted flares. Qasim sees the men clearly. They are Sikhs. Tall, crazed men wave swords. A cry: "Bole so Nihal" and the answering roar, "Sat Sri Akal." Torches unevenly light the scene and Qasim watches the massacre as in a cinema. An eerie clamour rises. Sounds of firing explode above agonized shrieks. (28)

Two persons escape the carnage: Qasim and a little girl who has lost her parents. Mistaking Qasim for her father, she clings to him. Qasim tries to shake her off but fails to do so. He finally accepts her as a substitute for the little girl he had lost and renames her Zaitoon after his dead daughter. The novel then follows Qasim and Zaitoon to Lahore where they attempt to make a new life for themselves. In the new land some people, including Qasim's new-found friend Nikka, make fortunes for themselves—not always honestly. And Sidhwa—as critic—depicts the corruption and coercion that Qasim experiences at second-hand. After a brief digression, which also includes a trip to Hira Mandi, the red-light district of Lahore, Sidhwa returns to the story of Zaitoon. Qasim, who hails from the hills, is nostalgic for the life of his youth, and he marries his adopted daughter to Sakhi, a distant nephew. Zaitoon, used by now to the freer, easier life in Lahore, chafes in the hills and runs away from her husband. Sakhi follows her, attempting to wipe out the dishonour she has brought upon him by killing her. While Zaitoon is more fortunate than the woman whose fate inspired Sidhwa to write this novel, she does not escape absolutely unharmed. She is raped and left torn and bleeding by some men who come upon her in the hills. Mushtaq, a young army officer—whose function until this point has been to seduce the American wife of a friend—sees Zaitoon and manages to rescue her from the wrath of her husband. The novel ends on a note of some happiness for Zaitoon. Though she can never go back to the adopted father who loves her, she might find some sort of happiness with Mushtaq's driver—aptly named Ashiq.

In this early novel, Sidhwa attempts to give a detailed account of the romantic side of purdah and to describe the whole code of behaviour that governs the relationship of men and women in a purdah society. Thus men and women do not look at each other or even address each other directly. This segregation, however, creates certain latent, almost at times, explosive sexual feelings. It is this repression that ventilates itself in vulgar dances—danced by innocent young girls at weddings where no men are allowed, but where they manage to enter occasionally. This repressed sexuality also helps prepare men and women to accept husbands and wives whom they have sometimes not even seen before the wedding day. However, Sidhwa points out through Zaitoon that the men whom they are married to are often brutal and expect to be served obediently and accepted a master. Sexual excitement is not enough, especially where women are nothing more than property.

Though *The Bride* fails to come up to the level of either *The Crow Eaters* or *Ice-Candy-Man,* its failure stems from the same motives that make *Ice-Candy-Mat* a success: to familiarize her audience with the writer's cultural, political milieu. In *The Bride,* however, Sidhwa is a little too anxious to show it all, the historical past as well as the anachronistic present. In *Ice-Candy-Man* to which she came via *The Crow Eaters,* she is both Parsi and

Pakistani at the same time. She returns to the Parsi world she had described so well in *The Crow Eaters* and focuses as she had in the second half of *The Bride,* on the fate of a young woman. By narrowing her canvas, she succeeded in writing a book which, even if not as successful as *The Crow Eaters*—this was, remember, the first of its kind—shows an exceptional literary talent. Furthermore, by blending the humour of *The Crow Eaters* with the theme of Partition and a feminist perspective, Sidhwa reveals herself as a writer of the rank of Ruth Jhabvala and Anita Desai.

In *Ice-Candy-Man* Sidhwa describes Partition through the eyes of the young Lenny. (Sidhwa denies that Lenny is a self-portrait, but Lenny suffers from an illness—as Sidhwa herself did—which prevented her from going to school.) The story of the growth of Lenny and her awakening into sexual awareness merges with her awakening into history. Sidhwa's humour blends with horror and pity as she tells the story of Partition through the perspective of a child. Lenny's comprehension of the events of Partition are told through the story of what happens to her beloved Hindu Ayah. When the story begins, Ayah is surrounded by many admirers, Hindu and Muslim. Among these many admirers is the Ice-Candy-Man after whom the novel is named. As Partition nears, Muslims and Hindus become enemies. Some Hindus in an attempt to save themselves become Christians. Some Hindus leave Lahore. Ayah is Hindu, but, protected by her Parsi employers, she assumes that she is in no danger. Unfortunately her charms lead to her abduction by a group led by the Ice-Candy-Man. Ice-Candy-Man keeps Ayah, renamed Mumtaz, hidden in Hira Mandi. Ayah begs to be rescued and she finally is by Godmother—in a departure from *The Bride* where the rescue of Zaitoon was effected by a man.

With a certain detachment Sidhwa sees the excesses to which religious intolerance takes one, shows how violence marks everyone, and yet—and this is where the Pakistani in Sidhwa comes in—she shows how Pakistanis have been unfairly treated. She stresses that Jinnah was no monster, and notes that in the atrocities committed during Partition, while both Muslims and Sikhs indulged in violence, the Muslim atrocities pale by comparison with those of the Sikhs. Sidhwa makes her Pakistani identity unmistakably clear in *Ice-Candy-Man* where she suggests how Partition favoured India over Pakistan.

> The Hindus are being favored over the Muslims by the remnants of the Raj. Now that its objective to divide India is achieved, the British favour Nehru over Jinnah. Nehru is Kashmiri, they grant him Kashmir. Spurning logic. Defying rationale, ignoring the consequence of bequeathing a Muslim State to the Hindus: while Jinnah futilely protests: 'Statesmen cannot eat their words!'
>
> Statesmen do.
>
> They grant Nehru Gurdaspur and Pathankot without which Muslim Kashmir cannot be secured. (159)

Shashi Tharoor objects to Sidhwa's use of the word "grant," noting that the British did not grant Kashmir to India.[4]

True, Lenny is not Sidhwa, but as Laurel Graeber points out, "Bapsi Sidhwa has attempted to give a Pakistani perspective to the Partition of India."[5] In a telephonic interview, Sidhwa told Graeber that the British glorified Mountbatten, the Indians Gandhi: "Gandhi really sowed the seeds of Partition and turned the whole Independence struggle into a Hindu movement. It's hard for people in the west, where he is deified, to regard him as a petty manipulative politician."[6]

As a Pakistani, Sidhwa feels it incumbent upon herself to defend Mohammad Ali Jinnah, the hiker of the Muslim nation. The reference to Jinnah is made aptly in the context of the Parsi family that is the focus of the novel. Lenny comes across the picture of an "astonishingly beautiful woman" and is told that it is the picture of Jinnah's wife. A Parsi, she married the Muslim Jinnah, braving her family's displeasure. The marriage was not a happy one, for the beautiful woman in the picture died of a broken heart. While Sidhwa cannot completely exonerate Jinnah here, she manages to blur the criticism by noting that Jinnah too died of a broken heart. She also makes it clear that she is on Jinnah's side.

> But didn't Jinnah, too, die of a broken heart? And today, forty years later, in films of Gandhi's and Mountbatten's lives, in books by British and Indian scholars, Jinnah, who for a decade was

> known as 'Ambassador of Hindu-Muslim unity,' is caricatured, and portrayed as a monster. (160)

Is this Lenny speaking or Sidhwa herself?

Sidhwa, however, rises above petty nationalism. *Ice-Candy-Man* does not stress the Two-Nation theory behind the creation of Pakistan. In other words, she does not stress the belief of Pakistani Muslims of the necessity of Partition and the creation of Pakistan. In fact, *Ice-Candy-Man* suggests that religious and cultural differences are artificially created and deliberately fostered. Through Lenny's perspective, Sidhwa shows how religious differences were deliberately exploited on the eve of Partition.

> Gandhi, Jinnah, Nehru, Iqbal, Tara Singh, Mountbatten are names I hear.
>
> And I become aware of religious differences.
>
> It is sudden. One day everybody is themselves—and the next day they are Hindu, Muslim, Sikh, Christian. People shrink, dwindling into symbols. Ayah is no longer my all-encompassing Ayah—she is also a token, a Hindu. Carried away by a renewed devotional fervour, she spends a small fortune in joss-stick, flowers and sweets on the gods and goddesses in the temples.
>
> Imam Din and Yousaf turning into religion zealots, warn Mother that they will take Friday afternoon off for the Jumha prayers. On Fridays they set about preparing themselves ostentatiously . . . . Sometimes, at odd hours of the day. They spread their mats on the front lawn and pray when the muezzin calls. Crammed into a narrow religious slot they too are diminished: as are Jinnah and Iqbal, Ice-Candy-Man, Masseur.
>
> Hari and Moti—the sweeper and his wife Muccho, and their untouchable daughter Papoo, become even more untouchables they are entrenched deeper in their low Hindu caste while the Shanthas and the Daulatrams, Brahmins like Nehru, are dehumanized by their lofty caste and caste-marks.
>
> The Roger's of Birdwood Barracks, Queen Victoria and King George are English Christians: they look down their noses upon the Pens who are Anglo-Indian, who look down theirs on the Phailbuses who are Indian-Christian, who look down upon all non-Christians.

> Godmother, Salvesister, Electric-Aunt and my nuclear family are reduced to irrelevant nomenclature—we are Parsee. (93-94)

At the beginning, Ayah is a cementing force. Hindu, Muslim, Sikh admirers flock around her. Gradually, however, things change, and this change is depicted in the dwindling of the group around Ayah. Though they still come it is no longer together, but in "twos or threes, or singly." (147) Things start turning ugly and violent. Houses are looted and burnt. There are riots, Lenny watches English soldiers being chased by a group of Sikhs, "their wild long hair and beards rampant, large fevered eyes glowing in fanatic faces . . . roaring slogans, holding curved swords, shoring up a manic wave of violence that sets Ayah to trembling as she holds me tight. A naked child, twitching on a spear struck between her shoulders, is waved like a flag, her screamless mouth agape she is staring straight up at me." (134-35) Lenny would like to attack the mob, but she knows it is useless: "the creature has too many stony hearts, too many sightless eyes, deaf ears, mindless brains and tons of entwined entrails." (135) The Sikh mob is followed by a Muslim one. And as Lenny watches she sees the destruction and the killing. "Every short while a group of men, like a whirling eddy, stalls, and like the widening circles of a treacherous eddy dissolving in the mainstream, leaves in its centre the pulpy red flotsam of a mangled body." (135) Ayah moans at the horror of the scene and collapses, but the violence excites many, among them Ice-Candy-Man: "the muscles in his face [are] tight with a strange exhilaration" that the narrator says she never wishes to see again. (135) Whole areas are set on fire. Shalmi, with its Hindu population, is set ablaze, and the watchers on the rooftops enjoy the spectacle. Even Lenny at first is mesmerized.

> It is like a gigantic fireworks display in which stiff figures looking like spread-eagled stick-dolls leap into the air, black against the magenta furnace. Trapped by the spreading flames the panicked Hindus rush in droves from one end of the street to the other. Many disappear down the smoking lanes. Some collapse in the street. Charred limbs and burnt logs are falling from the sky. (137)

When Lenny finally starts sobbing and screaming, Ice-Candy-Man tells her and Ayah, "You must make your hearts stout. . . . The fucking bastards! They thought they'd drive us out of Bhatti! We've shown them!" (137)

In a world gone topsy-turvy, friends turn into foes. In an attempt to save their lives, many convert. Some Hindus become Muslims, some Christian. Everyone is not saved. Hari is humiliated. Ayah, whom everyone had flirted with, is abducted. Masseur is killed. Personal scores are settled. Sidhwa brilliantly contrasts earlier, playful games with cruelty and brutality after religious differences begin separating Hindu from Muslim, Christian from Sikh. Thus, Hari is often teased by the Muslims who, intrigued by his wisp of a dhoti, tug at it, pretending that they will pull it off completely. The game, though boisterous and vulgar, is the beginning of just a game. Later, it ceases to be so. The dhoti does come off, and Hari is revealed in his pitiable nakedness, his very genitals shrunk with fear. Similarly, Ayah who has always attracted attention, once more becomes the focus of caressing hands. The situation has, however, changed. The amorous, playful caresses of the earlier scenes become lustful, threatening, violent. In minute detail, juxtaposing sexual images with images of violence, Sidhwa describes the scene of Ayah's abduction. "The men drag her in grotesque strides to the cart and their harsh hands, supporting her with careless intimacy, lift her into it. Four men stand pressed against her, propping her body upright—their lips stretched in triumphant grimaces." (18) For some time, Lenny is unaware of Ayah's whereabouts, believing that she is dead. It is soon revealed, however, that Ayah is alive and living in Hira Mandi, the Lahore red-light area. Ice-Candy-Man has married her. He tells Godmother who rebukes him for having been a party to her abduction: "I saved her. . . . They would've . . . killed her. . . . I married her." (249)

While violence *has* affected everyone, the Sikhs stand out in this respect. Sidhwa does not show a train massacre as she had earlier in *The Bride,* but she describes one briefly through the eyes of Ice-Candy-Man. "A train from Gurdaspur has just come in. . . . Everyone in it is dead. Butchered. They are all Muslim.

There are no young women among the dead. Only two gunny-bags full of women's breasts." (149) Ice-Candy-Man would like to avenge those deaths, those rapes, and mutilations. He cannot get the murderers but he can get Sher Singh. What does it matter that Sher Singh has not committed those atrocities? He is of the same faith as those who did. Masseur is one of the few to point out that Guru Nanak wore a shirt with inscriptions from the Koran and that the faith was an attempt to create Hindu-Muslim harmony. But in the passions let loose, the Sikhs wipe out entire villages, putting the men to the sword and raping the women.

Sidhwa describes the destruction of the Muslim village of Pir Pindo Lenny visited earlier during happier times. The villagers had been warned to leave, but they do not, and Ranna describes the mass murder that takes place. Sidhwa does not narrate this incident through Lenny but through Ranna:

> Ranna saw his uncle beheaded. His older brothers, his cousins. The Sikhs were among them like hairy vengeful demons, wielding bloodied swords, dragging them out as a handful of Hindus, darting about the fringes, their faces vaguely familiar, pointed out and identified the Mussulmans by name. He felt a blow cleave the back of his head and the warm flow of blood. Ranna fell just inside the door on a tangled pole of unrecognizable bodies. Someone fell on him drenching him in blood. (201)

Left for dead, Ranna comes to and hears the shrieks and wails of women. Outside their courtyard he hears the anguished sobs of a woman, and at intervals her screams "You'll kill me! Hai Allah. . . . Y'all will kill me!" (202)

Sidhwa took up the story of Ranna and retold it in a short story "Defend Yourself against Me." This short story, written after Sidhwa's fame led to appointments in the United States, also contains a new theme—that of the Indian-Pakistani-Bangladeshi Diaspora.[7] Away from Pakistan Sidhwa sees the Indian sub-continent from a wider perspective. The story is narrated by a Mrs. Jacobs from Lahore. Mrs. Jacobs is visiting - Houston, Texas, where the differences between the religious communities have been blurted. Hindus, Muslims, Sikhs seem to form one large "Indian" community. At a dinner, Mrs. Jacobs meets Sikander Khan, whom, she realizes, she knew long ago in Lahore. She recalls how she had met Sikander as a small boy when he and his mother had fled India during Partition and settled next door to her. The little boy had a deep scar and his mother had been raped and brutalized. It is several years later, but the hate, terror, pain of the past emerge again as the mother meets some Sikh friends of Sikander. In the explosive climax of this story, the Sikh men ask forgiveness for their fathers' sins. Ammijee, Sikander's mother, forgives the men—as, she says, she had forgiven their fathers, because without forgiving them she could not have survived. Thus, in this story Sidhwa also suggests that though the past cannot be forgotten, it can be forgiven. Let not the crimes of the fathers be visited on their sons—but then the sons must be conscious of their fathers' sins and ask for forgiveness. But one wonders whether it would have been possible for Sidhwa to suggest as easily that Pakistanis ask forgiveness for their crime of rape and genocide—in 1947 or 1971?

The United States enabled Sidhwa to give this "happy" ending to the story of Partition, but here too it may be seen how the victim is a Muslim woman, the perpetrators of the rape Sikhs. However, Sidhwa gives a different perspective on the story of Partition, emphasizing through Mrs. Jacobs the vulnerability of women, so that it is not the political stance that is focussed on at the end but the feminist one. "The vulnerability of mothers, daughters, granddaughters, and their metamorphosis into possessions; living objects on whose soft bodies victors and losers alike vent their wrath, enact fantastic vendettas, celebrate victories." (380) Nevertheless, significantly, it is Partition—and the atrocities perpetrated on Muslim women—that calls up intense passions.

Sidhwa is too good an artist to show only one side of the picture. Her overarching sense of compassion allows her an understanding of the pain of the "enemy." Her clear vision allows her to see that violence affects everyone. In both *The Bride* and *Ice-Candy-Man,* the riots affect Hindu and Muslim areas alike, Muslims attacking Hindu areas, Hindus attacking Muslim ones. Her sense of the absurd permits her to realize the meaninglessness of artificial divisions. "I am Pakistani. In a snap. Just like that." (140) Nevertheless, in all her writings Sidhwa reveals that, with all her love for truth, all her compassion, she sees Partition from the western side of the Indo-Pak border.

NOTES

1. Bapsi Sidhwa, *Ice-Candy-Man* (1988; Harmondsworth: Penguin, 1989), p. 140.
2. Bapsi Sidhwa, *The Crow Eaters* (1978; Glasgow: Fontana, 1982).
3. Bapsi Sidhwa, *The Bride* (1983; Karachi: Liberty Books, 1987).
4. Shashi Tharoor, "Life with Electric-Aunt and Slavesister," *New York Times Book Review,* Oct. 6, 1991, p. 11.
5. Laurel Graeber, "The Seeds of Partition," *New York Times,* Oct. 6, 1991, p. 11.
6. *Loc. cit.*
7. Sidhwa's successes brought her appointments at US Universities: Rice University, 1984-86; University of Houston, 1985; Columbia University, Spring 1989. Sidhwa has recently published a full-length novel which includes her US experience. The title of this novel is *An American Brat.* The novel, focussing on the experiences of a young Parsi girl, is set partly in Lahore and partly in the United States, thus combining Sidhwa's Pakistani and Parsi roots with her American experience.

Gender and Imagination in Bapsi Sidhwa's Fiction

K. NIRUPA RANI

It was only after the Second World War that women novelists transcended gender-related limitations in their thematic concerns and started writing about a range of experiences, including the squalid and the terrifying. In Sidhwa's work, the themes diverge from traditional to contemporary. The feminine imagination in her novels is presented with an incongruous humour to discuss serious socio-political issues even though, as Nirupa Rani argues, Sidhwa is not gender conscious in writing about any issue. She analyzes how Ice-Candy-Man, *despite possessing stylistic charm, vivacity and compelling themes, fails to achieve artistic synthesis. Though her language and narrative are refined, Sidhwa is unable to delve deep into the psyche of her female characters, consequently the sensations it generates are discordant and dishevelled.*

Editor

In the last thirty years there is a vigorous development in thinking about women and their role in society. For majority of women their gender has had some effect on their experiences, and their perceptions of the world, and this is reflected in the nature of the work they produce. Feminism has become a highly important issue in contemporary thought and has resulted in challenging the patriarchal assumption. The application of new ideas about women to their conceptions has produced extensive discussion of both how women have been represented in literature and their trend of writing, The 'gynocritics' theorize about women's literary production and women writers have responded in terms of 'colonization of the mind.' In the contemporary literary scenario in the Indian subcontinent, gender consciousness is not palpable in the phraseology of Western criticism. Women are not lagging behind in their input of literature—we have women writers writing in English from the nineteenth century onwards, not to mention regional writers. These writers with their distinctive talents, particular age of interests and individual style have proved that they are imaginative and are at par with women writers of the West.

It was thought before the First World War that a woman writer is at her best when she deals with the known domain of her womanliness, immediate surroundings and cognition of varied relationships that she creates for herself. But it was after the second World War that women novelists of quality have begun enriching literature, specially fiction, on the Indian subcontinent. Women writers are not always preoccupied with their personal lives; many of them are interested in large-scale social or intellectual questions. Novelists have started using a combination in varying proportions of what they have experienced, what they have discovered and what they have imagined. Their gender has not debarred women from writing about a range of experiences that include the squalid and the terrifying.

India and Pakistan have enjoyed a common literary and cultural heritage till 1947 and have parted ways in trends and achievements after Partition. In spite of Pakistani fragmentation and Sri Lanka's autonomy, India dominates the subcontinent due to its size and literature. The shared thought and heritage has produced in India many women writers whose work is copious and multifarious in its amplitude. But in Pakistan there is virtually only one established woman writer, Bapsi Sidhwa, and in Sri Lanka probably Yasmine Gooneratne.

Bapsi Sidhwa, born in Karachi and brought up in Lahore, is acclaimed by the *Times* as 'a powerful and dramatic novelist' and the *New Statesman* has described her as 'An affectionate and shrewd observer . . . a born storyteller.' In addition to writing and teaching in the United States, she is an active social worker and has represented Pakistan at the 1975 Asian Women's Congress. All her novels, *The Crow-Eaters* (1980), *The Pakistani Bride* (1983) and *Ice-Candy-Man* (1988), are experimentations in imagination with an aim to achieve artistic synthesis.

In Sidhwa's work themes diverge from traditional to contemporaneity. Her concern ranges from a pre-Independence social scene to Partition and its aftermath, and her time frame is fifty years. In this narrow canvas Sidhwa who experiences the pleasures of exile is in a more advantageous position than most of the writers. Her exile has given her an opportunity to laugh at the slogan 'Anatomy is destiny.' She could shed many inhibitions under this influence, but it is doubtful whether she has achieved artistic synthesis or not. Being a writer who is not gender-conscious, she relies more on her imagination than on values. As Pap Gems says: "Writing is individual. When you write you bring the whole of yourself to the meristem, to the growing point of your thought. You are an explorer. You try to push on, to find out. Writing is science, and like science, not entirely cognitive. In fact often hardly so at all."[1] Therefore, in most cases writing is a personal fantasy.

Sidhwa's first novel *The Crow-Eaters* is about Faredoon Junglewalla, a man of distinction and listed in the Zarathustra calendar of great men and women and whose motto in life is 'The sweetest thing/In the world is your need.' Through this narcissistic personality, in about forty-six chapters, Sidhwa takes us into the heart of the Parsi community, portraying its varied customs and traits. It is a straight narration without any twists in the plot and we travel through the book without much mental strain. At the age of twenty-three along with his wife Putli, mother-in-law Jerbanoo and an infant daughter Faredoon settles in Lahore, never to look back. In Lahore he continues to live till the end of the novel that is 1940. His family expands and with his pragmatic intelligence and fraud and arson in insurance he becomes a man of great consequence among the Parsis. People travelled thousands of miles to see him in Lahore, especially as they wished to escape the tight spots they had got themselves into. This successful worldly man encounters disappointment and personal loss in the death of his eldest son and a self-exiled second son. Within this straight conventional theme Sidhwa flings her feminine imagination with an incongruous humour to talk about serious issues like national politics, fraud, death-dealing of mother-in-law, Parsi superstitions, faiths, marriages, rites of death, romance, birth, multifaceted activities and forays to London. Not so much of action but so many incidents take place that one gets a feeling of contradiction. On the one hand the reader finds no link between the words on the page, and on the other the vision or experience is missing in the narrative.

The Pakistani Bride is about Qasim and his foster daughter Zaitoon. Qasim is a man who in the hands of fate had known no childhood. From infancy, responsibility was forced upon him and at ten he was a man conscious of rigorous code of honour by which his tribe lived. By the time he is ten, he is married to a fifteen-year-old girl, at sixteen he becomes a father and a widower at thirty-four. In the year 1947 he migrates to Jullundur which is in India after Partition and from there to Lahore, committing a murder at a slight provocation in Jullundur. If Freddy of *The Crow-Eaters* contemplates murder, Qasim executes it. On his way to Lahore he is impelled to adopt a little girl who is a riot victim like him and calls her Zaitoon. He also makes friendship with Nikkaa 'Pahilwan' and his wife Miriam in the refugee camp. Out of the thirty chapters in the novel, seven (from 4th to 11th) deal with Nikkaa's political connections and Zaitoon flowering into a young girl of sixteen, and as the years slip by Qasim gets nostalgic for the mountains and his memories become Zaitoon's fantasies. When a proposal comes from the mountains of Kohistani, Qasim decides to return to his tribe to settle his daughter. On their way to Kohistan they cross the Army Camp and encounter Major Mushtaq, his cousin Farukh and his American wife Carol. From here seven chapters explain the triangle involvement of Mushtaq, Farukh and Carol. The chapters dealing with this relationship are more authentic than the previous ones. Chapter 18 and 19 are about Zaitoon's incompatible marriage with Sakhi. In the next pan shot we come to know of the infatuation of Carol for Mushtaq and also her desire to understand Zaitoon: "Her life is different from mine, and yet I feel a real bond, an understanding on some deep level."[2] The American and the Pakistani brides become subjects of their husbands' suspicion and both take pragmatic decisions to overcome their crises. Carol decides to make it up to Farukh and contemplates to have a child to bring anchorage to her loveless marriage. Zaitoon decides to take a visionary course of action and runs away, knowing fully well that the punishment for such an act is death. There is a world of difference between these two women and Mushtaq explains to Carol:

> It wouldn't be easy for you really to understand her. You'd find her life in the Zenanna with the other women pitifully limited and claustrophobic—she'd probably find yours—if she could ever glimpse it—terrifyingly insecure and needlessly competitive. (180)

Though their paths are divergent, both Zaitoon and Carol take the same path to Lahore.

The title of the novel is to some extent misleading and cryptic. The novel is a combination of Qasim's personal difficulties and a diluted study of ideals and feelings about love and marriage. The area Sidhwa takes for her subject is a significant human experience, and in her treatment of it she does her best to make it a contemporary issue concerning the extent to which women are psychologically free to change their lives. No doubt Sidhwa has passionate interest in the depth and richness of human experience but to a certain extent her enterprise has become too much for her to cope with.

The third novel *Ice-Candy-Man* and its author have been acclaimed by Anita Desai: "There is no other writer I know on the subcontinent who combines laughter and ribaldry, a passion for history and for truth telling as Bapsi Sidhwa does in *Ice-Candy-Man.*"[3]

Sidhwa acknowledges that she is indebted to Rana Khan for sharing his childhood experiences at the time of Partition. Maybe the author's knowledge of Partition and the historical experiences in the novel is not all that authentic and could be only a borrowed experience. The book was written with the financial assistance of Bunting Institute and the National Endowment for the Arts. No doubt there is novelty and freshness in the book but how far it is artistic is the question.

Ice-Candy-Man comprises thirty-two chapters and gives us a glimpse into events of turmoil on the Indian subcontinent during Partition. Historic truth is only a backdrop of the novel and personal fate of the Ice-Candy-Man the focus. Ice-Candy-Man is a close associate and admirer of an eighteen-year-old ayah working in a Parsi household to look after Lenny, a polio child of four. As in other novels so also in this novel Sidhwa is meticulous in mentioning the age of her characters. It is through Lenny that we come to know of the action of the novel and the seriousness of the narration is marred because of this. It is an adult that speaks through the child's memory and keeps the reader on guard and creates a sense of impressions that the child is capable of reminiscing. The parallel theme in the novel is the slow awakening of the child heroine to sexuality and pains and pleasures of the grown-up and to the particular historical disaster that overwhelms her world. There is an element of exaggeration in all instances with regard to characterization and imagination.

Ayah has thirteen admirers and Sidhwa says: "Only the group around Ayah remains unchanged. Hindu, Muslim, Sikh, Parsee are, as always, unified around her." (97) Of this group Ice-Candy-Man is a man of varied interests. On bitterly cold days when ice sales plummet, Ice-Candy-Man transforms himself into a bird man: "News and gossip flow off his glib tongue like a torrent"; sometimes he quotes national leaders and does political analysis and finally he is a metamorphosed character adopting a poetic mould, confessing that he belongs to 'Kotha'—the royal misbegottens located in Hira Mandi. When Ayah becomes a riot victim it is Ice-Candy-Man that saves her and rehabilitates her in Hira Mandi and finally we come to know that she has left for Amritsar to be with her parents, leaving lovelorn Ice-Candy-Man to his fate. The vulnerable Ayah becomes virtuous gaining dignity and Ice-Candy-Man complimenting her says: "She has the voice of angel and the grace and rhythm of a goddess. You should see her dance. How she moves!" (247) and goes into a poetic outburst "Princes pledge their lives to celebrate her celebrated face!" Hitherto unknown talent of the Ayah is divulged. There are a number of characters in the novel but

Godmother alias Rodabai the social worker is the most mundane. She must have emerged from the depths of Sidhwa's personal experiences as a social worker. Some of the incidents in the novel, instead of being blended into the texture of the novel, are superimposed making the creativity of the author prosaic. After all, the novel is a statement about a thousand different objects and these elements are to be held in place by the force of the writer's vision, if the vision falters, the novel collapses.

A writer's imagination involves his creativity, enterprise, insight, inspiration and originality. To achieve artistic unity the writer has to realize that "Artistic creation is a process of synthesis; by effecting harmony in diffused elements, the artist creates a unity in diversity and imparts 'form' to the formless and the deformed."[4] No doubt Sidhwa is quite enterprising and she has dealt with hitherto untouched themes with a straight narration and her creativity is original but she has failed to achieve artistic synthesis. It is not enough for a writer to create sensation he has seen that there is a grain of truth even in malicious pleasure. "Experience is composed of sensations and it is never one solitary sensation but a system or pattern of sensations. When the sensations are co-ordinated and harmonized our experience is pleasant and when they are discordant and dishevelled the experience is unpleasant."[5] Some incidents in Sidhwa's fiction are quite incongruous and inconsequential. While reading her works one feels that it is a deliberate attempt of hers to give novelty to her writing. This deliberate attempt of hers in *The Crow-Eaters* to explore the erotic world and sentiments of the Parsi community is quite refreshing. In her narration in the first part of the novel, she explains her point of view and excels in the technique of description which is graphic and realistic.

Sidhwa's men have distinct personality traits but her women are not extravagant—they are ordinary, devoid of feelings. In their limited orbits they are socially active and lead only a superficial existence. Even though they are active, they are flat characters. In a novel like *The Pakistani Bride* where there is ample scope for the writer to explore, Sidhwa could not go deep into the psyche of her female protagonist, allowing methodical narration of events in sequential order. Jerbanoo, Rodabai and Carol are lively characters with natural instincts and imagination. They are more familiar to Sidhwa and are within her range of experience.

Sidhwa's language becomes quite refined, and her analytical faculties become sharp when she has to give insights into her statements.

Talking about Parsi community, which is her own community, Sidhwa makes appropriate statements:

> The endearing feature of this microscopic merchant community was its compelling sense of duty and obligation towards other Parsis. . . . There were no Parsi beggars in a country abounding in beggars. . . . Notorious misers, they are paradoxically generous to a cause.[6]

The characters in *The Crow-Eaters* are true to this statement. Her historic observation on the Parsi community's plight during Partition is also authentic. When Billy asks Freddy "Where will we go?" Freddy says softly, "We will stay where we are . . . let Hindus, Muslims, Sikhs or whoever rule. What does it matter?" (283) Likewise Lenny's family and Rodabai's family were not affected by the Partition. It is only the neighbours and close associates of these Parsis that got affected. She has given roots to her characters in Lahore and made Lahore the enchantress. *The Pakistani Bride* is about Muslim community and one realizes that Parsis are more stabilized and privileged and organized than the Muslims. Sidhwa made an honest attempt to explain Islamic sanctity about marriage: "We take marriage and divorce very seriously. It involves more than just emotions. It's a social responsibility." (181) The vision of the writer definitely creeps in the novel however much the author tries to maintain a distance from the subject. The third novel *Ice-Candy-Man* is about cosmopolitan context where there is no scope to think about a particular community. The problem in the novel concerns all the citizens of Lahore and its surroundings. There is no graphic description of Lahore in her works but for the mention of "Tower of Silence." In the first two novels she gave us a detailed account of the nocturnal activities that took place in Hira Mandi. It is only in the last novel that she has traced the original and historical significance of this leitmotif.

NOTES

1. *On Gender and Writing*, ed. Michelene Wandor (London: Pandora Press, 1983), p. 143.
2. Bapsi Sidhwa, *The Pakistani Bride* (Penguin India, 1990), p.180.
3. Bapsi Sidhwa, *Ice-Candy-Man* (Penguin India, 1990), p.180.
4. Bapsi Sidhwa, *Ice-Candy-Man* (Penguin India, 1989).
5. *Indian Aesthetics*, ed. V. Sethuraman, p. 271.
6. *Ibid.*
7. Bapsi Sidhwa, *The Crow-Eaters* (Penguin India, 1990), p. 21.

Ice-Candy-Man: A Feminist Perspective

SUBHASH CHANDRA

The article interprets Ice-Candy-Man *as a significant treatment of a gynocentric view of reality in which the feminine psyche and experiences are presented with a unique insight. The women characters of the novel are aware and confident of their individuality and cannot be easily subjugated. Lenny, her Ayah Shanta, her mother and Godmother affirm their autonomous selfhood and exhibit capability of assuming new roles and responsibilities. They also expose the patriarchal biases present in the contemporary social perceptions. Comparing the novel with Khushwant Singh's* Train to Pakistan, *the author clearly delineates Sidhwa's feminist credo and shows how feminist texts attempt at a radical restructuring of social thought.*

Editor

Ice-Candy-Man commands attention and admiration on several counts. It is the second novel by a woman writer (the first being *Sunlight on a Broken Column by* Attia Hosain), dealing with the theme of Partition of India, but it is the first by a non-partisan writer as Bapsi Sidhwa, being a Parsee, does not belong to either of the two communities which perpetrated mayhem on each other. Therefore, it is likely to be a more neutral and objective account of the traumatic event of Partition which caused divisiveness, disharmony, mutual suspicion, hardening and then tuning into hostility of feelings of friendliness and good-neighborliness and the eventual holocaust. While Attia Hosain does not delve deep into the gory details of the massacres, Sidhwa depicts the events overtaking the Partition in their naked cruelty and ruthlessness. It is a bold attempt on the part of a woman writer to take up a theme which is different from the traditional issues the women writers generally assay—the issues of romantic involvements and the sentimental stuff.

Also it is no mean achievement on Sidhwa's part to depict the process of sexual maturation of a young girl while living in a country like Pakistan where the measure of freedom for women is considerably less than it exists in India. But above all, the novel becomes a significant testament of a gynocentric view of reality in which the feminine psyche and experiences are presented with a unique freshness and aplomb. I shall attempt to demonstrate in the course of the paper how the gynocentric perspective determines the narrative strategy, resulting in the production of a truly feminist text. For the purpose of contrast, I shall posit a male discourse on the same theme, that is, Khushwant Singh's celebrated novel, *Train to Pakistan.* Strategy, even in the literary context "retains all its other inferences related to military strategy of skilful use of a stratagem, or a *maneuver* for obtaining a specific goal or result. Strategy is a move in a game, and the objectives are not available at the surface level of the narrative. It occupies a space between language and plot and between plot and character."[1] Through the structural device (as is done by Jane Austen in *Mansfield Pork* in which the moral control and power to order things passes from the male characters into the hands of Fanny Price who had been marginalized in the beginning of the book) Bapsi Sidhwa turns the female protagonists into the moral centre, while most of the male characters either remain apathetic or indulge in destructive violence and disintegrative action. The analysis of *Ice-Candy-Man* reveals that the female characters pulsate with a will and life of their own. While these characters are unselfconscious of the biological essentialism of their sex, they cut loose the constraints imposed by the gender which is a social construct (and can therefore be deconstructed), and which has come into existence through centuries of biased, motivated and calculated orchestration of the aggressive patriarchal postulates. In a "patriarchal social set up, masculinity is associated with superiority whereas 'femininity is linked with inferiority, and while masculinity implies strength, action, self-assertion and domination, femininity implies weakness, passivity, docility, obedience and self-negation."[2] *Ice-Candy-Man,* though ostensibly a hero-oriented novel, subtly but effectively subverts the ingrained elements of patriarchy, privileging female will, choice, strength along with the feminine qualities of compassion and motherhood.

The central consciousness of the fictional world *of Ice-Candy-Man* is represented by a young girl, Lenny, who is lame. The lameness of the narrator-protagonist becomes suggestive of the handicap a woman creative writer faces, when she decides to wield the pen, because writing, being an intellectual exercise, is considered a male bastion, outside the routine of a woman's submissive domesticity. Her recuperation symbolizes the overcoming of the constraint on the intellectual activity of writing by Bapsi Sidhwa. By making Lenny the narrator of the novel, the novelist lends weight and validity to the feminine perspective on the nature of surrounding reality.

II

An essential difference between a feminist text and a male discourse is that in the latter it is the male who is invested with the qualities of heroism, sacrifice, justice and action while generally the female protagonists remain the recipients of the male bounty and chivalry, in a feminist text, it is the woman who "performs" and controls and promotes the action by her active involvement and concern and in the process it is she who acquires the attributes of heroism and glory. In *Ice-Candy-Man,* the narrator's relationship with her cousin (he remains cousin throughout the novel, without the specific identity of a name) upholds the principle of equality (or even superiority of woman), as she does not allow him to manipulate her sexually and he remains a drooling figure, adoring her for her vivaciousness. In no way does Lenny's lameness become a source of self-pity or a constricting force on her psyche. She remains assertive, at times even aggressive and holds her own when it comes to the crunch. And who is the formative influence on Lenny? Her Ayah, Shanta.

The Ayah is a flame of sensuousness and female vitality around whom the male moths hover constantly and hanker for the sexual warmth she radiates. She acts like the queen bee who controls the actions and emotions of her male admirers: the Fallattis Hotel cook, the Government House gardener, the butcher, the compactly minded "head and body masseur" and the Ice-Candy-Man. The measure of Ayah's power is seen when she objects to the political discussion among her multi-religious admirers as she fears discord the Ice-Candy-Man defers to her wish and says, "It's just a discussion among friends . . . such talk helps clear the air . . . but for your sake, we won't bring it up again."[3] Epitomizing the strength of the feminity of a female, she infuses in Lenny the ideas of independence and choice. Flirtatious and coquettish, the Ayah is fully aware and confident of herself as an individual, who cannot be taken advantage of. At the same time, she is fiercely loyal to the interests of the family she serves and is extremely protective of Lenny, as a mother would be, besides being emotionally attached to her. She suffers during the Partition riots, she is abducted by the cronies of the Ice-Candy-Man, ravished and raped by the hoodlums, kept as the Ice-Candy-Man's mistress for a few months and then is forced to become the Ice-Candy-Man's bride. Her name is changed from Shanta to Mumtaz and she is kept at a *kotha* even after her marriage. During the interregnum between her abduction and marriage, she, in the words of Godmother, is "used like a sewer" by "drunks, pedlars, sahibs and cut-throats," with the connivance of the Ice-Candy-Man. But as soon as the opportunity presents itself, she seizes her freedom and gets away from the man she does not love. She is firm and decisive. "I want to go to my family. . . . I will not live with him," she tells Godmother. And this decision is in spite of the Ice-Candy-Man's love for her who weeps, snivels and pleads humbly with the Godmother to let her remain with him as he has married the Ayah. He receives a thrashing at the hands of the burly Sikh Guard at the Recovered Women's Camp gate, where Ayah is admitted and turns into a mad *faqir*, going to the extent of following the Ayah to Amritsar.

Lenny's mother conforms to the traditional Image of a fidel, faithful and serving wife who seems to be capable only of humouring things out of her husband. She submits to the moods of the man she is wedded to, tolerating in the process, the conventional hegemony given to the male of the species among human beings. And here it appears, the writer could not muster courage enough to invest her (Lenny's mother) with qualities different from those she does, considering the social ethos in the country of her habitat. But the feminist in Sidhwa cuts a caper, and achieves her end in a subtle and complex way. While in *Train to Pakistan,* it is Juggut Singh (Jugga) who, ennobled by his feelings of love for his beloved Nooran, saves, at the cost of his own life, the whole train-load of Muslims migrating to Pakistan in a bid to get away from the clutches of the violent riots, in *Ice-Candy-Man*, it is Lenny's mother and Lenny's aunt who play the sterling humanitarian and heroic role of fighting for the lives and property of Hindus. Clearing herself of Lenny's accusation that she has been helping in the communal conflagration, she says: "we were only smuggling the rationed petrol to help our Hindu and Sikh friends to run away. . . . And also for the convoys to send kidnapped women, like your ayah, to their families across the border." (242) Thus, it is the two women who undertake the risky job of saving lives in danger and the fact acquires significance in the fictional scheme of things.

Towering high among the women protagonists is the vibrant figure of Lenny's Godmother (one of her aunts) whose name is Rodabai. Godmother's personality sparkles with razor-sharp wit, her indefatigable stamina, her boundless love for Lenny, and her social commitment. Her sense of humour, her deer-like agility, in spite of her old age, and her power to mould, modify and order not only individuals but even the system, when she so desires, earn her respect and admiration of people around her. But besides these qualities she is endowed with profound understanding of human existence and her wisdom is revealed when she consoles the Ayah, in the aftermath of what has been done to her: "That was fated, daughter. It can't be undone. But it can be forgiven. . . . Worse things are forgiven. Life goes on and the business of living buries the debris of our pasts. Hurt, happiness . . . all fade impartially . . . to make way for fresh joy and new sorrow. That is the way of life." (262) The most glorious example of her self-confidence, authoritativeness, capacity to handle crisis-situations deftly is provided by her dealing with the Ice-Candy-Man and the rescue of the Ayah she effects after she has been kidnapped and is kept at a *kotha.* The Ice-Candy-Man is propped with the power of the pimp-community, consisting of lawless elements. Endowed with a glib tongue, he is not an easy person to deal with. I would like to quote snatches of the confronting conversation, in order to bring out, in full measure, the power to annihilate the adversary Rodabai possesses:

> Affected at last by Godmother's stony silence, Ice-Candy-Man lowers his eyes. His voice divested of oratory, he says, "I am her slave, *Baijee.* I worship her. She can come to no harm with me."
>
> "No harm?" Godmother asks in a deceptively cool voice—and arching her back like a scorpion its tail, she closes in for the kill. "You permit her to be raped by butchers, drunks, and *goondas* and say she has come to no harm?"
>
> Ice-Candy-Man's head jolts back as if it's been struck.
>
> "Is that why you had her lifted off—let hundreds of eyes probe her—so that you could marry her? You would have your own mother carried off if it suited you! You are a shameless badmash! *Nimakharam*! Faithless!"

Godmother's undaunted visit to the disreputable "Hira Mandi" (the area of *kothas*) and the rescue of the Ayah, once she is convinced that the Ayah is being kept by force against her will, are commendable indeed. Godmother concentrates in her character what the feminists feel is very important for a woman to realize her individuality: the feeling of "self-worth."

As against Sidhwa's novel, Khushwant Singh's *Train to Pakistan* is manifestly a male discourse in which it is the men who are in command and it is they who occupy the centre of the stage. The focus is on the hero, Juggut Singh mostly, and even though he is portrayed as a *budmash,* the writer's sympathy and admiration are obviously for him: for his devil-may-care attitude, his jauntiness, his physical stature (and later for his moral stature as well). When Juggut Singh has been arrested for the dacoity and the murder in the village of Mano Majra, the novelist comments: "Juggut Singh's head and shoulders showed above the turbans of the policemen. It was like a procession of horses with an elephant in their midst—taller, broader, slower with his chain clanking like ceremonial trappings."[4] There is hardly a woman character in the novel who matches the heights Juggut Singh reaches. It is a man's world of Juggut Singh, the budmash turned into a moral hero, Hukam Chand, the Magistrate and the Deputy Commissioner who tries his best to keep the situation under control in Mano Majra in the wake of turbulence caused by the Partition, Iqbal, the Marxist, whose ideology fails him in this time of crisis, Bhai Meet Singh, the priest of the village Gurdwara, who wants to keep on the right side of the police and the police sub-inspector, who is angry with the Sikhs of Mano Majra for not mauling the Muslims. The relationship between Juggut Singh and his beloved Nooran is that of an overbearing lover and submissive beloved. Once his lust overtakes him, he lays her, her protests notwithstanding, and he talks to her peremptorily. Nooran's words about him confirm this point: "*That is all you want. And you get it.* You are just a peasant. Always wanting to sow your seed. Even if the world were going to hell you would want to do that. Even when guns are being fired in the village. Wouldn't you?" (17, my italics) And when, frightened by the sound of gun-shots, and by the prospect of her absence being noticed, she tells him that she will never come to see him again, he says angrily, "Will you shut up or do I have to smack your face?" (17) Let us now compare the relationship between Lenny and Cousin. The latter's carnal cravings are thwarted determinedly by Lenny. "Ever ready to illuminate, teach and show me things, Cousin squeezes my breasts and lifts my dress and grabs my elasticized cotton knickers. But having only the two hands to do all this with he can't pull them down because galvanised to action I grab them up and jab him with my elbows and knees; and turning and twisting, with my toes and heels." (240) No woman character in *Train to Pakistan* attains heroic stature; they remain sex objects, on altars of grand sacrifice and macho love or remain consigned to the parameters of the conventional concept of womanhood. Clearly, the perception of woman is patriarchal and, therefore, women are not individually realized beings. They remain on the margin of the plot, while the task of furthering the action is given to the male protagonists. (Of course, Nooran indirectly galvanises Jugga into the significant humane act.) While Khushwant Singh's *I Shall Not Hear the Nightingale* portrays a fully realized, towering character in the person of Sabhrai, who remains an impressive figure throughout the book, with her qualities of faith in the Great Guru, moral uprightness, empathy and religious poise, the women characters in *Train to Pakistan* remain pale shadows of their male counterparts.

III

But then we come across the oppression and exploitation of her younger sister by Rodabai (Godmother). In spite of the younger sister's slaving obedience (she is called Slavesister), she is treated shabbily and frequently humiliated by Rodabai. Slave-sister's humiliation in the presence of others becomes unseemly and unpalatable. She is leading the life of a bonded slave, forced to suppress her self in every interaction (confrontation, to be precise) with the old lady; she is not allowed to exercise her discretion or her will in any situation. Does this relationship serve any creative purpose in the novel? On the face of it, it just appears to be a dispensable part of the plot, whose removal would not affect the coherence or the compactness of the structure. But I think, Sidhwa wants to convey an important message, or warning that the exploitation, manipulation and suppression of one individual by another are not confined to the male-female relationship. These can exist between a female-female relationship as well and become as vicious and debilitating for the victim as when a male dominates and exploits a woman. The feminists, it seems, are being made alive to the dangers of replicating the patriarchal principle and thus perpetuating the class of the exploiters and the exploited amongst themselves. This makes Sidhwa's feminist credo broader, fairer and more responsive to the human condition.

IV

Ice-Candy-Man, thus, becomes a feminist text in the true sense of the term, successfully attempting to bring to the centre-stage the female protagonists. These protagonists, while on the one hand, come alive on account of their realistic presentation, on the other, they serve as the means of consciousness-raising among the female segment of society. Literature is a powerful tool in the hands of creative writers to modulate and change the societal framework, and Sidhwa through her extremely absorbing and interesting work seeks to contribute to the process of change that has already started all over the world, involving a reconsideration of women's rights and status, and a radial restructuring of social thought. Sidhwa belongs to that group of women creative writers who have started to depict "determined women for whom the traditional role is inadequate, women who wish to affirm their independence and autonomy and are perfectly capable of assuming new roles and responsibilities." These writers wish to build a world which is free of dominance and hierarchy, a world that rests on the principles of justice and equality and is truly human.

NOTES

1. Jasbir Jain, "Gender and Narrative Strategy," in Iqbal Kaur, ed., *Gender and Literature* (Delhi: B.R., 1992), p. 48.
2. Iqbal Kaur, p. xi.
3. Bapsi Sidhwa, *Ice-Candy-Man* (Harmondsworth, Middlesex: Penguin, 1989), p. 92.
4. Khushwant Singh, *Train to Pakistan* (London: Four Square Books), p. 55.
5. Iqbal Kaur, p. vii.

Ice-Candy-Man: A Saga of Female Suppression and Marginalization

PALLAVI

Ice-Candy-Man *projects the violent and chaotic days of India-Pakistan Partition in 1947. Through the character of Lenny, Sidhwa has given graphic details of the political changes occurring in the country, as well as its effect on the citizens of India. The novelist has very realistically illustrated women's plight and exploitation in the patriarchal society. Men establish their masculine powers and hence fulfil their desires by brutally assaulting women. Men as aggressors feel elated and victorious whereas women endure the pain and humiliation of the barbarity enacted upon them. Sidhwa, as a novelist, talks of emancipation of women. Hence the novel ends on a positive note. Women strive to come out of their plight and finally move forward from their degraded and tormented state to start their lives afresh.*

Feminism as a movement has played a very vital role in projecting the suppressed status of women in the patriarchal society. In the domain of patriarchal culture, woman is a social construct, a site on which masculine meanings get spoken and masculine desires enacted. As Sushila Singh puts it in *Feminism and Recent Fiction in English*: "Human experience for centuries has been synonymous with the masculine experience with the result that the collective image of humanity has been one-sided and incomplete. Woman has not been defined as a subject in her own right but merely has an entity that concerns man either in his real life or his fantasy life."[1] Many contemporary writers have projected the plight of women based on caste, creed, religion, gender-prejudices, community and beliefs, and are trying to suggest some pragmatic solutions to them. Though the conservative social norms and myths of feminine behaviour are challenged all over the world yet a change in the attitude of patriarchal society towards woman is at a snail's pace. Bapsi Sidhwa's novel *Ice-Candy-Man* represents a series of female characters who have survived in a chaotic time of 1947 in India, which can be registered as the period of worst religious riots in the history of India.

Sidhwa has given a very realistic and transparent picture of carnage during Hindu-Muslim riots in 1947. The novel mirrors men becoming adversary on the basis of their religion and also represents the changing political scenario of the country. Emotional turmoil, individual weakness, barbarities of communal riots and the brutalities inflicted on women amidst this iconoclastic ruthlessness and communal frenzy have been very realistically projected by the novelist. The whole story has been narrated by the female protagonist Lenny who relates the horrors of violence and her personal observations and reactions. The protagonist not only observes but also analyses men's lascivious and degrading attention towards women, voraciousness of male sexual desires, women's plight as they are reduced to the status of sexual objects, and relates the peculiar disadvantages, social and civil, to which they are subjected.

Lenny as a narrator moves from one phase of her life, i.e., childhood to adolescence. During this journey, she understands the changes taking place in the society, men's attitude towards women and women's subjection. The whole phase helps her to develop a more mature vision towards life. She gives a closer look at the relationship between men and women which awakens her young mind to develop a vision of her own.

The narrator relates her life as "My world is compressed."[2] As a physically handicapped girl, her world is restricted to the four walls of the house. As a child she spends most of her time with her Godmother. She terms her Godmother's room as, "My refuge from the perplexing unrealities of my home on Warris Road." (1) As a child she had no inclination to have female possession though from time to time she was advised to have one by the women of her family. She recalls: "I can't remember a time when I ever played with dolls though relatives and acquaintances have persisted in giving them to me." (138) This reflects the sexual identity thrust upon her time and again. Her schooling is stopped as suggested by Col. Bharucha, her doctor, because she was suffering from polio. He concludes, "She'll marry—have children—lead a carefree, happy life. No need to strain her with studies and exams." (15) Lenny concludes that the suggestion made by Col. Bharucha sealed her fate. It reveals the limitations associated with a girl's life. Development of feminine virtues with female nature and carrying out the responsibilities associated with the domestic affairs are considered as the only aim for women. Patriarchal society considers women as physically weak to venture into the world outside the four walls of their houses and too deficient to make important decisions. Hence women are relegated to the domestic sphere where they have to accept the hegemony of a male counterpart. Since ages it is considered that it is a woman's duty to tend house, raise children and give comfort to her family. Shashi Deshpande, a contemporary novelist, suggests that women should be given enough space to realize their true personality. She points out in an interview to Geetha Gangadharan:

> The stress laid on the feminine functions, at the cost of all your potentials as an individual enraged me. I knew I was very intelligent person, but for a woman, intelligence is always a handicap. If you are intelligent, you keep asking, "Why, why, why" and it becomes a burden.[3]

Simone de Beauvoir also holds the same view about social conditioning. According to her, mothers are highly responsible for inculcating feminine traits of submission and self-abnegation in women. She writes in *The Second Sex* that the girl-child

> is often concerned in this way with motherly tasks; whether for convenience or because of hostility and sadism, the mother thus rids herself of many of her functions; the girl in this matter made to fit precociously into the universe of curious affairs; her sense of importance will help her in assuming her femininity. But she is deprived of happy freedom, the carefree aspect of childhood, having become precociously a woman, she leaves all too soon the limita-

> tions this estate imposes upon a human being; she reaches adolescence as an adult, which gives her history a special character.[4]

Lenny as a girl learns that marriage of girls is of utmost importance to their parents. Independence and self-identity are meant for men. The intense concern for her marriage even in her childhood puts Lenny in dismay. She states, "Drinking tea, I am told, makes one darker. I'm dark enough. Everyone says, 'It's a pity Adi's fair and Lenny so dark. He's a boy. Anyone will marry him." (81)

She recognizes the biological exploitation of women as she grows. As a child she cherishes her mother's love and her father's protection but the whole episode of Ice-Candy-Man and Ayah destroys all her conceptions about love. She was shocked to perceive Ice-Candy-Man pushing his wife Ayah into the business of prostitution. She concludes, "The innocence that my parents' vigilance, the servants' care and Godmother's love sheltered in me, that neither Cousin's carnal cravings, nor the stories of the violence of the riots, could quite destroy, was laid waste that evening by the emotional storm that raged around me. The confrontation between Ice-Candy-Man and Godmother opened my eyes to the wisdom of righteous indignation over compassion. To the demands of gratification and the unscrupulous nature of desire." (252) The site of Hindu and Muslim women being raped during the riots petrifies her. She watches men turning into beasts leaving no room for moral and human values. Women including Ayah were becoming prey of men. Lenny was shocked to see the human mind which was built of nobler materials getting so easily corrupted. Men were declaring superiority over each other by sexually assaulting women. Women had nothing in their favour. Envy, malice, jealousy, rage for personal power and importance in men were leading to violence and injury. Shashi Deshpande states:

> rape is for me the grossest violation of trust between two people. Whether it is someone in the family or your husband or any other man who commits a rape, it destroys the trust between men and women. It is also the greatest violence because it is not only the

> woman's body but it is her mind and feeling of her right to have a control on her body which is gone.[5]

Sidhwa has also projected the aftermath of such inhuman and barbaric acts against women after the riots. She has projected the farcical social behaviour which victimizes women alone for any bodily violence and leaves them to wail with their bitter experience which gives them a feeling of pain and sense of loss. Lenny is shocked to see the changing attitude of men towards one another. Religious enmity easily erased the threads of friendship. She concludes:

> And I became aware of religious differences. It is sudden. One day everybody is themselves—and the next day they are Hindu, Muslim, Sikh and Christian. People shrink, dwindling into symbols. (93)

She knows that men of different religions can never become friends again. To take revenge was their only motive in life. Lenny concludes, "Now I know surely. One man's religion is another man's poison." (117) Lenny is not ready to accept the prevailing social condition. As a grown up she analyses the whole situation and draws some conclusions. She decides to hunt for her lost Ayah, who also became a prey of the Hindu-Muslim riots. Lenny decides to talk to her mother regarding Ayah. She wants to save Ayah from the terrible profession of prostitution as told by her cousin. Lenny decides, "If those grown men pay to do what my comparatively small cousin tried to do, then Ayah is in trouble. I think of Ayah twisting Ice-Candy-Man's intrusive toes and keeping the butcher and wrestler at arm's length. And of those stranger's hands hoisting her chocolate body into the cart. . . . I decide it's time to confront Mother." (241) Due to Lenny's continuous persistence at home, she is informed about Ayah's whereabouts. The novel ends with Ayah being sent back to her parents' home.

Throughout the novel, Lenny appears as a courageous and bold girl who is not ready to succumb to the communal frenzy. She is inquisitive, daring, demanding and lively. Sidhwa has given a feminist touch to the character of Lenny who moves forward in life despite various hindrances and obstacles. As she observes the lives of various women around her, she understands the limitations associated with women's lives in patriarchal society. She is shocked to see men betraying and sexually assaulting women and exploiting them. Sidhwa as a writer encourages women to transgress the line of marginalization. She states in an interview:

> As a woman, one is always marginalised. I have worked among women to create an awareness of their rights and protested against repressive measures aimed at Pakistani women and minority community.[6]

Lenny's mother is another interesting female character of the novel. As a servile housewife, she limits her life to the four walls of her home. She reticently follows her husband, who is the decision-maker of the family. Lenny's mother is a representative of those traditional women who as subordinates never express their desire to establish themselves as better human beings. Sidhwa seems to illustrate through Lenny that men have to dilute their ego and women have to eschew the image of weaker sex or deprived femininity. Mindsets need to be changed in order to establish equality between the sexes. The patriarchal society should perceive women beyond the roles of daughters, wives and mothers. Traditional male fantasies have created a particular image of women to suit their interests—submissive, servile, docile and self-abnegating. These fantasies have become alive, as women have been meticulously trained by the patriarchal/social system to assimilate them. A big transformation is required at the social level, which will acknowledge women as human beings with souls, desires, feelings, ambitions and potentials. Simultaneously women should utilize their potentials beyond their domestic life to assert their individuality. The novel *Ice-Candy-Man* projects through Lenny's mother that women should have a purpose in life besides domesticity which should be developed by them to the best of their abilities. Women need to liberate themselves from the constraints of 'womanliness' which will erase the existing discrepancies regarding their marginalization.

Lenny's mother exhibits a change in her personality by the end of the novel. She becomes acquainted with the political changes occurring in the country during India-Pakistan division. She emerges as a social worker. Along with Lenny's Electric-Aunt, she helps the victims of 1947 riots. She provides people with petrol who wanted to cross the border and helps the raped and exploited women. Lenny's mother shows a lot of similarity with Bhabani Bhattacharya's female character Monju in *So Many Hungers*. Monju appears as a fuller and maturer woman by the end of the novel. In the beginning she projects the womanly traits of being happy and content with her life and family. But gradually, with the passage of time, the pathetic incidences of Bengal famine and pictures of human life transform her. She learns to think beyond the realms of her own life and as a human cannot remain blind to and detached from the miseries and traumas of others. With a soul to feel and a mind to think it is very difficult to shut oneself behind the door when people are screaming for help and rescue. Similarly Lenny's mother could not resist herself from helping the victims of 1947 riots.

Sidhwa exposes the patriarchal practices of the society which marginalize their growth and development and also represents women's psychology that has been toned by centuries of conditioning.

Hence, we can conclude that Sidhwa as a writer has a constructive approach towards women's predicament. Women may not just fill a place in the society but they should fit in it. By leading a contented life they paralyze their lives but if they desire they will have courage to break through their plight and afford opportunity for betterment.

NOTES

1. Sushila Singh, "Preface," *Feminism and Recent Fiction in English* (New Delhi: Prestige, 1991), p. 7.
2. Bapsi Sidhwa, *Ice-Candy Man* (New Delhi: Penguin, 1989), p. 1.

3. Shashi Deshpande, "Denying the Otherness," Interview with Geetha Gangadharan, *The Fiction of Shashi Deshpande*, ed. R.S. Pathak (New Delhi: Creative, 1997), p. 253.
4. Simone de Beauvoir, *The Second Sex*, ed. and trans. H.M. Parshley (1960; London: Four Square Books, 1961), p. 24.
5. Pallavi, Interview with Shashi Deshpande, "The Fiction of Shashi Deshpande: Women's Journey from Self-Effacement to Self-Actualization," Bangalore, 21 Aug. 2001.
6. Interview, *The Hindustan Times*, Sunday Magazine, 26 April 1998.

The Geography of Scars and History of Pain: A Study of *Ice-Candy-Man*

VANASHREE TRIPATHY

The article discusses the child protagonist's initiation in the adult world which is marked by a diverse and disparate cultural climate. It also analyzes the connotative interpretations of the title and shows how often the vast range of characters gives the narrative a caricature's edge and provides moments of pure mirth and hilarity. The article further equates Lenny's version of life with an authentic representation of the marginalized culture outside the mainstream as a part of history. Tripathy concludes that unlike other partition novels Ice-Candy-Man *transcribes the destructive impulse of the time with a humane and compassionate perspective.*

Editor

History, despite its wrenching pain, cannot be unlived. In *Ice-Candy-Man*, Bapsi Sidhwa conjures life and time in the sub-continent during the British Raj from 1935 to 1947, the period of the Partition of India and Pakistan. The narrative of the novel constitutes "the thick description of history"[1] in all its ramifications in the dramatic portrayal of interaction among diverse strata in various communities—their modes of the personality variants within a society by recording individual opinion, habit, belief, behaviour and psychological disposition in the context of cultural themes such as values, religion, politics and ethos. In seizing the lost truth—the "other" in history, the text reveals an intuitive grip of the events that makes it refreshingly different from the scores of other novels with similar concerns. Here I am inclined to attribute this version of history to the writer's view of history as a woman that makes the whole rendering further distanced from the stereotypes. The narrative encapsulates with compelling sensitivity and empathy the protagonist girl child Lenny's initiation in the adult world marked by a highly diverse and disparate cultural climate. The episodic structure of the novel describes within the framework of the larger theme of Lenny's growth and attainment of some understanding of human situations, the personal, political ideological pursuits, anxiety, pain, stupidity, suffering, joy possessing the epoch before and immediately after the Partition of India in Lahore. The shrewd but sensitive tendering of the past by girl child—its geography of scars, its history of pain—raises doubts about the credibility of the projection of the child's "point of view." One may find within the child's point of view a mature woman's perceptions or authorial omniscient point of view permeating and overlapping and as a result, a volitional blend of innocence and experience. In defence of this narrative approach, it could be observed that events of past really expand later and thus we do not have complete emotions about the immediate present. Only in the past we could invest meaning. Filled out in memory, the dead could take a final form only later. In the female infant Lenny's perceptions the living could be unformed, like herself in the making. Sliding into the adult's point of view, the narrative relates the random history of the female subtexts to the potential narratives of love and betrayal in a mode that enables both the narrator and the reader to discover patterns of cultural significance.

I

In versatile strokes of humour, fantasy, scatology and caricature, the upper middle class Parsee community—Godmother, Oldhusband, Slavesister, Mother, Father, Electric-Aunt, Cousin, Dr. Mody, Dr. Bharucha are portrayed. We are allowed to participate in their cultural codes, allegiances, insecurity, and political and human ideals. The Parsees situated in a metropolitan city of the then united India, sandwiched between two invidiously hostile Hindu/Sikh and Muslim communities—a delicate juncture, were more vulnerable in the contemporary political context because Lahore had to play a major part in the Partition of India. A period when such massive historical figures such as Gandhi,

Nehru and Jinnah loomed large, Lenny's immediate world is made of a Hindu Ayah Shanta, with whom she has developed a close bond, Imam Din, Masseur and Ice-Candy-Man, Shankar Haria, a Sikh neighbour Mr. Singh and his children, English Officer Mr. Roger, Anglo-Indian Mr. and Mrs. Pen etc. The narrative in its shifting focus makes us see the scene, hear the sound, and sense the flavour of a highly desperate cultural configuration coexisting in their intrinsic vulnerability, cruelty and ideological or religion-sanctioned logic. Hindu, Muslim, Sikh, Parsee and English are all seen in terms of experiences that are too versatile to be reduced to a category of funny, farcical, tragic or grand. While fundamentalist propaganda and politics rage, divided loyalties breed brutality and betrayal, arson, looting and the dislocation of common man. A poignant drama of personal loss and agony of young Ayah Shanta intrudes in the larger scenario and transmutes the whole tone of the novel. The awful profligacy, the ugliness, sordidness and deceit converge into an agony and ecstasy that transcend physical and rational levels and expose us to secret logic of human desire and depravity—the ghost of the past embodying inexorably the major character, Ice-Candy-Man. The novel, from being a shrewd satiric record of the history of India and Pakistan, becomes a lore of elegiac dimension that has already been anticipated in Iqbal's lines serving as a prologue: "The fire of verse gives us courage and bids me no more to be faint/With dust in my mouth. I am abject: to God I make no complaint/Sometimes you favour our rivals then sometimes with us. You are free/I am sorry to say it so boldly. You are no less fickle than we."[2] The last part of the novel centring on Ice-Candy-Man makes us recognize the teleos of history that has cast him in precarious times. His historical antecedents reveal skeletons on the cupboard of history. In the plight of this bastard—a derelict whom we identify not only a victim of history and his own doomed longings but also more significantly of the culpable, contemptible, misogynistic hypocrisy of the Moghul ruling class that gave social sanction to the sordid subjugation of women to pander to the lust and voyeuristic urges. And, subsequently, it bred a class of male and female bastards—dispossessed and disowned, whose perpetuation of pimping and prostitution in the facade of beauty, art and poetry concealed covetousness, helplessness and deceit. In the case of Ice-Candy-Man nonetheless, there has to be no more degradation. The disarray of history and his own fatal flaw assign him intense desolation but that also lift him to a sphere of spiritual plane. Rejection by his unwilling beloved transform him into "a moonstruck Fakir who has renounced the world for his beloved: be it a woman or God." (276). And Ice-Candy-Man's voice humming in our mind stirs a certain sense of awe;

> Don't berate me, beloved, I'm God-intoxicated:
> I'll wrap myself about you; I'm mystically mad. (277)

The opening chapters of the novel however do not provide a clue to understanding the significance of the title. It is at the end that the whole panorama of the novel attains a metaphoric image in the title. One may infer a similar implication of the title in Wallace Steven's "Emperor of Ice Cream." The poem evokes the image of a slatternly woman at her wake attended by a man who represents pleasure and by wenches who are apparently fellow prostitutes. The meaning suggests the power of death over physical satisfaction. While the novel affirms the supreme value of human freedom to make right moral choices, "Ice" in both the titles metaphorically suggests innocence, cruelty, betrayal and the ultimate power of death that divests life of all illusions.

Lenny's version of life is a truth telling project. Her affliction with polio in infancy has made her routine different from other children. She is in a privileged position and has also access to social and private gathering or the intimate lives of elders. She cannot be like others, she cannot lie. Says Godmother, "I'm afraid a life of crime is not for you. Not because, you aren't sharp, but because you are not suited to it. . . . A life sentence? Condemned to honesty??"(85) Since her truth telling brings about a disaster in some lives, she recognizes that she is "an animal with conditioned reflexes that cannot lie." (190) With ruthless candour, she describes her lameness, her exposure to her difference as physically handicapped and also as a female—the nature of male-female relationship—women as the object of lust, desire, the destructive outcome of sexuality. Lenny's parents, Ayah Shanta, her admirers, cousin make her sense the subterranean motives and urges both in political and personal lives. The city of Lahore in 1935 becomes alive, throbbing with life. Lenny pushed in a pram by her Ayah covers jail road, Queen Road, Past Y.M.C.A, past the Freemason's lodge (The Ghost Club) and across the mall to the Queen's statue in the park opposite the assembly chambers. She watches every scene, she loves it (18); Queen Victoria's statue imposes the English Raj in the Park, Felleti's Hotel Cook, the government house Gardener, and an elegant, compactly muscled head and body Masseur. Ayah Shanta and Lenny sit together. The Ice-Candy-Man of the title lurks in the background selling his popsicles lounging on the grass, a man who has to have an ominous significance in the story. In this Company, Lenny gathers knowledge of the pre-Partition politics in India, and also the mysteries of adult sexuality: "Masseur's knowing fingers, his voice gravelly with desire . . . consummate arm circles Ayah. Ayah's sound of pleasure." (18) Fine confident strokes describe the character: "Ayah, chocolate brown and short. Everything about her is eighteen years old and round and plump. . . . And as if her looks were not stunning enough, she has a rolling bouncing walk that agitates the globules of her buttocks under cheap colourful saree and the half spheres beneath her short saree-blouse. The English man no doubt had noticed." (3) Lenny notices things that love to crawl beneath Ayah's sarees: lady bird, glow worms and Ice-Candy-Man's toes: "They travel so cautiously that both Ayah and I are taken unawares. An absorbing gossip. I am sometimes bribed into commerce with the Ice-Candy-Man." (19) She senses tension among the competing admirers of Ayah: "They look as if each is a whiskered dog circling the other, weighing in and warning his foe." (151) The awareness of the subtle exchange of signals between man-man and man-woman mark her initiations into social-sexual codes. "I learn the human needs, frailties, cruelties and joys." (20)

Not only are the people inhabiting Ayah's world portrayed with vividness and spontaneity, the mother and father, Godmother—childless, abrasive are made to look real. Lenny's special relationship with the Godmother is recorded with genuine feeling: "The bond that ties her strength to my weakness, my fierce demands to her nurturing, my trust to her capacity to contain that trust-my loneliness . . . to her compassion . . . stronger than the bond of motherhood." (4) The Electric-Aunt, addicted to navy blue, swift moving cousin, her son who makes Lenny know herself as an object of sexuality—her difference. Adi, her brother, reminds her of her ugliness. "I am skinny, wizened, sallow, wiggly-haired ugly. He is beautiful." (22) The narrative varies from plain matter of fact to metaphoric that amaze and amuse because of the indigenous mode of perceptions: Lenny cannot imagine Ice-Candy-Man working alongside Ayah in her house. "Mother'd throw a fit! . . . with his thuggish way of inhaling from the stinking cigarettes clenched in his fist, his fleshy scarves and neck of jasmine altar . . . a shady almost disreputable type." (20) The sinister but charming implication of Ice-Candy-Man could be read in the portrait. "He talks news and gossip flow off his glib tongue like a torrent. He reads Urdu newspapers and the Urdu Digest. He can, when he applies himself, read the headlines of the Civil and Military Gadgets, the English daily. The rising German forces." (20) The very description constitutes spurious, promiscuous personality who, we learn later, is a bastard born in Kotha and can enact glibly the protocol of a Nawab as well as of a pimp. The focus on Shanta and Ice-Candy-Man serves Sidhwa's purpose of connecting the personal with the national concerns and expand the boundary of her fictional world. The novel is smoothly allowed to attain more space and contain not only the story of Ayah Shanta's love for Masseur, Masseur's murder in the riots, attrition, her abduction and cruel degradation but also the tense political scenario of the time. Things are happening at a charged pace. It is the time when the political agitations in the Raj are gaining momentum: "The European mystery is erased/ In secret of his conjuring trick is known." (111) The arrival and exaltation of Gandhi is received with mixed reaction—comic and wary: "Gandhiji reaches out and suddenly seizes my arm in a startling voice. What a sickly-looking child, he announces. . . . Flush her stomach! Her skin will bloom like roses." (87) He is a man who loves women. And lame children. And the untouchable sweeper . . . so he will love the untouchable sweeper's constipated girl child best . . . It wasn't until some years later . . . when I realized the full scope and dimension of the massacre . . . that I comprehended the concealed nature of the ice lurking deep beneath the hypnotic and dynamic femininity of Gandhi's non—violent exterior." (86)

Nehru however is inscribed with obvious awe and admiration and contrasted with Jinnah (159). The Nehru and Lady Mountbatten connection does not cease to excite most writers who deal with India's history. Jinnah's profile is summed up in a few succinct lines—austere, driven, pukka Sahib accented, deathly ill: Sidhwa's protagonist fancies a tragic-romantic story of Jinnah's love, marriage and loss—his Parsee wife and that he died because of heartbreak. Unlike the historiography, literature has chosen to conceive Jinnah in romantic terms. Sidhwa also takes his clue from Sarojini Naidu who paid tribute to Jinnah in gushing language: "preeminently the clam hauteur of his accustomed reserve, . . . an intuition quick and tender as a woman's humour gay and winning as a child . . . dispassionate in his estimate and acceptance of life." (161)

The conflict between Jinnah and Gandhi threatens the political climate. There is news of breaking the country. Ayah informs her: "They will dig a canal." (93) Lenny becomes aware of the catalytic power of religious differences. It is sudden, one day everybody in themselves and the next day they are Hindu, Muslim, Sikh, Christian. People shrink, dwindle into symbols. Ayah is no longer just my all-encompassing Ayah. She is also a token. A Hindu. (92-93) With the approaching climate of disquiet, the fundamentalism is provoked. While the Parsee community maintains caution, the Muslims Imam Din and Yusuf are turning into religious zealots: they take Friday afternoon off for the *Jumha* prayers. The vivid dramatic description illustrate Sidhwa's power of capturing moments with photographic accuracy.

> One Friday they set about preparing themselves ostentatiously. Squatting atop the cement wall of the garden tank . . . they wash their heads, arms, neck, the cans and noisily clear their throat and noses . . . crammed into a narrow religious slot they are diminished; as are Jinnah and Iqbal, Ice-Candy-Man and the Masseur. (93)

Equally realistic details evoke the low caste female child, Papoo and her family belonging to the sweeper class, they are alienated because of the caste hierarchy—"because they are entrenched deeper in their low Hindu caste. While the Sharmas and Daulatrams, Brahmins like Nehru, are dehumanized by their lofty caste and caste marks." (93) Sidhwa's pen sketches the heterogeneous configurations—caste—community with astute understanding: The Rogers of Birdwood Barracks, Queen Victoria and King George are English Christians. They look down their noses upon the Pens who are Anglo-Indian, who look down theirs on the Phaibus who are Indian Christian, who look down upon all non-Christians (94). The convoluted caste politics in colonial India, its grim implications—the will to power associated with deeply entrenched insecurity—form a cultural configuration from which Parsees as Sidhwa sees are fastidiously aloof: "In this milieu, Godmother, Slavesister, Electric-Aunt and my family are reduced to irrelevant nomenclature: "we are Parsee, what is God?" (91)

The easy flow of the narrative coordinates and incorporates a wide sweep of characters and episodes in interaction of diverse cultures, compulsions, implicated in the sociology and politics of culture. Punjabi abuses build up the ambience of the sweeper caste: Papoo an eleventh year daughter of Mucchoo shall be given to an older dwarfish man in marriage. Papoo is treated with sordid cruelty. Mucchoo screeching at Papoo: "I turn my back; the bitch slacks off? I say something, she becomes a deaf mute. I'll thrash the wickedness out of you." (94)

The scatology involved in story—telling intruding into the narrative here and there unobtrusively makes us grasp the displaced communal prejudice with ugly potentials. The butcher continues: "You Hindus eat so much beans and cauliflower. I'm no surprised your Yogis levitate. They possibly fart into their way right up to heaven." (97) Lenny observes Ayah Shanta is not laughing, she senses endemic hostility between different religions. Everybody is a party to it. With unrelenting accuracy Lenny describes a Brahmin: "our shadow glides over a Brahmin sitting cross legged, . . . our shadow has violated his virtue. . . . He looked at his food as if it is infested with maggots . . . and throws away the leaf.." (116-17) The interacting Sikh, Hindu, Muslim and Parsee give the narration a caricature's edge and provide some moments of innocent humour: "The little Sikh boys running about with hair piled in top-knots, are keeping mostly to themselves," or " Cousin tells Lenny that the twelve o'clock heat of the sun addles their brains" (96) or Muslim family with their burka-veiled women they too sit apart. Dressed in satins and high heels, the little Muslim girls wear make up." (96) Equally identifiable in the subcontinent is the scene: "A group of smooth skinned Brahmins and their pampered male offspring form a tight circle of supercilious exclusivity." (98) Lenny hears their yelling: Parsee, crow-eaters! (100) The mutual misinterpretation of the communities aggravates the confusion of the time.

The narrative's wittiest rendering is that of Parsee community, where slapstick and scatological references give a bounce and realism to the mimetic description and this is where the narrator feels most at home. The Parsee household, its cultural codes—patterns of communication, jokes—render characters like Godmother, old-husband, Dr. Manek Mody, Slavesister, Electric-Aunt, Cousin and Dr. Bharucha distinct individuality. Their idiosyncrasies, failings and convictions are vividly dramatized. The hilarious moments also neutralize the tense ambience of the outside world. Slavesister is often being subjected to reprimand. The narrator finds Godmother in a good form:

> His Sourship [Old Father] had his bath. Manek, you'd better take your term before Cleopatra [Slavesister] decides to settle down to her business on the commode. "Really, Rodabai. . . . I hate to say it, but you really are going too far . . . may I ask who you are to tell

Manek not to meddle? Are you somebody? Queen Cleopatra of Jail road perhaps?" (166-67)

Milan Kundera in his essay "63 words" defines obscenity as the root that attaches us most deeply to our homeland. This depiction tellingly brings to the fore the rootedness of the novelist as much in the description of Mother's prayer of the Great Trouble Easers, the angels Mushkali Assa and Behram Yazd.

II

The cultural praxis of the colonized people fighting hard to overthrow imperialism was already afflicted with an endemic inner malaise. Their movement for freedom and Independence was, in effect a combat between two nations, two races, two people, two cultures and two ideologies over a territory India. The fight was over who owns India, who rules India, who represents India. The rift makes itself apparent in the volatile moments of sloganeering much before the event of Partition in 1947, as the image figures in the mind of child Lenny:

> Adi and I slip past the attention of our vigilants and join the tiny tin pot processions that are spawned on Warris Road. We shout ourselves hoarse crying, 'Jai Hind! Jai Hind', or Pakistan Zindabad!' depending on the whim or the allegiance of the principal crier.

And as the time passes, the sectarian passion gains further momentum, every segment of the city life comes under the spell of sporadic violence of actions and words. DIG Police Roger is murdered—body found gutted. Muslim, Sikh, Hindu leaders rise for power and autonomy. Master Tara Singh is quoted as saying, "We will see how the Muslim swines get Pakistan: we will fight till the last man." (113) The arrival of Holi festival in 1947 is greeted with ominous ring by Muslims: Holi with their blood! Allah Ho Akbar—Pakistan Zindabad (134). Violence grows more gruesome. The narrative transcription of the lurking menace evokes a sense of fear, waste and vacuity. In terse, taut narrative the sinister design of the time is apprehended:

> 'Lahore is burning. . . . The abandoned houses of Sharmas, Daulatrams. . . . that Delhi Gate . . . There's Lahori Gate . . . There's Mochi Darwaza . . . Isn't that where Masseur lives? Ayah asks.
>
> 'Yes that is where your masseur stays' Ice-Candy-Man said, unable to mask his ire. 'It is a Muslim mohalla'. (134)

Lenny's observations tellingly register the demonstrations of invidious hatred between the communities:

> a mob of Sikhs, their wild long hair and beard rampant, large fevered eyes glowing in fanatic faces, pours into the narrow lane roaring slogans, holding curved swords, shoving up a manic wave of violence that sets Ayah to trembling as she holds me tight. A naked child, twitching on a spear struck between her shoulders, is waved like a flag: her screamless mouth agape she is staring straight up at me.
>
> And then slowly advancing mob of Muslim goondas: packed so tight that we can see only the top of their heads. Roaring: Allah o Akbar! Yaaaa Ali!' and Pakistan Zindabad!'
>
> The terror the mob generates is palpable—like an evil, paralyzing spell. The terrible procession, like a sluggish river, flows beneath us. Every short while, a group of men, like a whirling eddy, stalls—and like the widening circles of a treacherous eddy dissolving in the mainstream, leaves in its centre the pulping red flotsam of a mangled body. (135-136)

The violence further increases, the market places and residential area flash in explosions: "Trapped by the spreading flames, the panicked Hindus rush in droves from one end of the street to the other. . . . Some collapse in the street. Charred limbs and burnt logs are falling from the sky." (137) In Lenny's reflection, we discover the enormous desolation of this epoch:

> Despite the residue of passion and regret, and loss of those who have in panic fled—the fire could not have burned for . . . Despite all the ruptured dreams, broken lives, buried gold, bricked in rupees, secret jewellery, lingering hopes . . . the fire could not have burned for months and months. But in my memory it is branded over an inordinate length of time: memory demands poetic licence. (139)

And the Ice-Candy-Man is the medium of the news—his information/misinformation—horrendous tales of macabre violence threaten the world of Lenny: "There are no young women among the dead: Only two gunny bags full of women's breasts." (140) Lenny fancies: "I see mother's detached breasts: soft, pendulous, their beige nipples spreading," (140) a totem of female victimization. The stories of girls and women found naked in the ditches are too familiar. Ice-Candy-Man's stories grow more appalling as his shriveled dried up face looks possessed. In this milieu however bathing of buffaloes in Lenny's household, father's coming back by bicycle goes on as ever. Moti Mucchoo and Pappu (the untouchable) remain unruffled—themselves victims and victimizing each other, they belong to no community. While Lenny shares the troubled fears of Ayah Shanta and her knowledge that her lover Masseur was violently murdered, she does not have the resources to understand the depth of Ayah Shanta's inconsolable grief.

Ice-Candy-Man again appears on the scene, this time with a violent crowd and he manipulates the child into speaking truth about Ayah Shanta's whereabouts and gets her abducted:

> They drag Ayah out. They drag her by her arms stretched taut, and her bare feet—that want to move backwards—are forced instead. Her lips are drawn away from her teeth, and the resisting curve of her throat opens her mouth like the dead child's screamless mouth. Her violet Sari slips off her shoulder, and her breasts strain at her sari-blouse stretching the cloth so that the white stitching at the seams shows. A sleeve tears under her arm. (183)
>
> The last thing I noticed was Ayah, her mouth slack and piteously gaping, her dishevelled hair flying into her kidnapper's faces, staring at us as if she wanted to leave behind her, wide-open and terrified eyes. (184)

The multiple interconnected events fuse in the last part of the novel which along with describing the plight of Rana's laceration and mutilation in the wake of riots drive home the extremities of sadism let loose and the most brutal and barbarous illustration of violence figures in the suburban villages Kot Rahim Makipura. In a young boy Rana's predominantly Muslim village, the poor Muslim peasant families huddle, together, comforted by each other's presence, reluctant to disperse: "the villagers remained in the prayer yard as dusk gathered about them (199). But it is at the dawn the attack comes:

> the panicked women ran to and fro screaming and snatching their babies, and the men barely had the time to get to their ports . . . Tall men with streaming hair and thick biceps and thighs, roaring Bolay so Nihal! Sat Sri Akal. (199)

Rana abandoned by his mother and sisters halfway ran. In the frenzy of riots he saw his uncles beheaded. His older brothers his cousins, "some one fell on him, drenching him in the blood." (201)

Amidst the dead bodies, wailing women, raped and killed, Rana was running into the moonless night. He arrived at his aunt's village just after dawn. He watched it from afar, confused by the activity taking place, soldiers holding guns with bayonets sticking out of them, and was diverting the villagers. This village was not under any attack, perhaps the army trucks were there to evacuate the villagers and take them to Pakistan. The moment he caught the light of recognition in the eye of his Noni Chachi, the pain in his head exploded and he crumpled at her feet unconscious.

> Chachi washed the wound on his head with a wet rag. Clots of congealed blood came away and floated in the pan in which she rinsed the cloth.
>
> 'I did not remove the thick scabs that had formed over the wound', she says. 'I thought I'd see his brain!' The slashing blade had scalped him . . . . And old woman covered him with a white cloth, said, 'Let him die in peace!' (205)

He survived however and is now with Imam Din after the Partition settles.

III

The country divided on communal lines on the eve of Independence brought in its wake the twin traumas—the physical one of being dislocated and forced to migrate and the psychological one of living in 'alien' conditions—which millions of people experienced living on both sides of the religious divide. The riots subside, Ayah Shanta is found in Hira Mandi in the company of Ice Candy Man and we encounter the sordid concealed regions of our history and politics that subjected women and the poor to the worst kind of sadism and brutality and Ice-Candy-Man is the heir to this history. The historically insignificant portions buried in the backyard of history surface:

> The Mogul princes built Hira Mandi—to house their illegitimate offsprings and favourite concubines . . . who cares for orphans? . . . They are nothing but prostitutes . . . young girls kidnapped by pimps—forced into all kinds of depravities on pain of death. (246-47)

The narrative of this juncture of the novel grows heavy with the oppressive power of past history that vitiates the present. We share the narrator's apprehension: "Is Ayah Shanta's progeny doomed to this life wherein beauty, sexuality, sublimity and sordidness are mixed up? Since the Ice Candy Man recognizes in her "the rhythm of a Goddess, the voice of an angel. . . . How she moves (247). Like his ancestors he wants to celebrate her grace and the adolescent Lenny is mesmerized: "I am hypnotized by the play of emotions on the Ice-Candy-Man's plastic face, by the music in his voice. . . . Moghuls portrayed in miniature." (248) But this history need not be relived—it stinks. It reeks of a cultural politics in which the gross physical needs of the kings and the princes was the first priority. Lenny's Godmother is not going to abandon the mission of rescuing Shanta; she can see through the mouth of romantic love fostered by men with the support of the woman in a conspiracy of silence. Godmother is not going to be a party to the complicity in romanticizing and idealizing oppressive sexual relations. The event beginning with highly nostalgic, hypnotic, tone turns grotesque and frenzied, unmasking the cruelty beneath the facade of sentimental eulogy: "Is that why you had her lifted off—let hundréd of eyes probe her—so that you could marry her? You would have your own mother carried off if it suited you!—Badmash!" (248) Ayah becomes a living ghost: "can the soul be extracted from its living body." (260) Finally Ayah is dispatched with her scant belongings, wrapped in cloth bundle and a small tin trunk at the Recovered Women's camp. The broken bones and pimply influence of the Ice-Candy-Man and his cronies is of no avail. (259)

The Ayah's story ends exposing the latent cruelty and fetishes of history that always ominously appear to be in the grip of blind forces—the hegemonistic politics—endorsing the perpetuation of misinterpretation and appropriation of underprivileged and women. Getting to know Shanta, Pappoo, Hamida on the one hand, the Godmother and her own mother on the other, help the adolescent narrator reach an understanding of human situations. She must become the author of herself. The writer appears to be identifying herself with the character. The character speaking deeply, comes as close to the truth as fiction can come to the truth of the human heart. This however coincides with the loss of innocence. The experiences related are the "rite of passage" to her. Ingesting the pain of her world by facing it gives her strength and will to claim the power of her own moral position:

> The innocence that my parents' vigilance, the servant's care and Godmother's love sheltered in me, that neither Cousin's carnal cravings, nor the stories of the violence or the mobs could destroy, was laid waste that evening by the emotional storm that raged round me. The confrontation between Ice Candy Man and Godmother opened my eyes to the wisdom of righteous indignation over compassion—to the demands of gratification . . . and the unscrupulous nature of desire. (252)

Ice-Candy-Man is a sincere and successful effort to artistically portray the life in the subcontinent at a crucial juncture in history without indulging in hostile parodistic melodrama or extravagant, vociferous pyrotechniques one may find in the recent subcontinental fiction. While the latest novels by Rushdie, Tharoor or Khushwant Singh appear to be guided by a self-conscious, subversive ideology, Sidhwa's "truth telling" narration transcribes the destructive impulse of the time with such compassion in an unpretentious idiom that even most anaesthetized or cynical reader feels touched. Feeling flows in the narrative not intended to shock or to impress but to make us identify the marginalized culture outside the mainstream as a part of history. The text aligns diverse cultures, different epochs and captures a vast human context—socio political configurations, ideologies, spiritual longings, righteousness within and without in untheorized, un-formulated idiom, like a camera it impartially registers the subversive dynamics of time, in knowing it we hope to derive from it some knowledge of ourselves as the product of a common history/politics and common social constructs.

NOTES

1. See Geertz Clifford. "Thick Description: Toward an Interpretive Theory of Culture," *Interpretation of Culture* (London: ΘUP, 1973).
2. Bapsi Sidhwa, *Ice-Candy-Man* (London: Heinemann 1988), p. 1.
3. Milan Kundera, *The Art of the Novel* (London: Faber and Faber, 1988), p. 145.

Ice-Candy-Man: A Parsi Perception on the Partition of India

JAGDEV SINGH

Ice-Candy-Man *is, so far, the only novel written by a Parsi on the theme of Partition. Jagdev Singh points out that the prism of Parsi sensitivity through which the cataclysmic event of Partition is depicted is what distinguishes Bapsi Sidhwa's fiction. It portrays the noncommittal attitude of the Parsi community towards the flux in which the various communities of India found themselves. The article analyzes the changing pattern of communal relations during the period through the consciousness and point of view of Lenny, an usually precocious Parsi girl.*

Editor

The Partition of the Indian subcontinent in 1947 is one of the great tragedies, the magnitude, ambit and savagery of which compels one to search for the larger meaning of events, and to come to terms with the lethal energies that set off such vast conflagrations. There have been a number of novels written on the horrors of the Partition holocaust on both sides of the Radcliffe line: Khushwant Singh's *Train to Pakistan* (1956), Attia Hosain's *Sunlight on a Broken Column* (1961) and Chaman Nahal's *Azadi* (1975) present the Indian perception of the traumatic experiences while Mehr Nigar Masroor's *Shadows of Time* (1987) projects the Pakistani version of the tragic events, though both the versions are free from religious bias and written more in agony and compassion than in anger.

What distinguishes Bapsi Sidhwa's *Ice-Candy-Man* (1988)[1] is the prism of Parsi sensitivity through which the cataclysmic event is depicted. *Ice-Candy-Man* is, so far, the only novel written by a Parsi on the theme of Partition. While the novel shows in the beginning the noncommittal attitude of the Parsi community towards the flux in which the various communities of India found themselves in the beginning of the twentieth century, it distills the love-hate relationship of the Hindus and Muslims through the consciousness and point of view of Lenny, an unusually precocious five-year-old Parsi girl.

While the novel has attracted attention from Indian scholars and media persons, the studies themselves have been sketchy and inadequate. Madhu Jain in her review of the novel highlights the dilemma the Parsi community faced at the dawn of Independence: "The Parsi dilemma is: whom do they cast their lot with?"[2] But perhaps because of the limitations of space, she does not go beyond this observation to analyze how the pattern of communal relations were subjected to a maddening change during the Partition. Although Khushwant Singh's review[3] of the novel is comparatively longer, yet it, too, refrains from tracing at length the changing pattern of communal relations which form an integral part of this book.

In view of the obvious inadequacy of critical attention that this novel has received, this paper attempts to analyze the framework of the changing pattern of communal relations that continuously breathes underneath the narrative structure of this novel in order to evaluate its strengths and weaknesses as an aesthetic whole.

Set in Lahore, Bapsi Sidhwa's *Ice-Candy-Man* sets the tone and tenor of the events described in the very beginning of the novel. The tone of neutrality manifest in the narrator-character Lenny, in describing the climactic incidents of Partition, is anticipated in the Parsi get together for the Jashan Prayer, to celebrate British victory, at the Fire Temple in Lahore. While the Parsis have all along been loyal to the British government, they, however, fear the Partition of India and, consequently, are in a fix as to which community they should support. Col. Bharucha, the domineering Parsi doctor and the President of the 'Parsi Anjuman' sounds the note of caution: "There may be not one but two or even three new nations! And the Parsis might find themselves championing the wrong side—if they don't look before they leap!" (37) An "impatient voice" in the congregation replies sarcastically: "If we are stuck with the Hindus they'll swipe our business from under our noses, and sell our grandfathers in the bargain: if we are stuck with the Muslims they'll convert us by the sword! And God help us if we're stuck with the Sikhs!" (37) It is at this moment of Prufrockian dilemma that Col. Bharucha allays the fears of his community by advising them to cast their lot with whoever rules Lahore: "Let whoever wishes rule! Hindu, Muslim, Sikh, Christian! We will abide by the rules of their land!" (39) Thus the note is struck. The Parsis are going to be neutral in the tug of war among the three major communities of India. The neutral attitude of the narrator character, Lenny, has its roots in this racial psychology of the Parsis. In a way, the attitude of the Parsi community revealed here is the externalized collective sub-consciousness of Lenny.

As the action of the novel unfolds, we confront a pattern of communal amity where the three communities—the Hindus, Muslims and Sikhs—are still at peace with one another. But the intimations of an imminent death and destruction lurk in the symbolic significance of Lenny's nightmares at the break of dawn. In one of these nightmares she faces an immaculate Nazi soldier "coming to get me [Lenny] on his motorcycle." Another nightmare that she recalls from her childhood which is more telling and suggestive is that of "men in uniforms quietly slice(ing) of a child's arm here, a leg there." She feels as if the child in the nightmare is herself. She pictures her Godmother as stroking her head as they "dismember" her. She says: "I feel no pain, only an abysmal sense of loss—and a chilling horror that no one is concerned by what's happening." (22) The nightmare symbolizes the impending vivisection of India which was as cruel as the dismemberment of that child. Lenny's lack of pain, however, is suggestive of her community's indifference on account of its aloofness from the religio-political convulsion. This chilling horror that she feels over no one being concerned by what is happening sums up the lack of concern on the part of the authorities to check the unbridled display of barbarism during Partition.

Still another nightmare that Lenny has is that of a zoo lion breaking loose and mercilessly mauling her: "the hungry lion, cutting across Lawrence Road to Birdwood Road, prowls from the rear of the house to the bedroom door, and in one bare-fanged leap crashes through to sink his fangs into my stomach. . . Whether he roars at night or not, I awake every morning to the lion's roar. He sets about it at the crack of dawn, blighting my dreams." (23-24) The hungry lion which invariably appears at the crack of dawn seems to be a symbol of the flood of mutual hatred that the dawn of Indian Independence released to cause havoc to the Hindus, the Muslims and the Sikhs on both sides of the border. Thus, with these three nightmares that Lenny has, the novelist prepares the reader for the gruesome and gory pattern of communal discord that became blatantly obvious during Partition.

Having planted these two authorial guide posts in the structure of the novel, Sidhwa deftly hands over narration to Lenny, who narrates the story of the changing pattern of communal relations. As the action of the novel moves forward, we perceive the pattern of communal amity that still exists in rural India, between the Hindus, Muslims, Sikhs. On her maiden visit to Pir Pindo, a Muslim village thirty miles east of Lahore, Lenny has her first experience of rural life. She finds the Muslims of Pir Pindo and Sikhs from the neighbouring village of Dera Tek Singh sitting together and sharing their concern about the worsening communal relations in the cities. Sharing the village Mullah's concern about it is the Sikh priest, Jagjeet Singh. His words have the ring of the religious concord in Pir Pindo and adjoining villages: "Brother, our villages come from the same racial stock. Muslim or Sikh, we are basically Jats. We are brothers. How can we fight each other?" (56) As the conversation continues, we have a glimpse of the contrasting communal attitudes of townsmen and country-folk, in the words of the Chaudhry of Pir Pindo: "our relationships with the Hindus are bound by strong ties. The city folk can afford to fight . . . we can't. We are dependent on each other· bound by our toil; by Mandi prices set by the Banyas—they're our common enemy—those city Hindus. To us villagers, what does it matter if a peasant is a Hindu, or a Muslim, or a Sikh?" (56) The village Chaudhry's remarks have a historical authenticity. The Unionist Party of Punjab was a pro-farmer political party of the Hindus, Muslims and Sikhs struggling against the stranglehold of the Hindu money-lending class. That this party should have won at the hustings in the 1937 Provincial Elections, despite a stiff resistance from the Congress and the Muslim League, is indicative of the unstinted support that it got from the villagers of all the communities in Punjab. A renowned sociologist, M.L. Darling echoes the Chaudhry's remarks when he says: "A class of Hindu money-lenders had arisen in the Punjab which had enriched itself by exploiting the helpless peasantry."[4]

In fact, the roots of communal amity in rural Punjab go so deep that the members of the two communities are ready to sacrifice even their lives for protecting each other. "If need be, we'll protect our Muslim brothers with our lives!" says Jagjeet Singh. "I am prepared to take an oath on the Holy Koran," declares the village Chaudhry, "that every man in this village will guard his Sikh brothers with no regard for his own life!" (56-57) One gets the impression that rural Punjab is an oasis of communal fraternity in the desert of communal hatred that is ever expanding to spread its tentacles to engulf the two communities in the cities. At this stage of Indian history the pattern of communal relations between the two rural communities, despite buffetings from outside, was still that of harmony and concord.

The rumblings of communal discord soon reach Lahore. Lenny's parents often entertain guests who are drawn not only from their own community but also from the British and Sikh community. It is at one of these dinner parties that Inspector General Mr. Rogers expresses the view that the differences between the Congress under the leadership of Nehru and the Muslim League under Jinnah are pushing India to the brink of Partition. He feels that it is the English who are acting as a lid on this cauldron of flaming passions between the two communities. 'Mr. Singh, however, thinks that once India gains Independence, they will be able to settle all their differences, as these have been created by the British: "You always set one up against the other . . . you just give Home Rule and see. We will settle our differences and everything!" (63) Mr. Singh echoes the views of the Congress at that time that wanted to present the picture of a conflict-free society before the British so as to hasten the process of gaining Independence. The Congress was conscious that internal divisions would delay the liberation of the country as the British could justify their presence on grounds of maintenance of peace and stability. An Indian historian, Mujeeb, highlights Mr. Singh's views vis-a-vis the Congress approach at that time: "[these] considerations made the Congress hold that the minority problem could wait till the country became independent."[5]

Underlying the basic unity among the various religions of India is the Hindu Ayah and her multi-religious throng of admirers. Taking their turn one by one: the Mali Hari, the Ice-Candy-Man, the masseur, Sharabat Khan, Imam Din and Sher Singh, all converge on this focal point. The Ayah is undiscriminating towards all and it is in this that she becomes a symbol of the composite culture that India is. Interestingly enough, as the events roll ahead with a relentless speed, the group of Ayah's admirers begins to dwindle. A similar symbol of the unity of Indian religions is provided by the visitors to the Queen's Park where men of all religions and creeds rub shoulders with one another. With the imminence of Partition, the Park presents a picture of different religious groups keeping away from one another's company. The passions run high even when men of different religious communities talk and chat with one another. A reference to Gandhi, Nehru and Patel's influence in London evokes a retort from Masseur who feels that in ousting Vavell, they have got a 'fair man' sacked. The Ice-Candy-Man goes a step further:

> "With all due respect, malijee," says Ice-Candy-Man, surveying the gardener through a blue mist of exhaled smoke, "but aren't you Hindus expert at just this kind of thing? Twisting tails behind the scene . . . and getting someone else to slaughter your goats?" (90-91)

When the Government House gardener tries to cool the passions by imputing the differences between the Hindus and the Muslims to the English, the butcher with his "dead pan way of speaking" remarks:

> "Just the English?" asks Butcher. "Haven't the Hindus connived with the Angrez to ignore the Muslim League, and support a party that didn't win a single seat in the Punjab? It's just the kind of thing we fear. They manipulate one or two Muslims against the interests of the larger community." (92)

Thus the novelist shows the gradual emergence of the pattern of communal discord in urban India.

As the setting sun of the British Empire gathers its parting rays before sinking into oblivion, the lumpen element around Ayah meet less frequently at the Queen's Park and more at the 'Wrestler's Restaurant.' The geographical shift in their get-together is a premonition of the emergence of the pattern of communal discord. That British Queen whose statue stands abandoned in the Park, is soon going to relinquish her suzerainty over India and the Wrestler's Restaurant to which all flock now is a symbol of the wrestling ring that Partition is going to raise on the joint borders of India and Pakistan. Discussing the fate of the Punjab in the event of Partition, Masseur hopes that if the Punjab is divided, Lahore will go to Pakistan. The Government House gardener, however, hopes that this will not come true as the Hindus have much of their money invested there. At this the Sikh Zoo attendant, Sher Singh, shouts: "And what about us? The Sikhs hold more farmland in the Punjab than the Hindus and Muslims put together!" (120) When Masseur advises Sher Singh that it would be good for their community to cast their lot with one country rather than be divided into two halves and lose thereby their "clout in either place," Sher Singh, like the lions he tends, turns on him: "You don't worry about our clout! We can look out for ourselves . . . you'll feel our clout all right when the time comes!" (129) Seeing Sher Singh in a high temper, the butcher, with his professional mercilessness, cites the English, who call the Sikhs a "bloody nuisance." At this Sher Singh and the "restaurant owning wrestler" threaten the Muslims with dire consequences in the event of Partition. The verbal skirmishes between the butcher and the Masseur on the one hand, and the Government House gardener, Sher Singh and the restaurant-owner on the other, show how deep the pattern of communal discord among the Hindus, Muslims and Sikhs has become. The course of the changing pattern of communal relations seems to augur ill for the three communities as Partition looms large on the horizon.

Filtered, as these widening differences are, through the prism of the Parsi character-narrator, Lenny, her response to those relations becomes significant. Commenting on these changes, Lenny, and by implication, the novelist herself, remarks: "Gandhi, Jinnah, Nehru, Iqbal, Tara Singh, Mountbatten are names I hear. And I become aware of religious differences. It is sudden. One day everybody is themselves and the next day they are Hindu, Muslim, Sikh, Christian. People shrink, dwindling into symbols. Ayah is no longer just my all encompassing Ayah—she is also a token. A Hindu." (93)

That these changes should have sunk even into the mind of the tender and immature Lenny, speaks of the extent to which the various communities of India had become conscious of their individual identity at the cost of the composite culture they had evolved after centuries. As time passes, Lenny becomes aware of the newfound religious fervour among Ayah's admirers. Not only are the differences within the caste hierarchy of the Hindus accentuated but also the racial differences among the Christians heightened. The English Christians look down upon the Anglo-Indians, who snub the Indian Christians who, themselves, in turn, regard all non-Christians with a supercilious air. In this atmosphere of heightened communal consciousness, the Parsis are reduced to "irrelevant nomenclatures." Bapsi Sidhwa, thus, paints a miniature picture of the pattern of communal discord that then prevailed and simultaneously turns the neutrality of the Parsis. In the mock-epic manner, she holds up these differences to ridicule by showing how they had even affected the classification of jokes: "Cousin erupts with a fresh crop Sikh jokes. And there are Hindu, Muslim, Parsi and Christian jokes." The denudation that jokes undergo because of the communal differences derides the very essence of these differences.

By showing the adverse influence of an imminent Partition, the novelist draws a line between national politics and the relationship among different communities. Partition is shown to be the result of irreconcilability of the adamant and rash leadership of India. In the dinner party, that has been referred to earlier, Inspector General Rogers wonders how far Hindus and Sikhs will be able to settle their differences with the Muslims so long as they acknowledge the leadership of men like Master Tara Singh, Gandhi and Nehru. In fact, the malevolent nature of the differences between the Congress and the Muslim League on the ordinary people of India is rightly anticipated by Sharbat Khan when he cautions Ayah: "These are bad times—Allah knows what's in store. There is big trouble in Calcutta and Delhi: Hindu-Muslim trouble. The Congress-wallahs are after Jinnah's blood." (75) Ayah, however, shakes off this caution with a casual remark:

> "What's it to us if Jinnah, Nehru and Patel fight? They are not fighting our fight," says Ayah, lightly. (75)

However, Sharbat Khan does not agree with her assessment and is of the opinion that though that "may be true but they are stirring up trouble for us all." Here he becomes a persona of the novelist and comments that it was the intransigent sectarianism of the national leaders which wrought havoc on the pattern of communal amity existing in rural India.

As the fever of Partition runs high, Lenny notices "a lot of bushed talk." Everywhere "men huddled around bicycles or squat against walls in whispering groups." The fear of Partition and the violence it would unleash drives the common man to think about his safety. On her second visit to Pir Pindo, Lenny goes along with the members of Imam Din's family to Dera Tek Singh on the occasion of Baisakhi. As they reach the village, the festival is already in full swing. It is in the midst of these gay activities that Ranna senses the steel of suspicion and fear. Bapsi Sidhwa captures this feeling thus:

> And despite the gaiety and destruction Ranna senses the chill spread by the presence of strangers; their unexpected faces harsh and cold. A Ṡikh youth whom Ranna has met few times, and who has always been kind, pretends not to notice Ranna. Other men, who would normally smile at Ranna, slide their eyes past. Little by little, without his being aware of it, his smile becomes strained and his laughter strident. (106)

The apathy of Ranna's friends is symptomatic of the tension which the arrival of the "Akalis" in Dera Tek Singh has generated. Dost Mohammad, Ranna's father, too, has noticed the intrusion of a new factor in the communal atmosphere of Dera Tek Singh. When he refers to them during his conversation with the genial-faced Granthi, Jagjeet singh, he learns about their sinister designs from the affable Granthi:

> The Granthi's genial face becomes uncommonly solemn. . . . He says: ". . . The Akalis swarm around like angry hornets in their blue turbans. . . . They talk of a plan to drive the Muslims out of East Punjab. . . . They say they won't live with the Mussulmans if there is to be a Pakistan. . . . Trouble makers. You'll have to look out till this evil blows over." (107)

The patterns of communal relations between Lenny's first and second visit to Pir Pindo are, therefore, poles apart. While during her first visit, the Sikhs and the Muslims had pledged their lives to save each other from any intruders, during her second visit, that enthusiasm has evaporated in the heat of the violence that the Akalis hold out for anyone who comes in the way of their resolve. The pattern of communal harmony has been replaced by the pattern of fear and suspicion between the two communities.

It is in this surcharged atmosphere that the Akali leader, Master Tara Singh, visits Lahore. Addressing a vast congregation outside the Assembly chambers he shouts: "We will see how the Muslim swine get Pakistan! We will fight to the last man! We will show them who will leave Lahore! Raj Karega Khalsa, aki rahi na koi." (133-34) His address is greeted with the roar of "Pakistan Murdabad! Death to Pakistan! Sat Sri Akal! Bolay so nihal!" The Muslims, in turn, shout "So? We'll play Holi-with-their blood! Ho-o-oli with their blo-o-d!" (134) With both the communities having taken up their positions, the ensuing festival of Holi becomes a blood-soaked festival. The pattern of communal amity that existed before the Baisakhi of that year got shattered in the bloodbath of Holi during Partition.

What follows Partition is the unbridled ventilation of the pent-up rancour between the two communities on both sides of the border. While the Muslims of Pir Pindo—that fell on the Indian side of the border—are subjected to mass slaughter by the marauding gangs of the Akalis from the surrounding Sikh villages, the Hindus and Sikhs of Lahore undergo a similar harrowing experience. Their fate gets blighted when a trainload of corpses from across the border reaches Lahore. Ice Candy-Man's relations lie dead in the heap of carcasses in the ill-fated train. Imam Din's entire family has been wiped out in Pir Pindo. Ranna alone has survived to tell the gruesome tale. While the ambers of Partition goad Ice-Candy-Man to join the marauding hooligans out to kill and destroy the vestiges of the Hindu and Sikh presence in Lahore, Imam Din remains calm in the face of all calamities. The distinction between the two becomes marked when a gang of Muslim hooligans comes to abduct Ayah. Imam Din goes to the extent of telling a lie about Ayah: "Allah-ki-Kasam, she's gone." In contrast, Ice-Candy-Man not only abducts her and throws her to the wolves of passion in a Kotha but also kills out of jealousy his co-religionist Masseur. Thus, the novelist shows that the defenders of Islam who turned Lahore into a burning city were not even true proponents of Islam. Imam Din's character, therefore, shines in this novel as that of Kamala in B. Rajan's *The Dark Dancer* (1958).

While the flames of communal passions leap up in the skies of Lahore, the Parsis, who till now, have maintained a safe distance from this communal conflagration, act as the Messiah of the Hindus and Sikhs trapped in the burning city. They, as Lenny learns later on, help in their transportation to India. Even Ayah is rescued by Lenny's Godmother and is sent to her parents in Amritsar. Thus, inspired by a feeling of humanism, the Parsis shake off their passive neutrality and become the agents of a healing process.

The change from the pattern of communal discord to that of reconciliation is, however, traced in the person of the Ice-Candy-Man. Though his role in the cataclysmic events of Partition is painted in lurid colours, his growing passion and love for Ayah is shown to redeem him from the morass of senseless communal hatred. From a rough and rustic man, always ready to nudge Ayah, the Ice-Candy-Man becomes a person of refined sensibility; he steeps himself in poetry. When Ayah is wrenched away from him and sent to Amritsar, he follows her across the border. That the Ice-Candy-Man is willing to leave the land that he so much cherishes for the sake of his Hindu beloved is not only an example of self-sacrifice but also symbolic of a future rapprochement between the two warring communities—the Muslims and Hindus. Though Bapsi Sidhwa shows the possibility of the emergence of a harmonious pattern of communal relations between the Hindus and Muslims sometimes in the future, yet she leaves much unsaid about how the change in the Ice-Candy-Man's personality comes about.

Thus, the analysis of the changing pattern of communal relations shows a pattern of communal amity between the Hindus and Sikhs on the one hand and the Muslims on the other in the pre-Partition era, a growing impatience and mistrust between them on the eve of Partition culminating in the pattern of utter communal discord during Partition and the pattern of reconciliation in the breaking of the dawn of understanding between them in the distant horizon during the post-Partition era. Related very closely to these changing patterns of communal relations is the sea-change in the attitude of the Parsi community from the bald egg-shell of passive neutrality to an active neutrality towards the pattern of communal discord swirling around them during Partition.

Though Bapsi Sidhwa's novel does focus on the changing attitude of the Parsi community, it leaves out the exploration of the dilemma that the Parsi community had to resolve regarding its unnatural schismatic division between Indian and Pakistani Parsis. While the novel cannot be faulted for that, one does feel the need of yet another Parsi novel on Partition which would explore and express this vital aspect.

NOTES

1. Bapsi Sidhwa, *Ice-Candy-Man* (William Heinemann, 1988; London: Penguin, 1989).
2. Madhu Jain, "Sensitive Servings: Deshpande and Sidhwa Fetch Notice," *India Today*, September 15, 1989, p. 47.
3. Khushwant Singh, "*Ice-Candy-Man*: Partition Story," Saturday Plus, *The Tribune*, January 13, 1990, p. 1.
4. M.L. Darling, *The Punjab Peasant in Prosperity and Debt* (London, 1925), p. 116.
5. M. Mujeeb, *Indian Muslims* (London: 1967), fn. p. 7.

The Ice-Candy Man: Partition Revisited by a Parsi Woman Writer

V.L.V.N. NARENDRA KUMAR

The article underscores the subtle presentation of the human consequences of history in Ice-Candy-Man. *The device of the child-narrator enables Sidhwa to humanize history and place it in a postcolonial perspective. Sidhwa resorts to subversion to offer the points of view of the marginalized and chronicles the story of what happened to the poor when the politicians so heartlessly played around with their lives. Narendra Kumar traces how rejecting the British and pro-Hindu Indian versions of history, Sidhwa achieves the objective of dismantling notions of essence and authenticity. Besides analyzing* Ice-Candy-Man *as a postcolonial interpretation of history, the article also establishes it as a true bildungsroman in which Lenny learns to view the world from a heuristic perspective.*

Editor

Partition is an upheaval which transformed millions of hapless people on either side of the border in the subcontinent into refugees. If Partition is the cataclysm which Freddie predicts towards the end of the narrative in *The Crow-Eaters*, in *Ice-Candy-Man*, Partition becomes the moulding principle, a shaping force in the evolution of consciousness of Lenny, the Parsi child-protagonist. If Partition is a traumatic experience to Bhisham Sahni and Amrita Pritam, it is an integral part of Bapsi Sidhwa's consciousness. This narrative, complex as it is, marks a point of departure in Sidhwa's writing. For here, for the first time, she employs a child-narrator like Firdaus Kanga in *Trying to Grow* and Adam Zameenzad in *Gorgeous White Female*. The narrative depicts the growth of Lenny, her slow awakening to sexuality, and pains and pleasures of the adult world and to the cataclysmic event that tears her world apart. The process of Lenny's growth of consciousness against the backdrop of Partition becomes central to the narrative. Thus her progression is from one level of consciousness (Angra Mainyu) to the other (Spenta Mainyu).

According to Bapsi Sidhwa, she wrote *Ice-Candy-Man* from an "objective point of view," but like a Pakistani objective."[1] Sidhwa's treatment of history is typical of a postcolonial novel. Here history is richly humanized where Lenny's evolving consciousness integrates within itself the diachronic moment of her own growth, holistically, and conversely, the disintegration of the subcontinent. The Parsi attitude, rendered through Lenny, Godmother and other characters like Colonel Bharucha is that of a neutral disinterest. As they are not so much affected by the social, political or even economic consequences, they are near perfect, detached observers. Thus Sidhwa displays a fuller grasp of the 'human' consequences of history. In the narrative, action is internalized in the young, though fertile, mind of Lenny. Lenny thus becomes an eye-witness to, and a victim of, a topsy-turvy world.

Zoroastrianism enjoins that a Parsi should be loyal to the ruler. The Parsis are celebrated for their unflinching loyalty to the British. Referring to the loyalty of the Parsis to the British, Novy Kapadia observes that all the Parsis wanted from the ruling British authorities was religious autonomy and protection and they were granted both.[2] However, the sense of insecurity in the Parsi community was due to alienation brought about by the rejection of the coloniser and distrust of the nationalists. When objections are raised by some members of the Parsi community at a jashan meeting on the eve of Partition, Colonel Bharucha, the spokesman of the Zoroastrian community in Lahore, observes:

> I hope no Lahore Parsee will be stupid enough to court trouble. I strongly advise all of you to stay at the back—and out of trouble.[3]

He argues that it would be very difficult to predict the outcome of Partition. He cautions them:

> There may not be one but two—or even three—new nations. And the Parsis might find themselves championing the wrong side if they don't look before they leap. (37)

His word is almost a law for the Parsi community. He resolves that the Parsis of Lahore should cast their lot with whoever rules Lahore. He too, like Freddie in *The Crow-Eaters*, believes that there is no need for the Parsi community to leave Lahore. He tells them:

> Let whoever wishes to rule! Hindu, Muslim, Sikh, Christian! We will abide by the rules of their land. (39)

The proclamations of Colonel Bharucha at the community dinner reflect the stance of the majority in the Zoroastrian community in the pre-Partition context. He aptly predicts that Hindus, Muslims and even the Sikhs would jockey for power. He cautions the Parsis of Lahore not to jump into the middle. To Lenny, a child who is caught up in the whirlpool of religious disparities, Colonel Bharucha's proclamation is a revelation. Exiled several centuries ago, the Parsis adopted India as their homeland. Therefore, another migration would be truly unthinkable. They are attached to, and identified themselves with, the Indian soil.

Ayah, an eighteen-year-old Hindu, is at the centre of Lenny's scheme of things. The nexus between Lenny's world of childish pleasures and innocence and the fast-changing ambience is realised in Ice-Candy-Man whose presence is exhilarating for the young child. Ayah's amorous adventures become central to Lenny's perceptions. If the covetous glances of Ayah's admirers including the Masseur and Ice-Candy-Man awaken her to sexuality and passion, the passes of 'holy' men and dusty old beggars give her a glimpse of the adult life. Initially her world is made secure by strong, courageous and loving women like Rodabai and the young Ayah. Sidhwa very clearly establishes in the narrative that Parsi women are quite strong and their strength is revealed in moments of crisis. For Lenny, the process of growing up, of seeking to understand the adult world is largely an attempt to make sense of the senseless events of the Partition.

Colonel Bharucha who blames the British for bringing polio to India, seals the fate of Lenny. He declares:

> She'll marry—have children—lead a carefree, happy life. No need to strain her with studies and exams. (15)

Adi, her fair brother, is sent to school whereas she is denied several privileges which other Parsi children enjoy. She is reluctant to become a mere reproductive organism, a destiny designed for her by Colonel Bharucha, a man. Thus Sidhwa seems to disapprove of sexism which is part even of Parsi ethos. Speaking of the women's passive acceptance of the role allotted by the patriarchy, Susie Tharu observes: "As women we often believe our exploited, sexually passive, dependent role is best for us. We are contented, often exalted by its meagre rewards, its promised glitter. Further we have so identified with patriarchy's hostility to anything that challenges the established order we fear and even actively resist critical speech and radical action. Worst of all, we are ourselves so insecure in the system (the time between good and bad, and hence acceptable and totally unhoused, is slippery) that often we are the most vicious in our castigation of those who do not conform."[4] Tharu argues that there is a need for a 'real' consciousness. Women have not only internalized a bourgeois consciousness but also refuse to see themselves as victims. They are locked into a 'culture of silence' which they themselves contribute to the perpetuation of patriarchy that objectifies and destroys her.

Sidhwa's treatment of history is typical of a postcolonial novelist. Her fictional (and imaginative) rendering of historical figures and incidents is singular. Despite her admiration for Gandhi, she holds him, though partially, responsible for Partition. Gandhi was deified whereas Jinnah was caricatured in Indian films and biased accounts of the British and Indian historians. Sidhwa wrote *Ice-Candy-Man* since she felt that enough had not been written about Partition, although several novels including *Train to Pakistan*, *A Bend in the Ganges* and *Tamas* deal with Partition horrors. Her thesis is that most of these accounts, however moving, show a strong pro-Hindu bias. Thus Sidhwa sets out to 'dismantle' the 'Imperial purpose' in *Ice-Candy-Man*. In other words; she, to borrow Rushdie's expression, "writes back to the Centre."

Lenny's response to Gandhi is naive. He, a mythical figure, for her at least, emerges as a multi-dimensional reality. His presence is overwhelming:

> My brain, heart and stomach melt. The pure shaft of humour, compassion, tolerance and understanding he directs at me fuses me to everything that is feminine, funny, gentle, loving. He is a man who loves women,. And lame children. And the untouchable sweeper—so he will love the untouchable sweeper's constipated girl-child best. I know just where to look for such a child. He touches my face, and in a burst of shyness, I lower my eyes. This is the first time I have lowered my eyes before a man. (87-88)

Lenny truly comprehends the concealed nature of "ice" lurking deep beneath the hypnotic and 'dynamic' femininity of Gandhi's 'non-violent exterior' only after the communal frenzy starts. Sidhwa's description of Gandhi is a mixture of awe and irreverence. Her eulogy on Jinnah, on the other hand, is typical of a Pakistani, making it a moral obligation for her to defend him. When her mother tells her that Jinnah's wife, a Parsi, died heartbroken, Lenny reminisces:

> But didn't Jinnah too die of a broken heart? And today, forty five years later, in the films of Gandhi's and Mountbatten's lives, in books by British and Indian scholars, Jinnah who for a decade was known as 'Ambassador of Hindu-Muslim unity', is caricatured, and portrayed as a monster. (160)

This passage gives a clear indication of Sidhwa's anguish at the biased work of the British and Indian scholars. Taking a passage from Sarojini Naidu's tribute to Jinnah, Bapsi Sidhwa reinforces her argument:

> the calm hauteur of his accustomed reserve masks, for those who know him, a naive and eager humanity, an intuition quick and tender as a woman's, a humour gay and wishing as a child's pre-eminently rational and practical, discreet and dispassionate in his estimate and acceptance of life, the obvious sanity and serenity of

> his worldly wisdom effectually disguise a shy and splendid idealism which is of the very essence of the man. (161)

This is Sidhwa's glowing tribute to, and an assessment of, Jinnah, who, in her view, was discriminated against by the wily statesmen during Partition. She, however, rises above petty nationalism and presents the Partition horrors, not in the "red light of emotion" but in the "white light of truth." Her humanism permeates the narrative at all levels as she demonstrates, in effective fictional terms, how the religious disparities were deliberately exploited on the eve of Partition. Thus *Ice-Candy-Man*, like Khushwant Singh's *Train to Pakistan*, is the story of what happened to the poor when the politicians so heartlessly played around with their lives. They suffered the most. Bapsi Sidhwa, being a Parsi, did not suffer much during Partition. The fight was chiefly between Hindus, Muslims and Sikhs, people who were to gain by it and who were going to be empowered by it. It was their 'battle' and as a Parsi, her emotions were not aligned one way or the other. Lenny, at least to some extent, takes after Bapsi Sidhwa and most of the incidents did take place in her own life though she only fictionalised them.

Lenny who is incapable of lying, realises that to become corrupt or mimick others is no easy job. What she aims at is something which is natural to others but her efforts are an exercise in futility. She remains in an Edenic state whereas Adi and Cousin plunge into life with great gusto. One day Godmother catches her easily when she steals three jars. Her face and voice give her away. The resultant awareness brings only fresh pain:

> Adi can swear himself red in the face and look lovable—Rosy can curse steadily for five minutes, going all the way from 'Ullu Kay Pathay' to asshole; from Punjabi swear words to American, and still look cute. It's okay if Cousin swears—but if I curse or lie, I am told it does not suit the shape of my mouth or my personality or something. (85)

Her inability to accomplish what others do with effortless ease plunges her into fresh agony. Godmother comforts her:

> Some people can get away with it and some can't. . . . I'm afraid a life of crime is not for you. Not because you aren't sharp but because you are not suited to it. (85)

Godmother's remark is like 'life-sentence' to Lenny. Even her mother encourages her to speak the truth. When Lenny breaks a plate, she showers her daughter with the radiance of her approval:

> I love you. You spoke the truth. What's a broken plate? Break a hundred plates (85)

Lenny's realization at this juncture of life is significant:

> The path to virtue is strewn with broken people and shattered China. (85)

This truth, which is born of Lenny's tender experience acquires the magnitude of a cosmic truth in the narrative. Ironically enough, it is Lenny's probity which brings about the ultimate catastrophe—the abduction of Ayah by an irate Muslim mob led by Ice-Candy-Man, an occurrence from Sidhwa's childhood, though it was effectively dramatized in the novel.

The Hindu Ayah who sustains Lenny's life has a multi-religious throng of admirers but she does not discriminate. The Queen's Park becomes the locale where discussions throw light on the topic of the times—communal frenzy. As Partition becomes imminent, the admirers of Ayah become conscious of their communal identities. Communal loyalties too, which remain hitherto dormant, become sharper. Ayah too is slowly transformed into a 'token', an orthodox Hindu, whereas Imam Din, a fair and imaginative arbitrator, and Yousuf turn into religious zealots and take Friday afternoons off for the Jumha prayers. The initial optimism of Imam Din is superseded by anxiety and apprehension as his faith in the 'Sikh brothers' erodes slowly. However, he remains calm in the face of all calamities. Lenny's realization that he is 'not at ease with cruelty' indicates the effect of turbulent times on her tender psyche.

The widening disparities are filtered through Lenny's consciousness. She observes:

> One day everybody is themselves—and the next day they are Hindu, Muslim, Sikh, Christian. People shrink, dwindling into symbols. Ayah is no longer just my all encompassing Ayah—she is also a token—a Hindu. (93)

Sidhwa resorts to subversion in *Ice-Candy-Man* to offer the perspective of the marginalized. She comes close to Mistry who employs popular gossip and newspaper account to question the 'official' version of the infamous Nagarwala case. She introduces conversations among ordinary people in the novel. Her minor characters such as Masseur, the Government House gardener and Sher Singh perform, like Hardy's rustic characters, the role of a commentator and interpreter. They analyse and draw their own inferences which sometimes reflect the stand taken by the respective communal groups to which they belong. For instance, the discussions on politics in Queen's Park give ample scope for them to voice their feelings. At the same time, they curse the politicians in whose hands their destiny lies. The butcher's comment on Gandhi is typical of a Muslim in the pre-Partition context:

> That non-violent violence monger—your precious Gandhijee—first declares the Sikhs fanatics! Now suddenly he says: "Oh dear, the poor Sikhs cannot live with the Muslims if there is a Pakistan!" What does he think we are—some kind of beast? Aren't they living with us now? (91)

The Masseur's reply is equally sarcastic:

> He's a politician, yaar. It's his business to suit his tongue to the moment. (91)

Thus their comments on, and their interpretations of, the latest political developments in the subcontinent give Lenny a vivid idea of the crumbling familiar social order. Her realization that one man's religion is another man's poison is charged with profound significance. She closes her eyes and tries to shut out the voices. She remarks:

> I try not to inhale, but I must; the charged air about our table distils poisonous insights. Blue envy: green avidity: the grey and black

> stirrings of predators and the incipient distillation of fear in their prey. (131-32)

Lenny begins to play violent games, a gesture which she borrows from the adult world. One day Adi and she pull the legs of a doll and when the doll splits, she breaks down. In fury, Adi asks:

> "Why were you so cruel if you couldn't stand it?" he asks at last, infuriated by the pointless brutality. (139)

In Kapadia's view, Lenny's innocent act has symbolic significance. He observes: "It shows how even a young girl is powerless to stem the tide of surging violence within, thereby implying that grown-up fanatics emmeshed in communal frenzy are similarly trapped into brutal violence."[5]

Though Parsis were not victims of Partition, their agony was no less intense. Sidhwa highlights the quandary of the Parsi community on the eve of Partition. Forced to make a choice, (to opt for Hindu India or Muslim Pakistan), they were reduced to 'irrelevant nomenclatures'. They were mere detached observers of a bloody event which broke India into two. Her innocent query is typical of a child:

> India is going to be broken. Can one break a country? (92)

This strikes the keynote in the narrative. Sidhwa seeks to re-examine the role of the British in 'cracking' the country. She attempts to expose the 'illegitimate' part played by the British in the political process.

The birth of Pakistan leads to an identity-crisis in Lenny. She observes bitterly:

> I am a Pakistani. In a snap. Just like that. (140)

She takes another birth, though a symbolic one, as a Pakistani. *Ice-Candy-Man* is Pakistani in setting and sensibility. The perspective of Sidhwa is quite evidently Pakistani. According to her, Partition was a 'mistake', a tragedy which could have been averted. However, in the novel, she argues how Partition favoured India over Pakistan:

> The Hindus are being favoured over the Muslims by the remnants of the Raj. Now that its objective to divide India is achieved, the British favour Nehru over Jinnah. Nehru is Kashmiri, they grant him Kashmir. Spurning logic, defying rationale, ignoring the consequence of bequeathing a Muslim state to the Hindus. . . . They grant Nehru Gurdaspur and Pathankot without which Kashmir cannot be secured. (265)

Thus Sidhwa rejects the British and pro-Hindu Indian versions of history. She subverts the popular myth about Partition which was nursed and cherished by people on either side of the border in the subcontinent. *Ice-Candy-Man* is a typical postcolonial text which achieves the objective of dismantling notions of essence and authenticity. The experience which Sidhwa depicts in the narrative is 'real' which, hitherto has been regarded as 'inauthentic' and 'marginal'.

It is Lenny who unwittingly surrenders Ayah to the rioters led by Ice-Candy-Man. Even Imam Din's desperate lie fails to save her. Lenny's sense of guilt is acute:

> I am the monkey-man's performing monkey, the trained circus elephant, the snake-man's charmed cobra, an animal with conditioned reflexes that cannot lie. (184)

In disgust, she scours her 'truth-infected tongue' and even tries to wench it out. Sidhwa's narrative mode, like Narayan's, is ironic. Lenny's mother and Godmother set her firmly on the path of truth and it is her truthfulness that spells doom for Ayah.

The subsequent confrontation between Godmother and Ice-Candy-Man opens Lenny's eyes to the wisdom of righteous indignation over compassion, to the demands of gratification to the unscrupulous nature of desire and to 'the pitiless face of love'. Ice-Candy-Man who ravished the voluptuous Ayah however, repents and marries her. Even her name is changed to Mumtaz. Thus Sidhwa shows how patriarchy deliberately deprived women of liberty ultimately resulting in a crisis of identity. But Ayah rejects the new identity which her marriage offers. Lenny feels the pain of Ayah since it is she who perpetrates it, though in innocence:

> They have shamed her. Not those men in the carts—they were strangers—but Sharbat Khan and Ice-Candy-Man and Imam Din and Cousin's cook and the butcher and other men she counted among her friends and admirers. I'm not very clear how—despite Cousin's illuminating tutorials—but I'm certain of her humiliation. (253-54)

Thus Sidhwa effectively establishes how Partition affected the two nations in general, and women in particular. Urvashi Butalia raises a pertinent question about the predicament of women during Partition:

> Why was it that we heard so little about them? How had they experienced the anguish of the division, the euphoria of the newly-forming nations? My assumptions were simple: firstly, that these questions had remained unasked because of the patriarchal underpinnings of history as a discipline. I also believed (and this view has been considerably qualified since) that in times of communal strife and violence, women remain essentially non-violent, and are at the receiving end of violence as victims, and that they are left with the task of rebuilding the community.[6]

The task of building the community as pointed out by Urvashi Butalia is precisely what the strong women in the narrative—Rodabai and Lenny's mother—accomplish. When Rodabai confronts Ayah, now the wife of Ice-Candy-Man, she tries to comfort the hapless victim:

> It can't be undone. But it can be forgiven . . . worse things are forgiven. Life goes on and the business of living buries the debris of our pasts. Hurt, happiness . . . all fade impartially to make way for fresh joy and new sorrow. That is the way of life. (262)

But the traumatic experience leaves Ayah spiritually dead. She replies:

> I am past that. I am not alive. (262)

Her fractured self seeks relief in India where her roots exist. Lenny's realisation that Ice-Candy-Man is a 'deflated poet' and a 'collapsed pedlar' is symptomatic of her 'arrival.' She perceives the change which comes over Ice-Candy-Man:

> and while Ayah is haunted by her past, Ice-Candy-Man is haunted by his future: and his macabre future already appears to be stamped on his face. (265)

The eventual rehabilitation of Ayah which is chiefly the work of Godmother, the Good Samaritan as she is, and the repentance of Ice-Candy-Man give Lenny a glimpse of the power of love and the pain of separation.

Gayatri Chakravorty Spivak contends that the word 'subaltern' is packed with meaning. According to her, everything that has limited or no access to cultural imperialism is subaltern. She vehemently protests against the lack of cultural space for the subaltern. To work for the subaltern, she argues, is to bring it into speech.[7] Ayah in *Ice-Candy-Man* truly represents the 'subaltern' since she is denied some cultural space by Ice-Candy-Man, who in turn, is a victim of imperialism. Her humiliation is a concrete illustration of the subaltern's lack of access to the cultural imperialism.

Referring to allusion in the postcolonial literatures, Ashcroft, Griffiths and Tiffin write: "Allusion can perform the same function of registering the cultural distance in the postcolonial text, according to the extent to which the text itself provides the necessary context for the allusion."[8]

Thus in Bapsi Sidhwa's fiction in general, and in *Ice-Candy-Man* in particular, there are several intertextual references which not only enable her to register 'cultural distance' but also introduce the exotic to the western reader. This is one of the salient features of postcolonial fiction. *Ice-Candy-Man*, like Anita Desai's *In Custody*, provides the necessary context too for the allusion.

The Urdu couplets of Iqbal and Ghalib cited in the text are an evidence of Bapsi Sidhwa's passion for Urdu poetry. Ice-Candy-Man's anguish of separation is described in Iqbal's words:

> My passion has brought me to your street—
> Where can I now find the strength to take me back? (277)

While 'appropriating' the language of the coloniser, Sidhwa, at the same time, maintains 'Otherness' which gives a distinct identity to the text. Thus she challenges some of the assumptions which hitherto ordered 'reality'. Ice-Candy-Man's newborn wisdom is a mystery to the young mind of Lenny. She realises the power of love only when he too disappears across the newly-created border into India.

Ranna's nightmarish experience at Pir Pindo is closely modelled on a personal experience of Ranna Khan, a friend of Bapsi Sidhwa. His survival in the carnage is a miracle, yet he takes a comic-ironic view of his own predicament:

> It's funny. . . . As long as I had to look out for myself, I was all right. As soon as I felt safe, I fainted. (205)

His endurance teaches Lenny the importance of being whole. His 'instinct for survival' and his ready ability to forgive a past which could not be controlled are in sharp contrast to her frivolous ways of life.

Discussing the treatment of Partition and its effects in fiction, Susie Tharu observes: "By representing the Partition in 'Universalist' terms as outrageous, and its effects as a metaphysical disorder that can be restored to an equilibrium only by the artist who is imaged as a magician-healer, these texts inaugurate a narrative and a subjectivity that translates history and politics into a failure of humanity.[9]

She argues that the trauma and suffering of people during Partition is largely due to degeneration of politics leading to sub-human acts. The tragedy of Ayah and the trauma of Ranna are the result of what Tharu calls 'failure of humanity'. Lenny at one juncture cries out:

> I feel so sorry for myself—and for Cousin—and for all the senile, lame and hurt people and fallen women—and the condition of the world—in which countries can be broken, people slaughtered and cities burned—that I burst into tears. (217)

Lenny's 'education' is a growth of consciousness, a phenomenon which is hastened by events and situations at once tragic and brutal.

When a novelist attempts to develop a philosophical conception of history, the point of view as a literary strategy assumes great significance. Bapsi Sidhwa avoids the pitfall of employing omniscient narration in *Ice-Candy-Man*. This work marks a new phase in her writing in the use of narrative voice. She is true to history, by and large, though there are a few aberrations in providing historical signposts. Ralph Crane argues that Lenny's unreliable narration proves to be reliable in its own way, since it causes us to question the British and Indian versions of the truth that have hitherto been accepted.[10] Sidhwa, in fact, employs two narrative voices for rendering the account of Partition. The first is that of Lenny, a child and the other is that of authorial omniscient narrative voice. Lenny's rendering is through her dreams and nightmares. It is more subjective, though not involved or enlightened about its consequences. The other is an implied adult narration trying to objectify what is child's narration, however precocious she may be. Sidhwa's success lies in an excellently maintained restraint and impartial, disinterested, near-factual description. She maintains balance so that the voice remains childlike but sophisticated enough to involve the adult reader. There is no authorial comment, yet Sidhwa's narrative brings out the full fury of Partition horrors, through electrifying scenes and dramatic use of language.

Sidhwa's *Ice-Candy-Man* invites comparison with Firdaus Kanga's *Trying to Grow* and Adam Zameenzad's *Gorgeous White Female*. All the three protagonists are children endowed with fertile imagination. They are precocious whose sharp perceptions are out of proportion to their age. If Sidhwa's Lenny tries to interpret the actions and events connected with Partition, though she is too young to accomplish it, Lahyayani, Zameenzad's eleven-year-old protagonist, the offspring of a Bengali babu and an English woman, attempts to live an intense life. His aspiration to be reborn stands in glaring contrast to the struggle of Kanga's Brit whose passage to adulthood is necessitated by his Osteogenesis imperfecta. Interestingly enough, however coincidental it may seem, Lenny is a victim of polio whereas Brit is an invalid by birth. Lahyayani, on the other hand, transcends the barriers of race, gender and age in order to achieve his objective of rebirth. Zameenzad, like Sidhwa, is an expatriate writer exploring the themes of rootlessness (which is the result of his mixed origin), colour and sexuality through the volatile mind of his child-protagonist. Childhood is the 'country' which all the three protagonists—Lenny, Brit and Lahyayani—try to leave behind in their journey to adulthood. If Brit succeeds in establishing nexus with the adult word, Lenny and Lahyayani, despite their intense struggle, fail to acquire an identity of their own. Lenny's predicament is qualitatively different from that of Brit in that she is a girl. Brit's identity which he achieves after a heroic struggle within himself is Kanga's triumph as well. The singular achievement of Sidhwa and Kanga is that they provide a true look into the depths of childhood memory which Zameenzad fails to achieve in his *Gorgeous White Female*.

Bapsi Sidhwa's *Ice-Candy-Man* was retitled *Cracking India*. Born in Pakistan, and teaching in U.S.A., Sidhwa has a 'dual literary heritage'. If Ghalib and Iqbal fascinated her, writers like Eugene O'Neill influenced her writing to a considerable extent. An early reference in the text links Sidhwa's title to O'Neill's play, *The Ice-Man Cometh*:

> Ice-Candy-Man is selling his popsicles to the other groups lounging on the grass. My mouth waters. I have confidence in Ayah's chocolate chemistry . . . lank and loping the Ice-Candy-Man cometh. (18)

Thus by referring to the influence of American writers like O'Neill, Sidhwa reflects on the influence of America on Pakistani history. Commenting on the change of title, Sidhwa remarks:

> This novel was published as *Ice-Candy-Man* in Germany and in Britain. But here the publishers wanted to change the title. My publisher said that the American readership will not relate to *Ice-Candy-Man*, because apparently Ice and Candy are euphemisms for drugs here. So they felt it would be better to give a title based on what the narrator says in the novel about the Partition. I feel that not enough has been written about the Partition.[11]

The new title is suggestive, no doubt, but as Robert Ross aptly points out, it diminishes the centrality of Ice-Candy-Man and blurs his symbolic role.[12] Ice-Candy-Man, in Sidhwa's view, stands for wily politicians whose work it was to 'crack' the once unified country. He symbolises evil for which stand the statesmen of the times, leaders who were responsible for the unmitigated suffering of ordinary people on either side of the border. Through Lenny, Sidhwa demonstrates how absurd it is to break a country. The new title thus suggests the notion of quest, of discovery.

In *Ice-Candy-Man*, allegory is the structural principle controlling the narrative. Some Indian scholars regard this work as a moral allegory. According to Nilufer Bharucha, the Hindu Ayah is symbolic of the Indian earth[13] whereas Shirin Kudchedkar observes that Ayah represents the innocent, natural sexuality of women who becomes the prey of debauched male desire.[14] Sidhwa herself admitted in an interview:

> Ayah, for instance, is not symbolic of anything, but on reflection, I felt that she could be representing India in a way. These are people who desire her so much, and each one of them, when he has a chance, ravishes her.[15]

Sidhwa's *Ice-Candy-Man* foregrounds the Partition, its horror and consequences. Though Sidhwa was not aware of the allegorical reference, at least when she was writing, perceptive readers pick up the resonances. Thus in the ultimate analysis, Ayah and Ice-Candy-Man emerge as personifications of ideas—the former standing for Mother Earth and the latter for Evil.

Thus *Ice-Candy-Man* is a novel of education in which Lenny's growth of consciousness takes place against the backdrop of Partition. Khushwant Singh's *Train to Pakistan* is racy and down-to-earth whereas Balachandra Rajan's *The Dark Dancer* employs myth as a structural parallel. The Hindu-Muslim riots are viewed as a re-enactment of the fratricidal battle of Kurukshetra. It is an allegory since the allegorical reference is sustained and unbroken. Manohar Malgonkar's *A Bend in the Ganges* projects the value of love which transcends violence and non-violence and brings about freedom and fulfilment to individuals. Bhisham Sahni's *Tamas* is a grim reminder of the human tragedy suggesting that those who forget history are condemned to repeat it. For all these Indian novelists and Sidhwa, Partition is not a mere historical event but an all-pervasive emotional experience.

The worldview which serves as the controlling point of the narrative here is characteristically Zoroastrian. In Lenny's consciousness, there is a gradual and purposeful shift from scepticism to faith. It is a tale of 'arrival,' a true bildungsroman in which Lenny learns to view the world from a heuristic perspective. Her enlarged consciousness results from her experiment with truth of which Ayah is the victim. Lenny's passage from a state of bliss to the adult world of pains and pleasures constitutes the core of the narrative. The progression of her mind is thus a positive movement in which she reaches the plenitude of her being.

In *Ice-Candy-Man*, Sidhwa presents a diachronic world where the life of Lenny and her growth at all levels is in a parallel time order. In other words, there is the history of Lenny and there exists the chronology of subcontinental Partition tale. As historical time is linear and colonial which is nothing but a record of depravity, cultural, economic, political and emotional, each postcolonial novelist creates his own 'space' of authenticity and belongingness by his 'english'. By doing so, he is 're-placing' the text in the postcolonial context. New 'spaces' are sought to be created for redefining the native sense of history. Thus in Sidhwa's fiction too, there is this tug between history and the hapless protagonist in such a history. He/She is an 'insider' in history, yet without his/her own autonomy of self. Hence he/she seeks to break out of this 'history' and creates his/her own world with temporal autonomy through his own 'english'.

NOTES

1. Chelva Kanaganayakam, "Interview with Bapsi Sidhwa," *The Toronto South Asian Review*, p. 45.
2. Novy Kapadia, "The Parsi Paradox in *The Crow-Eaters*," *Commonwealth Fiction*, ed. R.K. Dhawan, p. 130.
3. Bapsi Sidhwa, *Ice-Candy-Man* (Penguin, 1989), pp. 36-37.
4. Susie Tharu, "Patriarchy and Feminism: The Birth of a Consciousness," *Modern Thought and Contemporary Literary Trends*, ed. Narsing Rao and Kadir Zaman (Hyderabad, 1982), p. 50.
5. Novy Kapadia, "Communal Frenzy and Partition: Bapsi Sidhwa, Attia Hussain and Amitav Ghosh," *Indian Women Novelists*, ed. R.K. Dhawan (New Delhi: Prestige, 1993), p. 83.
6. Urvashi Butalia, "Community, State and Gender: Some Reflections on the Partition of India," *Oxford Literary Review*, Vol. 16, Nos. 1 & 2, pp. 33-34.
7. Leon de Kock, "Interview with Gayatri Chakravorty Spivak: New National Writers Conference in South Africa," *Ariel*, Vol. 23, No. 3, 1992, pp. 45-46.
8. Ashcroft, Griffiths and Tiffin, *The Empire Writes Back*, p. 57.
9. Susie Tharu, "Rendering Account of the Nation: Partition Narratives and other Genres of the Passive Revolution," *Oxford Literary Review*, Vol..16, Nos. 1 & 2, 1994, p. 78.
10. Ralph J. Crane, "A Passion for History and for Truth-Telling: The Early Novels of Bapsi Sidhwa," *The Novels of Bapsi Sidhwa*, ed. R.K. Dhawan and Novy Kapadia, p. 55.
11. Chelva Kanaganayakam, "Interview with Bapsi Sidhwa," *The Toronto South Asian Review*, Vol. II, No. 1, 1992, p. 44.
12. Robert Ross, "Cracking India: A Feminine view of Partitoin," *The Novels of Bapsi Sidhwa*, p. 185.
13. Nilufer Bharucha, "The Parsi Voice in Recent Indian English Fiction," *Indian English Fiction 1980-90: An Assesment*, ed. Vilas Sarang and Nilufer Bharucha (New Delhi: B.R., 1994), p. 81.
14. Shirin Kudchedkar, "The Second Coming: Novels on the Partition," *Indian English Fiction 1980-90: An Assesment*, p. 69.
15. Chelva Kanaganayakam, "Interview with Bapsi Sidhwa," p. 48.

Ice-Candy-Man: A Reassessment

REENA MITRA

While re-evaluating Bapsi Sidhwa's classic novel Ice-Candy-Man, *eminent critic Reena Mitra relates the novel to an important segment of Indian English fiction that has focused on the theme of India's Partition in 1947. The novelist in this work shows the Parsi attitude to the various political happenings at this juncture. Though much has been written on the theme of Partition, Sidhwa's account of the holocaust is a tale with a difference. Caught between the conflicting demands of the major communities of the country, the Parsis being a pathetic minority did not have much of a choice to make. Apart from expressing this predicament, Sidhwa, unlike other Partition novelists, explores the world of women rather than men. In this respect, Sidhwa is innovative and highly refreshing.*

Editor

The Indian English novel has its roots in history and in the Indian consciousness, for it began as a vehicle of political awakening during the national struggle for Independence and thus, initially, the principal inspiration was not creative but expository. Now that Indian English fiction has come of age, and more than come of age, the possibilities of retrieving experiential moments of history through fictional strategies are innumerable. From vast, comprehensive and exhaustive papers, I am narrowing my focus down to a short, intensive one, more thought-provoking, perhaps, than any write up with an expansive sweep. For the Indian novelist writing in English, the theme of India's Partition is imbued with the magical quality of a reflection in a mirror—it is true and yet not true. Every novelist has his own blend of fact and fiction to offer, the guiding factor being what Rushdie calls "memory's truth," which is a process of selection and elimination creating its own reality, but usually presenting a coherent version of events. This qualifying factor of "memory's truth," I believe, is a cardinal principle prevailing as a determinant in all fictional art and applies to all creative works.

The road from life to art, from author to creation, can mean turning the past alive by providing a transparent window on reality rather than an indecipherable code. The literary artist proceeds through craft sophistication to an optimum level of fictive reality, a reality that is "true-to-life." Nothing is explained, what is shown must be perceived, apprehended and the reader's pleasure is often in proportion to what is left unsaid, or ambiguously hinted at.

Bapsi Sidhwa, a Parsi domiciled in Pakistan, is a novelist who has an abundance of inventive and narrative energy manifested in her fiction, which warrants the careful critical attention of those interested in new possibilities for imaginative prose which resorts to viable fictional means—largely realistic—for tracing the compelling force of historical events on individual lives and presenting a collage of the lives and experiences of men and women caught in the web of history. It is Sidhwa who gave to the Pakistani novel in English a distinct identity.

Bapsi Sidhwa's novels are notably different from one another in content and form, in subject and treatment. Her first novel, *The Crow-Eaters*, published in 1978, deals with the lives and fortunes of the Parsi Junglewalla family in British India. The narrative adroitly adopts comic and ironic modes directed towards the realization of Zoroastrian values in the lives of the members of the community. The novel is also an exposition of the anglicized Parsi way of life in Pakistan as Dina Mehta's *And Some Take a Lover* (1992) is a comment on the upheaval in the world of the community caught in the political welter of the Quit India movement.

Sidhwa's second novel, *The Pakistani Bride* (1983), is very different from her first in that it makes no assertion of the Parsi identity. In fact, it has no Parsi character at all. It is about a young Pakistani girl, a Muslim refugee, who is adopted by a Pathan during the Partition turmoil. The novel testifies to Sidhwa's understanding of and insight into the Pakistani ethos, no doubt, but when released it did not really make waves. Next came *Ice-Candy-Man* (1990) which was followed by *The American Brat* in 1994. *The American Brat* dramatizes the conflict of the value systems of the East and the West and this conflict of cultures has its impact not only on the social plane but on the personal life of the protagonist as well.

Coming back to *Ice-Candy-Man*, the response to this novel was absolutely mind blowing. The author in this work showcases the Parsi attitude—the Parsis, here representing a minority community—to the imminent Partition and to the concept of 'Swaraj'. Set in pre-Partition Lahore, in the period which Subhash K. Jha in his review of the work refers to as the period of "The satanic rites of fragmentation in the Indian subcontinent,"[1] the novel clearly highlights the vulnerability of human relationships that can be torn asunder at the slightest pretext. Also, here again, as in Dina Mehta's novel and in Bapsi Sidhwa's earlier novel, *The Crow-Eaters*, we see the ambivalent attitude of the Parsis towards the British. They find it difficult to choose their loyalties—"Swaraj or the British Raj?" At a special meeting organized at the Temple Hall in Warris road an irresolvable battle-of-words on the political situation ensues. Col. Bharucha's advice to the Parsis is to keep their distance from the slush of the nationalist agitation. Dr. Mody, on the other hand, pleads for commitment to the cause of the freedom struggle for the transparent reason that "our neighbours" will think we are betraying them and siding with the English."[2] And finally, at the instance of Toddywalla, the banker, the Parsis decide to opt for a path of compromise. Here, it may be relevant to point out that Sidhwa's novels voice the views of the particularly affluent, urban, middle-class Parsis.

Reams have been written on the Partition—in resentment, in anger, in affliction, in erudition or as a cathartic exercise, or again, even as an attempt to exorcise ghosts, phantoms of the agonizing past that refuse to be ignored. Bapsi Sidhwa's account of the holocaust is a tale with a difference—it is a concatenation of events seen through the insouciant eyes of an eight-year-old Parsi girl Lenny (who could very well have been Bapsi Sidhwa herself), who is baffled and perplexed by the adult world of turnabouts and shifting loyalties as also by changing emotions and widening gulfs. Caught between the conflicting demands of the major communities of the country, the Parsis in a pathetic minority have no misconceptions regarding the choices they confront. Under their affluence and prosperity won by competence and industry lurks a sense of insecurity when the country is on the verge of a painful partition: "If we are stuck with the Hindus, they'll convert us by the sword. And God help us if we are stuck with the Sikhs!" (37) Finally, under the mature guidance of Col. Bharucha the Parsis of Lahore decide to stay on there and cast their lot with whoever rules Lahore—Hindu, Muslim, Sikh, Christian. "People now shrink dwindling into symbols" (93) and human beings suddenly turn on one another.

Lenny, polio-stricken in infancy, is cared for by her eighteen year old nubile, voluptuous, buxom, chocolate-brown Ayah, who is mostly spending time with her ward under Victoria's statue in Queen's Park. Interestingly, she is always surrounded by a host of male admirers—the Fallettis Hotel cook, the Government House gardener, the elegant, compactly-muscled Masseur and the "lank and loping" Ice-Candy-Man, later additions to the community of suitors being the Chinaman and the Pathan, Sharbat Khan. "Ayah's presence," we are told, "galvanizes men to mad sprints in the noon heat" (32) and she brazenly succumbs to the advances of each in turn—and each is conscious of the fact that "a whiff off Ayah carries the dark purity of creation." The group surrounding her "remains unchanged, . . . as always unified around her." (97) Primarily, however it is the Masseur and the Ice Candy Man who vie for Ayah's attention though it is the former who happens to be more privileged of the two .

The easy familiarity, the bawdy humour and the friendly banter in the narrative soon undergo a change in tone and direction and each one has an acrimonious dig at the other's religion and nation. Every verbal exchange involuntarily slips into talk of India and Pakistan. Attitudes crystallize and the earlier distinction at Queen's Park between "baba-log" with their starchy Ayahs and the native children with their Ayahs in limp cotton saris soon dissolves and now are seen only Muslim women in 'purdah' separated from the Sikh community that breaks away from Hindus.

In Lenny's house, too, the placid harmony amongst servants from different communities disintegrates and each concentrates on surer signs of his own religion. Ayah never forgets to burn joss sticks around the statues of her own gods. The pogramme begins and takes on a vertiginous speed with the perpetrators of the crime never being tracked down. The "we are brothers" theory fails. Gandhi visits Lahore and Lenny, seeing him, is distressed at what she calls "this improbable toss up between a clown and a demon."[3]

Nothing works—the nation is in flames, Lahore is burning, Mazang Chowk is turned to ashes. The Muslim mob comes to Lenny's house to assault the Hindu servants but Ayah is safely hidden at the back of the house. Lenny, with her penchant for truth is, however, soon cajoled into disclosing Ayah's hideout to the Ice-Candy-Man, who, despite promises to protect her, has her dragged out and carried away only, perhaps, to be made an inmate of a brothel . Later it is heard and believed that the police rescue her from the Ice-Candy-Man who had forcibly married her and sends her back to her family in Amritsar. The irresolvable end leaves us guessing as to whether Ayah was accepted into the family at home or did life become for her "the torture of Sisyphus," never ending.

Bapsi Sidhwa, in *Ice-Candy-Man*, experiments with the reality of the times to create a timeless reality of her own universe. History undertaken by the fiction writer and explored as material, refers always to the particular in which there is an attempt to present history as sensory detail, as visual image, as time which reverberates in our time.

Sidhwa, does not, in her novel resort to the immediacy of journalistic methods. Images in the novel do not, like in a journalistic report, follow a conveyor-belt succession. She takes the slant of humour and the obliqueness of satire. The humour is sometimes mistaken for ribaldry but an in-depth analysis of the novel shows that all the humour, laughter and mirth employed is with a purpose. It is through their ribald humour and rustic wisdom that Ayah's as also Lenny's companions enable the little girl to chronicle the tragedy of the Partition.

The novelist's satire is of a characteristically cruel and unforgiving nature—Lenny's world centres around her relationship with her loving Ayah, and ardent cousin suitor (who transposes Lenny from dolls to condoms) and a Godmother with her companion connotatively referred to as Slave sister. Lenny grows up when she learns on her own the lesson that divides her Hindu Ayah, from her Parsi employers and her Muslim revengers. To put it broadly, the novel is "about the slow awakening of the child heroine both to sexuality and grown up pains and pleasures and to the particular historical disaster that overwhelms her world."[4] T.N. Dhar's conclusion in his book, *History-Fiction Interface in Indian English Novel* that "the novelist deals with history by using narrative modes which are essentially non-mimetic, such as comedy, satire and allegory"[5] is unflinchingly applicable to Sidhwa's *Ice-Candy-Man* for in it the non-mimetic mode represents a "reality" that transcends historical space for it is "memory's truth" again as Salim Sinai in *Midnight's Children* calls it and in the end "it creates its own reality."[6] Thus, there is no knowable reality. Only personal observations. It is these personal observations that make Lenny grow up and interpret her perception of the duplicities and deceptions of a savage adult world. Wading through the sea of events and experiences, she soon acquires a heuristic perspective in life which enlarges her consciousness and awareness of things around. Her experiment with truth has ended in misery.

Even though *Ice-Candy-Man* is primarily a novel of the Partition, the Partition as a historical event and not an emotional convulsion, one may, for an observation, turn to R.K. Narayan's emphatic statement that "a mere story is not the point of fiction; people and emotions are what's important."[7] Emotion in this novel is conspicuous by its absence in the man-woman relationship and it is this very absence that is a comment on the image of woman as portrayed in this work.

Ice-Candy-Man skilfully recreates the ethos of the Partition as a historical event affecting the lives of the characters in the novel but apparently, the novelist, in her bid to crystallize objective reality has markedly ignored the experimental realm of the highly victimized woman—the Ayah of the Parsi family at Lahore—who suffers excruciating pain and agony at the hands of the mob that tears her apart. As if this physical abuse by the mob was not enough, the Ice-Candy-Man clinches her lot by condemning her to prostitution. Though later he tries to make amends by marrying her, the harm has been done. She is, one presumes, left with a lacerated heart and mind but nowhere does the novelist elaborate on her injured psyche. And yet, we may absolve the novelist of this charge for, perhaps, this was not a part of her scheme of things.

The Parsi world in the novel is clearly more about women than men. Characters like Lenny's father, Old Husband and even Manek Mody are relatively insignificant when compared to Godmother and Mother. But it is the men, and especially the Ice-Candy-Man, who perpetrate the suffering of the women. Lenny's father's indulgence in adultery and his lashings endured by her mother are instances that make strong the case against the victimization of women. But none speaks out, and Ayah, too, moves "from speech to silence."[8] Silence in the novel is designed to be more eloquent than speech.

The combination of laughter and ribaldry, wit and wisdom is in the novel an unmistakable pointer to the degree of levity with which a woman is treated. As mentioned earlier, each one of the suitors in the novel makes frivolous advances to Ayah but none treats her as an individual in her own right.[9] She remains throughout a symbol of sex, an "object" to be ogled rather than an individual to be regarded and respected.

There is no attempt on the novelist's part to show her as an approximation to the Indian concept of the female "Shakti." There is no attempt either, as in Jayanta Mahapatra's poem, "Temple," to plumb the agony and the enigma in the Indian woman, "a riddle on its pedestal' (as Mahapatra refers to her). Apparently, there is no agitation regarding her, anywhere in the novel—there is only raillery and reporting of a dispassionate kind. Deep down, however, there is something very unnerving about the betrayal of the Ice-Candy-Man who, Sidhwa tells us "appears to have grown shades darker, and his face is all dried up and shrivelled-looking." (149) The supposedly staid and cool narrative operates at a plaintive decibel mixing illusion and reality, fiction and fact as the flow of events demands. Thus, underlying the thematic historical perspective of *Ice-Candy-Man* is the trauma of reassessing the past in terms of experiential reality underpinning the larger historical reality.

Sidhwa conceives of historical representation not only as a welter of statistical events but as a repertoire of inexhaustible possibilities in terms of happenings as well as human experience, central and peripheral—all merging into an organic totality which forbids a linear interpretation of the past and offers instead an entirety of existence.

NOTES

1. Subhash K Jha, "Dipped in Ribaldry," *The Times of India*, 5 Nov. 1989, p. 2.
2. Bapsi Sidhwa, *Ice-Candy-Man* (London: Heinemann, 1988), p. 37
3. Subhash K. Jha.
4. Book review in *Observer*; cited in cover blurb (New Delhi: Penguin, 1989).
5. T.N. Dhar, *History-Fiction Interface in Indian English Novel* (New Delhi: Prestige, 1999), p. 33.
6. *Ibid.*
7. Book review of R.K. Narayan's *The World of Nagaraj*, Sunday 11-17 Nov. 1990.
8. Chelva Kanaganayakam, "Allegory and Ambivalence in Bapsi Sidhwa's *Cracking India*," *Parsi Fiction*, Vol. 2, ed. Kapadia, Dodiya and Dhawan (New Delhi: Prestige, 2001), p. 43.
9. Shirin Kudchedkar, "The Second Coming: Novels on the Partition" *Indian English Fiction 1980-90: An Assessment*, ed. Vilas Sarang and Nilufer Bharucha (New Delhi: B.R., 1994), p. 69. Compare Nilufer Bharucha's view that the ravishing of Ayah is symbolic of the abuse of the Indian earth: "The Parsi Voice in Recent Indian English Fiction," *Indian English Fiction, 1980-90: An Assessment.*

Ice-Candy-Man: The Dehumanizing Effects of Communalism

NAGENDRA KUMAR

The article highlights the changes wrought upon the destiny of the individuals by one of the cruellest exchanges of population in modern times caused by the Partition of India in 1947. The Partition led to the outburst of communal riots and thousands of people lost their valuables and even lives. Thousands were rendered homeless and rootless overnight. The friends turned foes overnight and their individual relationships were sucked by the ebbing surge of communal feelings and religious fanaticism. The paper shows how the dehumanizing effects of communalism reduced human beings to the stature of haunting beasts who drenched in the blood of their own fellow beings.

Editor

> I was a child then. Yet the ominous roar of distant mobs was a constant of my awareness, alerting me, even at age seven, to a palpable sense of the evil that was taking place in various parts of Lahore. The glow of fires beneath the press of smoke, which bloodied the horizon in a perpetual sunset, wrenched at my heart. For many of us, the departure of the British and the longed-for Independence of the subcontinent were overshadowed by the ferocity of Partition.[1]

The above statement very potently sums up the harrowing recollection of partition by Bapsi Sidhwa 'a Pakistani-Parsi Woman' and the leading diasporic writer of Pakistan today (Bapsi Sidhwa in an interview with Julie Rajan). Bapsi Sidhwa is a Parsi who was born in undivided India and grew up in Lahore, Pakistan, married to a Parsi from Mumbai, India, divorced after a couple of years, married a second time to a Pakistan-based Parsi and moved to the U.S.A., thus having experiences of a lifetime in a comparatively short span of time. She has been a precocious polio-ridden child with an uncanny knack for life around her. As a young girl, Sidhwa witnessed first-hand the bloody Partition of 1947, in which seven million Muslims and five million Hindus were uprooted in the largest, most terrible exchange of population that history has known. The Partition was a result of a complicated set of social and political factors, including religious differences and the end of colonial rule in India. Sidhwa was also a witness to these evils, including an incident in which she found the body of a dead man in a gunnysack at the side of the road. Characteristically succinct, she recalls the event, "I felt more of a sadness than horror."[2] Her home city of Lahore became a border city in Pakistan, and was promptly flooded by hundreds of thousand of war refugees. Many thousands of these were victims of rape and torture. Due to lasting shame and their husbands' damaged pride, many victims were not permitted entry into their homes after being "recovered." There was a rehabilitation camp with many of these women adjacent to Sidhwa's house, and she states that she was inexplicably fascinated with these "fallen women," as they were described to her at the time. She realized from a young age that "victory is celebrated on a woman's body, vengeance is taken on a woman's body. That's very much the way things are, particularly in my part of the world."[3] These events left a permanent scar on the psyche of the child Bapsi and years later she could not resist her powerful urge to record that decisive moment in the history of the two nations and the result was her most influential and much-acclaimed narrative—*Ice-Candy-Man/Cracking India*.

Ice-Candy-Man (1988) is one of those few books which have captured the events leading to Partition so vividly and authentically the others being *Train to Pakistan* (1956) by Khushwant Singh, *A Bend in the Ganges* (1964) by Manohar Malgonkar, Chaman Nahal's *Azadi* (1975) and Salman Rushdie's *Midnight's Children* (1980). The novel is considered by many critics to be the most moving and essential book on the Indian Partition. Told from the awakening consciousness of an observant eight-year-old Parsi girl, the violence of the Partition threatens to collapse her previously idyllic world. The issues dealt within the book are as numerous as they are horrifying. The thousands of instances of rape, and public's subsequent memory loss that characterize the Partition are foremost. In the hatred that has fueled the political relations between Pakistan and India since that time, these women's stories were practically forgotten. In one of her infrequent bursts of poetry, Sidhwa writes, "Despite the residue of passion and regret, and loss of those who have in panic fled—the fire could not have burned for. . . . Despite all the ruptured dreams, broken lives, buried gold, bricked-in rupees, secreted jewellery, lingering hopes . . . the fire could not have burned for months."[4] Sidhwa replaces flowing, poetic sentences with forceful criticism when she theorizes about what caused the fires to keep burning. Sidhwa repeatedly condemns the dehumanizing impact that religious zealotry played in promoting mob mentality, separation, and revenge during the Partition.

It is a book of many voices, poignant, humorous, and desperate. It is a tale of upheaval in which every friend and enemy will be displaced. Eight-year-old Lenny, the spirited and imaginative daughter of an affluent Parsi family, narrates the story of the *Ice-Candy-Man* during the 1940s, as she witnesses Muslims, Hindus, Christians, and Sikhs fight for their land and their lives. As rumours of riots, fires, and massacres in distant cities become a reality, Lenny's tale follows the course of her quickly shifting life.

This multi-dimensional novel evoked a very good response from the critics and won many accolades for the author. Khushwant Singh, the celebrated author of *Train to Pakistan*, one of the most powerful accounts of Partition, commends Sidhwa: "*Ice-Candy-Man* deserves to be ranked amongst the most authentic and best [books] on the Partition of India"[5] Another noted Indian woman novelist Geetha Hariharan finds a contemporary relevance in the novel as she comments: "Sidhwa captures the turmoil of the times, with a brilliant combination of individual growing-up pains and the collective anguish of a newly independent but divided country. Sidhwa's work, particularly the dehumanizing effects of communalism, she movingly reveals in *Ice-Candy-Man* is painfully relevant to our present-day India."[6]

Sidhwa's narrator is Lenny, a Parsi girl with a 'truth-infected tongue' who turns eight on the day Partition is announced. Lame in one foot and indulged by her reasonably well-off parents, Lenny is ferried around Lahore by her beloved Hindu Ayah (nanny) whose 'spherical attractions' draw a varied group of suitors eager to dispense ice-lollies, silk doilies, massages and other gifts. Here's how we first meet Lenny:

> Lordly, lounging in my briskly rolling pram, immersed in dreams, my private world is rudely popped by the sudden appearance of an English gnome wagging a leathery finger in my ayah's face. But for keen reflexes that enable her to pull the carriage up short there might have been an accident: and blood spilled on Warris Road. Wagging his finger over my head into Ayah's alarmed face, he tut-tuts: "Let her walk. Shame, shame! Such a big girl in a pram! She's at least four!"
>
> He smiles down at me, his brown eyes twinkling intolerance. I look at him politely, concealing my complacence. . . .
>
> "Come on. Up, up!" he says, crooking a beckoning finger.
>
> "She not walk much . . . she get tired," drawls Ayah. And simultaneously I raise my trouser cuff to reveal the leather straps and wicked steel callipers harnessing my right boot.
>
> Confronted by Ayah's liquid eyes and prim gloating, and the triumphant revelation of my callipers, the Englishman withers. (2)

Lenny's deformed foot sets her proudly apart from other children, spares her the tedium of school—she receives private tuition by the odorous Mrs. Pen—and gives her entry into the world of adults. Cared for by Ayah, she observes her romances and admirers as well as the lives of other servants and relatives. There is Cousin who thinks he has turned into a honeycomb when he discovers ejaculation and is besotted with Lenny, or Dr. Manek who can fart on cue.

With her throng of characters, Sidhwa paints a microcosm of Pakistani society, filtered through Lenny's irreverent and innocent eye which values people regardless of their social standing and rejoices in their lusts and longings. Born into the tiny Parsi community, Lenny is outside the communal frenzy that follows, but emotionally torn by the violence engulfing her friends. If

Sidhwa is partisan, it is in her contempt of politicians pursuing separatist agendas, dividing maps in state rooms.

The vortex of violence that soon follows sucks up Ayah and her Muslim admirer Ice-Candy-Man just as it rips apart other lives. But Sidhwa stays true to her characters: they refuse to give up on life, stop joking or turn into tragic symbols. All of which brings home the horror of what they survive. As men lose their senses, raping, killing, and looting, women reveal their strengths, building links across the divided communities, sheltering survivors, insisting on continuity.

The novel captures the dispirited effects of communal frenzy that follows the Partition through the innocent eyes of Lenny, much more like her creator, polio-ridden, precocious and a keen observer of the happenings around. Lenny's disadvantage, as she is physically handicapped, turns out to the benefit of the readers. She is looked after by her Hindu ayah, "chocolate-brown and short. Everything about her is eighteen years old and round and plump. Even her face. Full-blown cheeks, pouting mouth and smooth forehead curve to form a circle with her head. Her hair is pulled back in a tight knot . . . she has a rolling bouncy walk that agitates the globules of her buttocks under her cheap colourful saris and the half-spheres beneath her short sari-blouses." (3) As the above description suggests, her ayah is exceptionally beautiful and sensuous, capable of attracting people. Lenny is conscious of this fact as she reveals: "The covetous glances Ayah draws educate me. Up and down, they look at her. Stub-handed twisted beggars and dusty old beggars on crutches drop their poses and stare at her with hard, alert eyes. Holy men, masked in piety, shove aside their pretences to ogle with her lust. Hawkers, cart-drivers, cooks, coolies and cyclists turn their heads as she passes, pushing my pram with the unconcern of the Hindu goddess she worships." (3) Among her admirers Ayah has Ice-Candy-Man, Masseur, Imam Din, Hari and many more. It is through her that young Lenny gets a feel of the life of the cross-section of Pakistani society. They feed and cater to her idyllic world of romances. They are what they are to her—human beings, full of human strengths and weaknesses. She loves them, their company, their frailties, little disputes, jokes, funny stories and their jealousies to command the love and attention of Ayah. She never cares for their religious faith, their distinct loyalties and political talks till she hears the disturbing talk of Partition of the nation. Things don't remain the same as this news spreads like a bush fire in her town. Her idyllic world of childhood innocence gives way to the tormenting adult world of Partition riots. The individual identities merge with the identities of the community and soon the society is sharply divided on the communal lines. Lenny cannot understand it, as she reflects:

> There is much disturbing talk. India is going to be broken. Can one break a country? And what happens if they break it where our house is? Or crack it further up on Warris Road? How will I ever get to Godmother's then?
>
> I ask Cousin.
>
> "Rubbish," he says, "no one's going to break India. It's not made of glass!"
>
> I ask Ayah.
>
> "They'll dig a canal . . ." she ventures. "This side for Hindustan and this side for Pakistan. If they want two countries, that's what they'll have to do—crack India with a long canal"
>
> Gandhi, Jinnah, Nehru, Mountbatten are names I hear.
>
> And I become aware of religious differences.
>
> It is sudden. One day everybody is themselves—and the next day they are Hindu, Muslim, Sikh, Christian. People shrink, dwindling into symbols. Ayah is no longer just my all-encompassing Ayah—she is also a token. A Hindu. Carried away by a renewed devotional fervour she expends a small fortune in joss-sticks, flowers and sweets on the gods and goddesses in the temples. (92-93)

The news of atrocities on Muslims near Amritsar and Jullundhar are heard in Lahore. The details are so brutal and bizarre that it is hard to believe. After a fortnight or so an army truck dumps a family outside the gate of Lenny and she recognizes them to be the distant kins of Imam Din from a village in Punjab. The process of uprooting has started. The familiar faces have started dwindling or have changed beyond recognition. The people who were simply friends have now turned Muslims, Hindus, Sikhs or Christians, fighting for their land and faith even at the cost of their established social relationships. Lenny has a bitter realization by now: "*One man's religion is another man's poison.*" (117, my italics) Suddenly the whole atmosphere is charged with religious slogans. The Sikhs are wielding their *kirpans* shouting '*Pakistan Murdabad!* Death to Pakistan! *Sat Siri Akaal! Bolay se nihaal!*' (134) And Muslims are roaring: '*Allah-o-Akbar! Yaaaa Ali!*' and '*Pakistan Zindabad.*' (135) The Hindu houses are put on fire in Lahore in retaliation to what happens in Punjab. Sidhwa captures this poignant moment in a very touching paragraph of the novel:

> Trapped by the spreading flames the panicked Hindus rush in droves from one end of the street to the other. Many disappear down the smoking lanes. Some collapse in the street. Charred limbs and burnt logs are falling from the sky.
>
> The whole world is burning. The air on my face is so hot I think my flesh and clothes will catch fire. I start screaming: hysterically sobbing. Ayah moves away, her feet suddenly heavy and dragging, and sits on the roof slumped against the wall. She buries her face in her knees. (137)

Communal frenzy has rocked the two sides and geographical division has led to division in souls of the people. People are being butchered, men, women, children, old, young, handicapped, diseased, indiscriminately on the either sides. Houses are set on fire, looted. Women have been the worst sufferers as they have been raped brutally and their limbs amputated. Ice-Candy-Man is no more the simple admirer of Ayah whom she scolds at times for his unruly behaviour, he has become a militant Muslim fighting the cause of his faith and land. One day he comes breathless in sweat and dust to announce the worst outcome of these communal riots:

> 'A train from Gurdaspur has just come in' he announces, panting. 'Every one in it is dead. Butchered. They are all Muslim. There are no young women among the dead! Only two gunny-bags full of women's breasts!' (149)

One by one most of the Hindus and Sikhs in Lahore have either left, killed or forced to convert in this bloody battle. Hari, the gardener, has been forced to adopt Muslim faith and has now become Himat Ali. Even Ayah is not spared and is kidnapped by a mob with the help of Ice-Candy-Man, her lover, to suffer humiliation, defilement and mental torture. At that instant she is not the woman whom Ice-Candy-Man always desired, she is a Hindu woman who deserves to be treated the way Muslim women have been treated by Sikhs and Hindus. She is forced to become Mumtaz, the wife of Ice-Candy-Man and also to dance and sleep with numerous people until she is recovered from that hell by Godmother. Masseur's body is found by the roadside in a gunny sack. Thus this surge of communalism spoils the harmony and peace of Lahore completely. Thousands have been uprooted and rendered homeless, thousands have lost their lives, thousands have been compelled to leave a legacy of lifetime in that one moment. Lenny realizes this change as she goes to the Victoria Park with her new ayah Hamida. The whole atmosphere has changed; she is not able to find any familiar face among those who are occupying her favourite spot. As she narrates: "Beaden Road, bereft of the colourful turbans, hairy bodies, yellow shorts, tight pyjamas, and glittering religious arsenal of the Sikhs, looks like any other populous street. Lahore is suddenly emptied of yet another hoary dimension: there are no Brahmins with caste-marks—or Hindus in dhotis with *bodhis*. Only hordes of Muslim refugees." (175) Lahore is seething with aliens who have lost their settled homes in India and have been forced to go to Pakistan. Having lost their property, prestige and nearest and dearest ones in this riot they are struggling hard to recover from this sudden jolt. They are occupying the abandoned houses of Hindus and Sikhs who have left Lahore to meet the same fate at the other end.

The novel describes the horrors of the Partition very well and the reader is drawn into the tale. The fears, the insecurity, and the hatred that was bred in the people by the politicians of that time for their own vested interests is very much caricatured in the novel. The changing loyalties of the circle of friends who in the end become fiends brings forth the true horror of Partition when friends became traitors. The description of the massacre of

Ranna's village shows how humans behaved like savages, killing their own countrymen. The Ice-Candy-Man sees a perfect opportunity to claim what he thinks is his. The Partition also psychologically affects the Ice-Candy-Man as his family is murdered brutally on the train. It turns him into a cruel person, he then joins in the fray and kills Hindus, some of them his friends. All in all the Ice-Candy-Man is very much affected by the Partition and he uses the violence as a mechanism to claim Ayah but it backfires.

Thus here a sad tale of Partition is shown, where the crimes of the people killed the national spirit and no matter what was tried, it still remains as a deep scar on the psyche of the people. As Jinnah himself put it, 'Pakistan has been the biggest mistake of my life.' Partition of India is truly the sorest point in the subcontinent's history, when a new nation was born amidst turmoil and violence that later both countries have regretted and will do so for the rest of their existence. So will the Ice-candy-man regret his deeds for the rest of his miserable life.

The Ice-Candy-Man shows us the naked human emotions that are revealed whenever passions run high and it also shows how they can be good and evil in the same person. The novel has a simple narrative, enhanced by the use of humour, which effectively tells us the story of the Ice-Candy-Man. It precisely captured that decisive moment in history when 'one day everybody is themselves—and the next day they are Hindu, Muslim, Sikh, Christian', when identities that existed side-by-side get sharpened like swords against each other. It is a story which has been repeated in various attempts at genocide and 'ethnic cleansing' the world over, and which, in the case of India and Pakistan uprooted seven million Muslims and five million Hindus and Sikhs as they fled from massacres to cross newly-created borders. The legacy of this tumult is the continual chafing of Muslims, Hindus and Sikhs, with periodic eruptions of violence stirred up now-and-then by political interests and local gangsters. So supposedly sensitive is the issue that government media in India will often demurely speak of 'attacks by members of one community against members of another'. This is a story in which individuals and their community identities are inseparable, a story of emerging nations as well as a story of single characters. Not only Lenny, but everyone in this novel experiences substantial change in the context of the Partition. Ayah's traumatic transformation at the hands of Ice-Candy-Man, the suitor, who finally possesses her, and Ice-Candy-Man's own moral erosion through the Partition, figure the situation of all people involved in the ill-planned Partition, which resulted in migration, deaths, and incidents of rape and torture, all on a massive scale.

The links between individuals and nations are emphasized both by multiple plots and points of view. Specifically, while Lenny is the clear protagonist and narrator for most of the novel, Ranna, a Muslim child, whose experiences were particularly violent and traumatic, tells his own story. A significant aspect of the novel is the marginality of Britain and the Raj in the plot; colonialism sets this trauma in place, but postcolonial characters are its focus.

Thus the novel *Ice-Candy-Man* to a great extent focuses on the dehumanizing effects of communalism. The novelist is aware of the sensitivity of her readers on the two sides and has quite skilfully interwoven a gripping tale of everlasting impact. Being a Parsi, a microscopic minority, Sidhwa for the most part of the action has been a neutral observer and has at the same time a license to comment on the events without being termed a propagandist or communalist. As she herself says in one of her interviews: "The struggle was between the Hindus and the Muslims, and as a Parsi (member of a Zoroastrian sect), I felt I could give a dispassionate account of this huge, momentous struggle."[7] Again at another place she almost reiterates the same thing: "As a Parsi, I can see things objectively. I see all the common people suffering while the politicians on either side have fun."[8] But this does not mean that Parsis were silent spectators in this grimmest and most cruel human drama. They had their own share of things. Bapsi Sidhwa also wants people to know what Parsis had to offer during that period. We find Lenny's mother and Godmother helping the suffering women even at the risk of their own lives. It is ultimately Godmother who rescues Ayah from the clutches of Ice-Candy-Man and manages to send her to her family. Lenny's mother helps her Hindu and Sikh friends with gasoline etc. so that they can safely leave Pakistan. Lenny is suspicious of her mother's activities, as she secretly slips out of the house at odd hours, and charges her for her involvement in the bloody battle at that she explains her mission and her voice is not intended for Lenny alone it is for the whole world: "I wish I'd told you . . . we were only smuggling the rationed petrol to help our Hindu and Sikh friends to run away. And also for the convoys to send kidnapped women, like our Ayah, to their families across the border." (242) The novel, apart from being a classic of partition novel, is a celebration of writer's own community and its humanity and loyalty for the nation and the people it inhabits and shares things with.

NOTES

1. Bapsi Sidhwa. "New Neighbors." (11 Aug. 1997) n.pag.Online. Time. Internet.2 Apr. 1997. http://www.pathfinder.com/time/maga zine/1997/int/970811/spl.neighbors.html
2. An Interview with Bapsi Sidhwa', *Massachusetts Review,* 1990, p. 523.
3. Laurel Graeber, "The Seeds of Partition," Review of *Cracking India*, *New York Times Book Review*, 6 Oct. 1991, p. 6.
4. Bapsi Sidhwa, *Ice-Candy-Man* (New Delhi: Penguin, 1989), p. 139.
5. Khushwant Singh, 'A Review of *Ice-Candy-Man*,' *The Tribune*. http://members.aol.com/_ht_a/bsidhwa/crack_India_Indian.html?m tbrand=AOL_US
6. Geetha Hariharan, 'A Review of *Ice-Candy-Man,' The Economic Times*. http://members.aol.com/_ht_a/bsidhwa/crack_India_Indian. html?mtbrand=AOL_S
7. Ruth Gutman, "Visiting Prof.'s Novel to be in Film" (27 Feb. 1997) 4 par.Online. *The Mount Holyoke News*. Internet. 2 Apr. 1997. http://www.mtholyoke.edu/org/mhnews/S97/feb27/news/Nn ovel.html
8. "Writer-in-Residence Bapsi Sidhwa Takes Laughter Seriously." (28 Mar. 1997) 6 par. Online. *The College Street Journal. Internet.* 2 Apr. 1997. http://www.mtholyoke.edu/offices/comm/csj/970328/ sidhwa. html

A Postcolonial Appraisal of Sidhwa's Fiction

RAHUL SAPRA

Ice-Candy-Man *is no mere Partition novel; it has great significance as a literary work from postcolonial point of view. Sidhwa, in this novel, rewrites history from the Pakistani angle and also demonstrates the neutral stance adopted by the Parsi community to the freedom struggle of India. Rahul Sapra compares the novel with the fiction written by other postcolonial novelists like Chinua Achebe and Ngugi, and brings out several similarities between them. In a subtle fashion, Sidhwa questions the British and Indian versions of the subcontinent's history and provides an alternate version of history which has assumed great significance as a chronicler of a minority's role and viewpoint.*

Editor

Bapsi Sidhwa's fiction deals with both the pre- and post-colonial period of the Indian subcontinent. Her fiction not only brings to life the horror of the Partition but also vividly portrays the complexities of life in the subcontinent after Independence. What makes her work interesting from the post-colonial point of view[1] is the way in which she re-writes the history of the subcontinent. In *Ice-Candy-Man*,[2] Lenny, the young narrator, in the process of narrating the story of her family re-writes the history of the subcontinent, thereby undercutting the British view of history imposed on the subcontinent. In *An American Brat*,[3] Sidhwa highlights the predicament of the Pakistani people in general and of the Parsi community in particular vis-a-vis the emerging fundamentalist politics in Pakistan. Thus, while in *Ice-Candy-Man* Sidhwa grapples with the realities of the pre-Independence period, in *An American Brat* she highlights the phenomenon of neo-colonialism in Pakistan. What is most remarkable about her work is her dual perspective, which is based on both the Pakistani and the Parsi point of view. She speaks both for the Pakistanis and the marginalized Parsi community.

I

Sidhwa's re-writing of history in *Ice-Candy-Man* is far more complex than it appears to be, since she re-writes history not just from the Pakistani but also from the Parsi point of view. In order to highlight the Parsi dilemma at the time of the Partition she goes back thirteen hundred years to the significant moment in Parsi history, when they "were kicked out of Persia by the Arabs" and "sailed to India." (37) After waiting for four days on the Indian coast they were visited by the Grand Vazir, with a glass of milk filled to the brim, symbolizing that his land is full and prosperous and in no need of "outsiders with a different religion and alien ways to disturb the harmony." (38) However, the Parsi forefathers, intelligently, "stirred a teaspoon of sugar into the milk and sent it back," (39) symbolizing that the Parsis "would get absorbed into his country like sugar in the milk. And with their decency and industry sweeten the lives of his subjects." (39) The short account, whether true or not, highlights the dilemma the Parsis have faced over the centuries—the dilemma of assimilating themselves into an alien culture and risking the loss of their identity. The impending partition of the country, as depicted in the novel, might prove that all the efforts the Parsis have made over the centuries to assimilate themselves into Indian culture are futile since the community all of a sudden faces the threat of extinction/annihilation in the wake of the Partition. Thirteen hundred years ago, the Parsis had tried to accept Indian culture with all its diversities, but now at the moment of Partition they might be forced to take sides with one of the dominant communities/religions in India—Hindus, Muslims or Sikhs. Thus Sidhwa undercuts the received historical view that the Parsis were totally indifferent to the partition of the country. Instead of indifference the Parsis had a complex attitude towards Partition, as brought out in the main-hall meeting in the Fire Temple. Col. Bharucha, the president of the community in Lahore, argues that the Parsis should shun the anti-colonial movement and stick to their long standing stance of loyalty to the British Empire. He warns the Parsis that once we get Swaraj, "Hindus, Muslims and even the Sikhs are going to jockey for power: and if you jokers jump into the middle you'll be mingled into chutney!" (36) However Dr. Moody points out that it is not so simple. The Parsis cannot remain uninvolved and will have to take a stance otherwise, "our neighbours will think that we are betraying them and siding with the English." (37) This, however leads to a further complication, as voiced by a fellow Parsi, when he asks: "Which of your neighbours are you going to betray? Hindu? Muslim? Sikhs?" (37) This remark brings to the foreground the bitter fact that even after thirteen hundred years the Parsis feel alienated in the subcontinent. Their alienation from all the major communities in India ultimately forces them to support "whoever rules Lahore." (34) Col. Bharucha suggests, "Let whoever wishes to rule! Hindu, Muslim, Sikh, Christian. We will abide by the rules of the land." (39) Thus Sidhwa by giving voice to the marginalized Parsis demonstrates that their choice of remaining neutral in the context of the Partition was not out of indifference but forced upon them by a complex historical reality.

Sidhwa, further, demonstrates that the neutral stance adopted by the Parsi community vis-a-vis the freedom struggle did not prevent them from participating in the freedom struggle in whichever way they could. M.F. Salat observes that Sidhwa contradicts the received discourses by showing the "silent but positive role played by Lenny's parents in helping both the Hindu and the Muslims,"[4] suggesting that "the Parsis too were involved in their own ways in the events of the time and that they were not just indifferent and passive onlookers to the awful human tragedy." (102) Salat observes that it is a revelation meant not only for Lenny but also for all those who are ignorant of the Parsi involvement in the Partition when Lenny's mother explains the secret of her suspicious outings. (102) She explains: "I wish I'd told you . . . we were only smuggling the rationed petrol to help our Hindu and Sikh friends to run away. And also for the convoys to send kidnapped women, like our Ayah, to their families across the border." (242)

This theme is further developed in her next novel.*An American Brat*, where the Parsi community is shown actively participating in Pakistani politics. Instead of keeping a neutral, detached stance, Ginwalla family is passionately involved in the country's current political crisis. Zareen at one point voices her concern over her daughter's intense involvement in "Bhutto's trial." (30) Her concern for her daughter, however, does not stop her from working in "many women's committees with Begum Bhutto." (175) Feroza, even when she is in America, remains acutely concerned about the crisis in her country. She is totally shocked to hear of Bhutto's hanging: "Asshole! Douchebags! Fools! Donkeys!' Feroza shouted, her voice breaking, and, repeating the swear words again and again, began to weep." (182) On coming back to Pakistan, she voices her disappointment at being inadequately informed about Pakistan's current political scenario: "I want to know what's going on here. After all, it's my country!" (237) Thus Sidhwa exhibits that the Parsis, both in the pre- and post-Independence period, instead of showing indifference to the country's politics, have been actively involved in it.

Sidhwa in *Ice-Candy-Man*, as mentioned earlier, rewrites history from the Pakistani point of view also. In an interview with David Montenegro, she clearly states this agenda:

> The main motivation grew out of my reading of a good deal of literature on the partition of India and Pakistan . . . what has been written by the British and Indians. Naturally they reflect their bias. And they have, I felt after I'd researched the book, been unfair to the Pakistanis. As a writer, as a human being, one just does not tolerate injustice, I felt whatever little I could do to correct an injustice I would like to do. I have just let facts speak for themselves, and through my research I found out what the facts were.[5]

To counter the British and Indian versions of the Partition, Sidhwa in *Ice-Candy-Man* not only tries to resurrect the image of Jinnah but also demystifies the image of Gandhi and Nehru. Jinnah in the novel is highlighted as an ambassador of Hindu-Muslim unity: "Today forty years later, in films of Gandhi's and

Mountbatten's times, in books by British and Indian scholars, Jinnah who for a decade was known as an 'ambassador of Hindu-Mislim unity,' is caricatured and portrayed as monster." (160) To substantiate this image of Jinnah, Sidhwa quotes the Indian poetess Sarojini Naidu:

> The calm hauteur of his accustomed reserve masks, for those who knew him, a naive and eager humanity, an intuition quick and tender as a woman's, a humour gay and winning as a child's—pre-eminently rational and practical, discreet and dispassionate in his estimate and acceptance of life, the obvious sanity and serenity of his worldly wisdom effectually disguise a shy and splendid idealism which is of the very essence of the man. (161)

The sublime image of Gandhi constructed by British and Indian historians is totally undercut when he is seen through the eyes of the seven-year-old narrator, Lenny: "He [Gandhi] is small, dark, shrivelled, old. He looks just like Hari, our gardener, except he has a disgruntled, disgusted and irritable look; and no one'd dare pull off his dhoti! He wears only the loincloth and his black and thin torso is naked." (86) Unlike most of the Indian historians who credit Gandhi for single-handedly ousting the British from India, in *Ice-Candy-Man* Sidhwa reduces him to the role of an eccentric dietician, who advises every woman to "flush" (87) their systems with enemas. According to Masseur, Gandhi "is a politician" and "it's his business to suit his tongue to the moment." (91) Similarly Nehru is a shrewd politician who in spite of all the efforts of Jinnah "will walk off with the lion's share." (131) Nehru, according to the Ice-Candy-Man is "a sly one. . . . He's got Mountbatten eating out of his one hand and the English's wife out of his other what not. . . . He's the one to watch!" (131)

Even though Sidhwa tries to depict the atrocities committed by Hindus, Muslims, and Sikhs without partiality, being a Pakistani writer she makes it obvious that her sympathies are with the Muslim victims. Not only is the Sikhs's attack on Muslim villages in Punjab described vividly, but also it is seen through the eyes of the Muslim child Ranna, which shifts the reader's sympathy towards the Muslims. In an interview with David Montenegro, Sidhwa observes, "the Sikhs perpetrated the much greater brutality—they wanted Punjab to be divided. A peasant is rooted in his soil. The only way to uproot him was to kill him or scare him out of his wits." (50-51)

Thus we see that Sidhwa not only shifts the blame of the Partition on to the Indian leaders, but also makes the reader sympathise with the Muslim victims of the Partition by accentuating the violence inflicted upon the Muslims by the Sikhs. However, in *An American Brat*, Sidhwa is not so sympathetic towards the Pakistani leaders. *An American Brat*, as mentioned earlier, deals with the post-Independence scenario when the army under General Zia-ul-Haq seized control in 1977. The erstwhile president Zulfikar Ali Bhutto was tried for corruption and murder and sentenced to death in 1978. In spite of worldwide appeals for clemency, the sentence was carried out in 1979. As a result, Pakistan was totally under the grip of fundamentalist politics. Zareen attacks the "mullah-ish mentality" (13) that had begun to effect their normal day-to-day life:

> Could you [Cyrus] imagine Feroza cycling to school now? She'd be a freak! Those goondas would make vulgar noises and bump into her, and the mullahs would tell her to cover her head. Instead of moving forward, we are moving backward. What I could do in '59 and '60, my daughter can't do in 1978! Our Parsi children in Lahore wouldn't know how to mix with Parsi kids in Karachi or Bombay. (11)

It is this suppression that forces Zareen to send her daughter to "the mind-broadening and character-building" (38) America. It is thanks to this ever-increasing interference of the state in peoples' life that in Pakistan, unlike in America, politics concerns everyone. Sidhwa observes that in spite of "Martin Luther King Jr.'s and the Kennedy's assassinations" (171) "the tenor of her [Jo's] life and that of her parents remained the same: full of opportunity for those with ambition to grab it." (171) In Pakistan, on the other hand:

> Politics concerned everyone—from the street sweeper to the business tycoon—because it affected everyone, particularly women,

> determining how they should dress, whether they could play hockey in school or not, how they should conduct themselves even within the four walls of their homes. (171)

What is the way out of this neo-colonial chaos? Does Sidhwa offer any solutions? On the news of Bhutto's death, Zareen had anticipated large processions "to protest the injustice: to establish a martyr's claim to his martyrdom," (178) but unfortunately there was "no main crowd, no large procession . . . no venue to vent their rage, hurt, and grief." (178) At this point Zareen realizes the bitter fact "that there is no such thing as a spontaneous uprising unless it is sanctioned!" (178) Thus Sidhwa does not offer a peoples' revolution as a solution simply because it is impossible. In this regard her stance is not very different from that of Chinua Achebe in *A Man of the People*, where he portrays a society in which a mass movement seems to be an impossibility. The society depicted in *A Man of the People* has helplessly adapted itself to the neo-colonial situation, for instead of condemning the corrupt leaders, the people hope to get a share out of the "National cake."[7] The society depicted in Sidhwa's *An American Brat* is not very different: Bhutto's death was possible because "General Zia had the support, open or covert, of all the major political forces in the country and all the country's major institutions—the military, the civil bureaucracy, and the judiciary." (178) The only way in which a common man can deal with the situation is by converting it into a joke: "Most catastrophes were converted into jokes. How else could ordinary people tolerate what was happening to the country and to them?" (138) Instead of revolting against the system, people end up tolerating the system. However, Achebe, unlike Sidhwa, does offer a solution. In *A Man of the People*, even when he undercuts the possibility of a peoples's revolution, he does not deny the individual's responsibility towards the society. In his next novel *Anthills of the Savannah* (1987), he puts the responsibility on the leaders: "the whole point of being a leader is that, in spite of the cynicism or the despair of the masses, it is [the leader's] job to do something for them."[8] Sidhwa, on the other hand, refuses to give any solution for the dismal state of affairs in Pakistan. Her major contribution is that she has been able to draw attention towards the social and political chaos in Pakistan, which, if not a solution in itself, might lead to one. Achebe once said that a writer does not necessarily have to provide solutions: "The fact that you are talking about it implies some optimism that somebody may listen, that there is still a possibility of change. One has to bring these problems out as forcefully as possible to draw attention to them."[9]

However, though Sidhwa describes the neo-colonial situation in Pakistan, she does not analyse the significance of the neo-colonial role of the United States in the subcontinent's politics. Unlike the Kenyan writer Ngugi wa Thiong'o, who in his novel *Devil on the Cross* (1982) exposes the way in which the neo-colonial elite in Kenya are strengthened and encouraged by the western powers; Sidhwa does not deal with this aspect. This is not to say that there is no mention of the United States' neocolonial role, for at one point she does mention that the United States deals in "death" (315) by selling the "most lethal weapons to impoverished countries" (315); and, at another point, she states that no matter "how many weapons the United States and the Soviet union manufactured or countries they bullied or bombs they rained down, the threat of war would be profitably maintained and kept remote from their part of the world." (170) In spite of such references, there is no suggestion of the United States' interference in the subcontinent's politics. In fact Sidhwa's stance vis-a-vis the United States's neo-colonial role is far more tolerant than that of most postcolonial writers. Even while she criticizes the United States for selling "the world's most lethal weapons to impoverished countries," she is quick to add that the United States "simultaneously absorbed the dispossessed of the chronically dispelling world." (313) The United States, in the novel, is used as a contrast to Pakistan. While Pakistan is fundamentalist, confining and controlled by "fundos" (305)—the United States is land of "generosity," (316) "opportunities" (119) and "free economy." (140) Towards the end of the novel, Sidhwa compliments the United States as "a New World, the future in microcosm, the melting-pot in which every race and every creed was being increasingly represented, compelled to live with and tolerate the 'other'." (313)

II

Another interesting feature of Sidhwa's writing from the postcolonial perspective is her use of the English language. In fact, language is a major preoccupation of the postcolonial writer. Should the writer write in the language inherited from the imperial power or should he/she revert to the native language? An opposing stance has been taken by the two African writers Chinua Achebe (Nigeria) and Ngugi wa Thiong'o (Kenya) vis-a-vis language in postcolonial literature. Ngugi after writing his earlier works in English has rejected the language and now writes in his native language Gikuyu. Explaining his stance in *Decolonising the Mind*, Ngugi asks: "What is the difference between a politician who says that Africa cannot do without imperialism and the writer who says that Africa cannot do without European languages?"[10] Ngugi's point is that language has been always used by the colonizer to mentally and spiritually control the colonized: "The domination of a peoples' language by the languages of the colonizing nations was crucial to the domination of the mental universe of the colonised." (16) By continuing to write in the colonizer's language, one is colonized on the cultural level, and instead of enriching one's own native language and culture, one only ends up enriching the European traditions. However, writers such as Chinua Achebe and Gabriel Okara disagree. Achebe argues: "I feel that the English language will be able to carry the weight of my African experience. But it will have to be a new English, still in full communion with its ancestral home but altered to suit new African surroundings."[11] He best demonstrates this new English in his much acclaimed work *Things Fall Apart*.

Sidhwa's stance is in line with that of Chinua Achebe. In her interview with Feroza Jussawalla, she states:

> My first language of speech is Gujrati, my second is Urdu, my third is English. But as far as reading and writing goes I can read and write best in English. I'm a tail end product of the Raj. This is

> the case with a lot of people in India and Pakistan. They're condemned to write in English, but I don't think this is such a bad thing because English is a rich language. Naturally it is not my first language; I'm more at ease talking in Gujrati and Urdu. After moving to America I realized that all my sentences in English were punctuated with Gujrati and Urdu words.[12]

So, even though Sidhwa writes in English, it is a new English—an English punctuated with words from the native language. However, it is not a simple addition of words from the native language to English. While the writer translates a number of words from the native languages, a large number of words are also left untranslated. For instance, the following words, in *Ice-Candy-Man*, have been translated: "pahailwan, a wrestler" (27), "Choorail, witches" (21), "Shabash, Well Said!" (245), "Ghar ki Murgi dal barabar. A neighbour's beans are tastier than household chickens" (232), "Khut putli, puppets" (222), "Mamajee [Uncle]." (77) In *An American Brat*, almost every word and phrase of the native language employed in the novel is translated by the writer in a "Glossary" at the end of the novel. For instance: "Badmash: scoundrel," "Gora; white, in Urdu," "Heejra: eunuch or transvestite." What such a translation of individual words does? Bill Ashcroft et al in The Empire Writes Back observe that such translation of individual words is the most obvious and most common authorial intrusion in cross-cultural texts. Juxtaposing the words in this way suggests that the meaning of a word is its referent. But the simple matching of words from the native language with its translated version in English reveals the general inadequacy of such an exercise. (61) The moment a word from a native language is juxtaposed with its referent in English, instead of clarifying the meaning, it shows the gap between the word and its referent. Bill Ashcroft et al argue that the implicit gap between the word from the native language and its referent, in fact, disputes the "putative referentiality" of the words and establishes the word from the native language as a cultural sign. (61) For instance, let us take the word "Kotha" (267) from *Ice-Candy-Man*, which is translated as "Roof" (267) in the novel. However, it is made clear in the novel that the Hindi word

"Kotha" does not simply mean "roof," but is a place of prostitution. This gap between the word "Kotha" and its English translation "roof" establishes "Kotha" as a cultural sign.

Apart from these words, in *Ice-Candy-Man*, there are certain other words from the native language which are not translated, such as: "sarkar" (157), "yaar" (91), "doolha" (180), "chachi" (199), "Arrey Bhagwan" (26), "Angrez" (28), "Haramzadi" (45), "Haramkhor" (95), "chaudhary" (198). What purpose is served by not translating words of the native language? The use of untranslated words "is a clear signifier that the language which actually informs the novel is an other language."[13] Even though the *Ice-Candy-Man* is written in English, the untranslated words remind the reader that the language of conversation of the characters is not English but Hindi, Urdu and Punjabi. The untranslated words are part of the strategy of the postcolonial writer to highlight the cultural difference.

Apart from using the strategies discussed above, Sidhwa, to highlight Muslim culture, quotes various Urdu poets in her narrative. In fact, *Ice-Candy-Man* opens with Iqbal's poem "Complaint to God." (1) At the beginning of chapter 13, the quote from Iqbal's poetry is a good example of the poet's anticolonial stance:

> The times have changed; the world has changed its mind.
> The European's mystery is erased.
> The secret of his conjuring tricks is known:
> The Frankish wizard stands and looks amazed. (111)

Iqbal demystifies the notion of the Whites as a superior race by exposing the secret of its "conjuring tricks."

III

To conclude, Sidhwa through the *Ice-Candy-Man* successfully questions the British and Indian versions of the subcontinent's history and provides an alternate version of history based on the Pakistani point of view. In *An American Brat*, she voices the social and political chaos in Pakistan generated by the forces of neo-colonialism. In both the novels, she has succinctly adapted the English language to suit her purposes. Further, she has not just provided the marginalized Parsi community with a voice but also a large number of Pakistani readers. She is justified in saying:

> I think a lot of readers in Pakistan, especially with *Ice-Candy-Man*, feel that I've given them a voice, which they did not have before. They have always been portrayed in a very unfavourable light. It's been fashionable to kick Pakistan, and it's been done again and again by various writers living in the West. And I feel, if there's one little thing one could do, it's to make people realize: We are not worthless because we inhabit a poor country that is seen by Western eyes as primitive, fundamentalist country only.[14]

N0TES

1. Bill Ashcroft et al in *The Empire Writes Back* (1989) use the term postcolonial to "cover all the culture affected by the imperial process from the moment of colonization to the present day." (2) Consequently the literature written in the colonized countries from the moment of colonization till the present day can be termed as postcolonial literature. The literature of African countries, Australia, Bangladesh, Canada, Caribbean countries, India, Malaysia, Malta, New Zealand, Pakistan, Singapore, South Pacific Island countries and Sri Lanka, are all postcolonial literatures. What makes each of these literatures distinctly postcolonial is that "they emerged in their present form out of the experience of colonization and asserted themselves by foregrounding the tension with the imperial power, and by emphasizing their differences from the assumptions of the imperial centre." (2) For more details see Bill Ashcroft, Gareth Griffiths and Helen Tiffin, *The Empire Writes Back: Theory and Practice in Postcolonial Literatures* (London: Routledge, 1999), p. 61. However, there are various interpretations of the term. For a detailed analysis of the subject, read Paul Brians' essay "'Postcolonial Literature': Problems with the Term" (7 Aug. 1998). Online. Internet. 10 Oct. 1998.
2. Bapsi Sidhwa, *Ice-Candy-Man* (New Delhi: Penguin, 1989).
3. Bapsi Sidhwa, *An American Brat* (New Delhi: Penguin, 1994).

4. M.F. Salat, "Magic Writings of Bapsi Sidhwa," *The Parsis: Madyan to Sanjan*, ed. Novy Kapadia and A.G. Khan (Delhi, 1997), p. 102.
5. David Montenegro, *Points of Departure: International Writers on Writing and Politics* (1989), p. 36.
6. According to Shashi Tliaroor, Sidhwa is not good when it comes to handling politics. He observes that some of the incidents described in the novel lack historical accuracy:

    > What she [Bapsi Sidhwa] doesn't handle as well is politics: when her characters discuss the issues of the day, Ms. Sidhwa's deftness collapses in cliches. Don't look for historical accuracy in this seemingly realistic tale: Mahatma Gandhi's march to the sea protesting the British tax on salt is displaced by a decade and a half, and when Ms. Sidhwa uses her authorial authority to inform the reader that "the British favour Nehru over Jinnah. Nehru is Kashmiri, they grant him Kashmir," it is not simply wrong (the Maharajah of Kashmir acceded to India a year after Partition), it undermines her narrator.

    See Tharoor's review of the novel "Life with Electric-Aunt and Slavesister."
7. Chinua Achebe, *A Man of the People* (London: Heinemann, 1958), p. 145.
8. Qtd. Anuradha Dingwaney Needham, "Articulating the Postcolonial Writers' Social Responsibilities: The Example of Chinua Achebe," *South Asian Responses to Chinua Achebe*, ed. Bernth Lindfors and Bala Kothandaraman (Delhi: Prestige, 1993), p. 26.
9. Ibid., pp. 24-25.
10. Ngugi wa Thiong'O, *Decolonising the Mind: The Politics of Language in African Literature* (London: James Curry, 1986).
11. Qtd. Ngugi, p. 8.
12. Feroza Jussawalla and Reed Way Dasenbrock, ed., *Interviews with Writers of the Postcolonial World* (1990), p. 214.
13. Ashcroft et al, p. 64.
14. Montenegro, p. 51.

The Narrative Techniques in *Ice-Candy-Man*

PASHUPATI JHA & NAGENDRA KUMAR

Bapsi Sidhwa relives the trauma of Partition carnage and communal riots through the innocent, and hence objective, impressions of Lenny, an eight-year old, polio-inflicted child. What enriches the thematic pattern of the novel is its narrative design—though filtered through the innocent eyes and mind of a girl child, there are layers of subtle and sophisticated narrative ploys adopted by the novelist to make the plot more poignant and gripping.

Editor

Bapsi Sidhwa, the internationally-acclaimed Pakistani Parsi writer, has secured an enviable position for herself among the literary circles today. She has proved that her minority experience as the member of a tiny Parsi community in Pakistan, far from being a visible trouble-spot on her creative psyche, offers her enough to celebrate her talent. She feels that it has given her a unique sense of 'detached attachment' for her country and its people. Her creative odyssey, which started with *The Crow-Eaters* (1978), has grown from strength to strength in her successive works like *Pakistani Bride* (1983), *Ice-Candy-Man* (1988) and *An American Brat* (1994).

Bapsi Sidhwa's third and till date the most celebrated and widely quoted novel *Ice-Candy-Man/Cracking India* (1988) is one of the most powerful narratives of recent times. The novel captures one of the most decisive moments in the history of India and Pakistan—Partition—in a very compelling way through the eyes of an eight-year old disabled girl, Lenny. As Tariq Rahman comments in a review: "The novel is an imaginative response to the traumatic events of the Partition of India in 1947, and Sidhwa has used surrealistic techniques, somewhat like Salman Rushdie, to make it an adequate symbol for the effect of external events on human beings." Another very perceptive comment comes from Shashi Tharoor, a noted columnist and novelist: "*Ice-Candy-Man* is a novel in which heartbreak coexists with slap-stick . . . and jokes give way to lines of glowing beauty ("the moonlight settles like a layer of ashes over Lahore"). The author's capacity for bringing an assortment of characters vividly to life is enviable. In reducing the Partition to the perceptions of a polio-ridden child, a girl who tries to wrench out her tongue because it is unable to lie, Bapsi Sidhwa has given us a memorable book, one that confirms her reputation as Pakistan's finest English language novelist."[1]

Lenny's development from childhood to adolescence coincides with India's struggle for independence from Britain and the partitioning of the country into India and Pakistan. The skilfully interwoven plots give each other substantial meaning. Partly because Lenny comes from a Parsi family, a religious and ethnic minority that remained relatively neutral in post-Partition religious conflicts, she has access to people of all ethnicities and religions, both within Lahore and in other locales. More significantly, she has access to a wide variety of viewpoints, both pre- and post-Partition, through her Ayah, a beautiful woman whose suitors are ethnically and religiously diverse. From the lap of her beautiful Ayah, or clutching her skirts as Ayah is pursued by her suitors through the fountains, cypresses and marble terraces of the Shalimar Gardens, little Lenny observes the clamorous horrors of Partition. It is 1947. Lenny lives in Lahore, in the bosom of her extended Parsi family: Mother, Father, Brother Adi, Cousin, Electric-Aunt, Godmother and Slavesister. Working for them, or panting after Ayah, are Butcher, the puny Sikh zoo attendant, the Government House gardener, the favoured Masseur, the restaurant-owning wrestler and the shady Ice-Candy-Man—Muslims, Christians, Sikhs, Hindus, friends and neighbours—until their ribald, everyday world disintegrates before the violence of religious hatred.

Lenny's passionate love for Ayah, and the loss of innocence that accompanies their changing relationship through the Partition, is an energetic centre to the plot. Lenny's relationships with her mother, her powerful Godmother, and her sexually invasive cousin are also important to the novel. Lenny's polio forms a significant early narrative thread. Other minor but compelling subplots include Lenny's parents' changing relationship, the murder of a British official, Ranna's tragic tale, and the child marriage of Papoo, the much-abused daughter of one of Lenny's family's servants.

Sidhwa's focus in this symbolic novel is not so much on the story as it is on the narrative techniques, for they contribute to the work's total effect. Foremost among them is the first-person present-tense narration. Lenny, like Saleem Sinai in Rushdie's *Midnight's Children,* is—or was—a child when the events described take place, and the events are seen through her consciousness, the present tense providing immediacy and a certain simultaneity between past and present. By the end of both the novels, the narrator knows much about human treachery, mainly through the impact of external events. Lenny learns of the perverse nature of amorous human passions from her experiences with her cousin, who courts her with a determination comparable only to the Ice-Candy-Man's pursuit of Ayah. How religious fanaticism can breed hatred and violence is evident in the killing of the Hindus in Lahore and the Muslims in the Punjab of the Sikhs. The dehumanizing impact of communal riots is reflected in the story of Lenny's friend Ranna, a harrowing account of the human atrocities that can be perpetrated when all civilized restraints are removed through external events or political propaganda.

Bapsi Sidhwa chooses Lenny, a polio-ridden, precocious child as the narrator of the novel because she provides her with a scope for recording the events leading to bloody Partition riots with utmost objectivity, without an air of propaganda. Moreover, she comes from a Parsi family and so is free from any religious or ethnic bias. Like most of the children of her age, she has a truth-infected tongue. In many respects, she resembles her creator who had a bad polio, which affected her normal movement compelling her to stay at home under the care of an Ayah for the most part of her childhood life, busy in delicately nursing her world of idyllic romances. Bapsi was of the same age when the nation was divided into two and had the first hand experience of the Partition-riots. As she recalls: "I was a child then. Yet the ominous roar of distant mobs was a constant of my awareness, alerting me, even at age seven, to a palpable sense of the evil that was taking place in various parts of Lahore. The glow of fires beneath the press of smoke, which bloodied the horizon in a perpetual sunset, wrenched at my heart. For many of us, the departure of the British and the longed-for Independence of the subcontinent were overshadowed by the ferocity of partition."[2] The events of Partition had left an indelible mark on the psyche of child Bapsi and kept compelling her to unburden herseif from the harrowing experiences of those days. Lenny, in fact, is the personae, voicing the inner urge of the author. Bapsi Sidhwa herself explains why she chose Lenny as the narrator of the novel: "I'm establishing a sort of truthful witness, whom the reader can believe. At the same time, Lenny is growing up—learning, experiencing, and coming to her own conclusions."[3] Though it sounds cautioning to identify the narrator with the author, the intersections of the two at various points of the narrative seem to be deliberate and not a mere coincidence, because the novel is as much about personal history as it is about memory and imagination. The author has no secrecy whatsoever regarding her resemblance with the narrator as she admits in an interview, "the scene where people ride into the house to kidnap Ayah did happen in real life, although I have fictionalized it."[4]

In *Ice-Candy Man*, Lenny is the narrative persona. Her narration starts in her fifth year and ends after her eighth birthday. She recalls her first conscious memory of her Ayah thus: "She passes pushing my pram with the unconcern of the Hindu goddess she worships."[5] She also remembers her house on Warris Road in Lahore and how she used to find refuge in her Godmother's "one-and-a-half room abode" and succeeded in getting away from the "gloom" and the "perplexing unrealities" of home. These perplexities include her own polio affliction, which she uses as an armour against a "pretentious world," her mother's extravagance, her father's dislike of it, her strain to fill up the "infernal silence" during her father's "mute meals" by "offering laughter and lengthier chatter" ("Is that when I learnt to tell tales?"). These perplexities also involve the household staff. It includes her very dear Ayah, an eighteen-year-old dusky beauty, Shantha, Imam Din, the genial-faced cook of the Sethi household, Hari, the high-caste Hindu, Moti, the outcaste gardener, Mucho, his shrew of a wife, Papoo, his much abused child—and the Ice-Candy-Man, a raconteur and a "born gossip" who never stops touching Ayah with his "tentative toes"—and masseur, a sensitive man who loves Ayah and is loved by her, much to the chagrin of Ice-Candy-Man; and last but certainly impressive Ranna, the boy whom Lenny befriends when she visits his village with Imam Din and numerous others. Lenny leads us on, dwelling on interesting facts mingled, as it were, with picturesque language. The main events, besides the end of the Second World War, India's Independence and Partition of the subcontinent into Pakistan and India, revolve around Ayah. She is—not unlike India itself—a symbol of larger-than-life reality, truly "perplexing." Lenny also notices that, "beggars, holy men, hawkers, cart-drivers, cooks, coolies and cyclists" lust after her (3). Hasn't India been a much-looted country, which finally is forced to make a new beginning? With such emerging connotations, the novel sustains our interest at the personal and political levels.

For Lenny, in a few years' time a whole world, which is also her world, undergoes a sea change marked by "blood dimmed anarchy." Her focus switches from her own "sense of inadequacy and unworth" and the "trivia and trappings" of her learning, to the world outside, which she finds is dark and dangerous. With greater perception, she notes the fast, unstoppable and violent changes that leave her and those around her, particularly Ayah, "wounded in the soul."

As observed by Iyengar, in a novel "Action, passion, contemplation, feeling, even the unconscious mind find place."[6] In Sidhwa's novel, one finds different shades of human thought, feelings and behaviour truthfully voiced. Every character in the novel lets us glimpse into his inner reserves and we are constantly surprised at the reality of it. Passages describing bloodshed and murder highlight the brute in human beings. After Master Tara Singh's rousing address against the division of Punjab, the mob turns "maniac." Even the police were targeted. And then there is towering inferno in Lahore. Lenny observes:

> The whole world is burning. The air on my face is so hot. I think my flesh and clothes will catch fire. I start screaming: hysterically sobbing—how long does Lahore burn? Weeks? Months? (137, 139)

The working of native psyche is well brought out by an ingenious use of various devices by Sidhwa in this novel. She shows us, with graphic clarity, how little Lenny's mind sees, grasps and ponders over the world around her through her nightmares, witticisms, description of people, their mannerisms and feelings in idioms and metaphors, both homegrown and alien. An enslaved country's total plight is shown in the line

> Queen Victoria's statue imposes the English Raj in the park. (18)

Before the conflict, Muslims and Sikhs lived in peaceful harmony. They celebrated and participated in each other's festivals such as Baisakhi and Id. But once the big trouble started "One man's religion is another man's poison." (117) All this scuffle between two countries was caused and furthered when "the Radcliff commission deals out Indian cities like a pack of cards." (140) And at the end of a gory day "the moonlight settles like a layer of ashes over Lahore." (137)

Besides idioms which evoke a terrible national tragedy, Bapsi Sidhwa also makes use of devices such as nightmares (21, 22), jokes involving bathroom humour, (30, 35) poetry by the popular Urdu poet Iqbal, Parsi entrance into India (37, 38), their customs, prayers, fire temples, and funerals in Towers of Silence (37, 38), elaborate discussions and debates on national politics by the haves and the have-nots (91, 93, 131), detailed accounts of villages such as Pir Pindo inhabited by people of different religions (105-11), and the bitter change of later times, forced conversions (180), forced child marriages (188) and many other minute yet grave details, which succeed in bringing to the reader a whole gamut of tragi-comic and tragic incidents.

As the narrative progresses, everything is filtered through the consciousness of Lenny. Her interest in things around her is somewhat unnatural as we find her recording each and everything like a video camera. There are no restrictions on her movements and she seems to be enjoying all the happenings around. She can attend the Parsi meeting to discuss the future course of action in the wake of Partition conflicts and can also loiter around parks, cheap hotels, and such other places along with her ayah and can have access to the popular opinion. Because of her physical disability and precocious nature, she is loved and cared by all, and even her parents do not keep restrictions on her. She is even allowed to accompany Imam Din in his visits to Pir Pindo, a village in Punjab. This visit provides her with an opportunity to meet Ranna, the boy who later becomes a tool in the hands of the novelist to detail the events of inhuman brutality heaped on the Muslims across the border by the Sikhs, thus complementing the account of Partition narrated by Lenny.

The narrative design that Bapsi Sidhwa follows in the novel apparently looks very simple and straightforward, but on a closer look one realizes that its simplicity is merely deceptive. Although the main narrator is Lenny, the voice that emerges from the novel is far from being a monologue. There are moments when it is hard for the readers to believe that a little girl like Lenny can utter the words that have been put into her mouth. Like the one that is quoted here:

> I am held captive by the brutal smell. It has vaporized into a milky cloud. I float round and round and up and down and fall horrendous distances without landing anywhere, fighting for my life's breath. I am abandoned in that suffocating cloud. I moan and my ghoulish voice turns me into something despicable and eerie and deserving of the terrible punishment. But where am I? How long will the horror last? Days and years with no end in sight. (6)

And again:

> My nose inhales the fragrance of earth and grass—and the other fragrance that distils insights. I intuit the meaning and purpose of things. The secret rhythms of creation and mortality. The essence

> of truth and beauty. I recall the choking hell of milky vapours and discover that heaven has a dark fragrance. (19)

Passages like this make the reader aware of the presence of the author in the child, Lenny voicing her adult reactions to her childhood situation. Of course Sidhwa narrates the novel in the first person putting everything in the mouth of the child protagonist, but one thing is for sure that she does it with a serious purpose. She does not want to sound political and controversial, yet cannot turn herself back from the purpose at hand, i.e., to present the other side of the truth regarding the Partition riots—the Pakistani or in her own right the neutral point of view. It is another thing that at times she sacrifices even the decency and decorum of a literary artist, just flaunting the emotions of millions of people. Like we find in her observations and comments about Gandhi and Nehru. Lenny reflects on Gandhi:

> He is small, dark, shrivelled, old. He looks just like Hari, our gardener, except he has a disgruntled, disgusted and irritable look, and no one'd dare pull off his dhoti! He wears only the loincloth and his black and thin torso is naked.
>
> Gandhijee is certainly ahead of his times. He already knows the advantages of dieting. He has starved his way into the news and made headlines all over the world. (86)

Despite the occasional limitations like the one we have noticed above, this goes without saying that "no other novel catches as this one does India's centuries-old ways of living with religious difference before Partition."[7] Lenny is inquisitive and notices everything: clothes, smells, colour, the patina of skin, sex everywhere, and eyes—olive-oil-coloured, sly eyes, fearful eyes. In writing which is often lyrical, always tender and clever, with a nuance here, a touch there, Sidhwa shows us the seedbed of the Partition massacres—an abused Untouchable, the ritual disemboweling of a goat, a priest shuddering over the hand of a menstruating woman. This laughing, gentle tale, told through the eyes of innocence, is a testament to savage loss, and a brilliant evocation of the prowling roots of religious intolerance.

Thus though Bapsi has been accused by some diehard Indian nationalists of presenting a Pakistani view of history, we must not forget that this is a novel and not a work of social documentation; it limits itself to one child's perspective through which the dissenting, disagreeing voices she hears are refracted; and what Aamer Hussein says, "insofar as a novel can be objective, Bapsi is in the grand tradition of the Progressive writers on both sides of the border, scrupulously fair to all parties concerned, approaching politics with the empathy and compassion of a humanitarian feminist."[8] In fact the point of view Bapsi adopts, is one of the novel's most successful ploys. We believe we are witnessing the events of Partition through the eyes of an innocent child, but strategically placed flash-forward signal, in a subtle manner, that the adult Lenny is actually reliving the past in order to make sense of the events that baffled her when she was too small to comprehend; simultaneously, she restricts herself to the experiences and sensory perceptions of the child she was. Thus we are given a double—even dialogic—perspective that layers innocence on experience, introspection on hindsight.

NOTES

1. Shashi Tharoor, "Review of *Cracking India" New York Times Book Review*: October 6, 1991. (Sunday, Late Edition-Final)
2. Bapsi Sidhwa, "New Neighbors." (11 Aug. 1997) Online. Time. Internet. 2 Apr. 1997. http://www.pathfinder.com/time/magazine 1997/int/970811/spl.neighbors.html
3. David Montenegro, *Points of Departure: International Writers on Writing and Politics* (Michigan: Univ. of Michigan Press, 1991), p. 32.
4. Chelva Kanaganayakam, *Configurations of Exile* (Toronto: TSAR, 1995), p. 86.
5. Bapsi Sidhwa, *Ice-Candy-Man* (New Delhi: Penguin, 1989), p. 3.
6. K.R. Srinivasa Iyengar, *The Adventure of Criticism* (Bombay: Asia, 1962).
7. Carmen Callil and Colm Toibin *The 200 Best Novels in English Since 1950* (London: Picador, 1999).
8. Aamer Hussein, "Bapsi Sidhwa, Storyteller" http://members.aol. com /_ht_a /bsidhwa/rev_aamer_hussein.html

Select Bibliography

A. Primary Sources

I. Fiction

The Bride. London: Jonathan Cape, 1983. New York: St. Martin Press, 1983. Karachi: Liberty Books, 1987. Rpt. as *The Pakistani Bride*. New Delhi: Penguin, 1990. London/Sydney: Futura, 1994.

The Crow-Eaters. Bombay: Sangam, 1978, 1980. London: Jonathan Cape, 1980. London: St Martin Press, 1982. Glasgow: Fontana, 1982. Harmondsworth, Middlesex: Penguin, 1989.

Ice-Candy-Man. London: Heinemann, 1988. New Delhi: Penguin, 1989. Rpt. as *Cracking India* in the U.S. Minneapolis: Milkweed, 1991.

An American Brat. Minneapolis: Milkweed, 1993. Delhi: Penguin, 1994.

II. Non-Fiction

"Why Do I Write?" Dhawan and Kapadia, *The Novels of Bapsi Sidhava*. New Delhi: Prestige, 1996.

"The ABCD of Alienation ("American born confused Desi)," *Indian Express*, 8 May 1994.

"New Neighbors." (11 Aug. 1997) n.pag.Online. *Time*. Internet. 2 April 1997. http://www.pathfinder.com/time/magazine/1997/int/970811/spl.neighbors.html.

"Writing as an Immigrant," *The Atlantic Literary Review*, vol. 1, No. 2, Oct.-Dec. 2000.

III. Interviews

Afzal-Khan, Fawzia. An Interview with Bapsi Sidhwa. "Ties That Bind" by Edward Hower in *The World and I* (Magazine of *Washington Times*). March 1994,

Butalia, Urvashi. "Community, State and Gender: Some Reflections on the Partition of India," *Oxford Literary Review*, Vol. 16, nos. 1-2.

Hussain, Naila. An Interview with Bapsi Sidhwa. *Nation, Midweek*, 26 May 1993

Jussawalla, Feroza. An Interview with Bapsi Sidhwa. *Interview with Writers of the Post-Colonial World*, ed. Feroza. Jussawalla and Reedway Dasenbrock. Jackson: University Press of Missisipi, 1992.

Kanaganayakam, Chelva. Interview with Bapsi Sidhwa. *The Toronto South Asian Review*. Vol. II, no. 1, 1992.

Khan, Rahim. An Interview with Bapsi Sidhwa. *Weekend Post*, 23 Oct. 1991.

Mohsin, Jugnee. An Interview with Bapsi Sidhwa. *Friday Times*, July 1989.

Montenegro, David. An Interview with Bapsi Sidhwa. *Points of Departure: International Writers on Writing and Politics*.

Rajan, Julie. "Cracking Sidhwa: An Intimate Chat with Pakistani, Parsi Writer Bapsi Sidhwa on "Life, Words and all the Cracks In-between," http://www.monsoonmag.com/interviews/i3inter sidhwa.html.

B. Secondary Sources: Critical Works

I. Books

Butalia, Urvashi. *The Other Side of Silence: Voices from the Partition of India*. New Delhi: Penguin, 1998.

Dhawan, R.K. and Novy Kapadia, ed. *The Novels of Bapsi Sidhwa*. New Delhi: Prestige, 1996.

Kapadia, Novy, Jaydipsingh Dodiya, R.K. Dhawan, ed. *Parsi Fiction*. New Delhi: Prestige, 2001.

II. Research Articles

Asaduddin, M. "Against Forgetting: Memory as Metaphor in 'Dream Images'," *Translating Partition*, ed. Ravikant and Tarun K. Saint. New Delhi: Katha, 2001.

Bharucha, Nilufer. "The Parsi Voice in Recent Indian English Fiction," *Indian English Fiction 1980-90: An Assessment*, ed. Vilas Sarang and Nilufer Bharucha, New Delhi: B.R., 1994.

Chandra, Subhash. "Bapsi Sidhwa's *Ice-Candy Man*: A Feminist Perspective," *The Commonwealth Review*, 6.1 (1994-95).

Cowasjee, Saros. "The Partition in Indo-English Fiction," *Explorations in Modern Indo-English Fiction*, ed. R.K. Dhawan, New Delhi: Bahri, 1982.

Crane, Ralph J. "A Passion for History and for Truth Telling," *The Early Novels of Bapsi Sidhwa*. Dhawan and Kapadia, ed. *The Novels of Bapsi Sidhwa.*

Daruwala, K.N. "Of Parsis and their Literature," *Critical Practice*, vol. VII, no. 1.

Dhawan and Novy Kapadia. "Entrée: The Fiction of Bapsi Sidhwa." Dhawan and Kapadia, ed. *The Novels of Bapsi Sidhwa.*

Didur, Jill. "Cracking the Nation: Gender, Minorities and Agency in Bapsi Sidhwa's *Cracking India*," *Ariel*, 29.3 (1998).

Hai, Ambreen, "Border Work, Border Trouble: Postcolonial Feminism and the Ayah in Bapsi Sidhwa's *Cracking India*," *Modern Fiction Studies*, Volume 46, number 2, Summer 2000.

Havely, Cicely. "Patterns of Migration in the Works of Bapsi Sidhwa." Dhawan and Kapadia. *The Novels of Bapsi Sidhwa.*

Jussawalla, Feroza. "Navjote Ceremonies: The Location of Bapsi Sidhwa's Culture." Dhawan and Kapadia, *The Novels of Bapsi Sidhwa.*

Kapadia Novy, "Communal Frenzy and Partition: Bapsi Sidhwa, Attia Hosain and Amitav Ghosh." Dhawan, *Indian Women Novelists*, Set II, Vol. 1.

Kudchedkar, Shirin. "The Second Coming: Novels on the Partition," Vilas Sarang and Nilufer Bharucha. *Indian English Fiction 1980-90: An Assessment.*

Mann, Harveeen Sachdeva. "Cracking India: Minority Women Writers and the Contentious Margins of India National Discourse." *Journal of Commonwealth Literature*, 29.2 (1994).

Needham, Anuradha Dingwaney, "Multiple Forms of (National) Belonging: Attia Hosain's *Sunlight on a Broken Column*," *Modern Fiction Studies*, Vol. 39, number 1, Winter 1993.

Paranjape, Makarand. "The Novels of Bapsi Sidhwa," Dhawan, *Commonwealth Fiction*, Vol. 2.

Pathak, R.S. "Problematizing the Minority Discourse: Inlets to the Parsi Sensibility," Points of View, vol. V, no. 2, Winter 1998.

Piciucco, Pier Paolo. "The Hidden Strength of Women: A Key to the Reading of Bapsi Sidhwa's *Ice-Candy-Man*," *The Atlantic Literary Review*, Vol.1, no.1, July-September 2000.

Rani, K. Nirupa. "Gender and Imagination in Bapsi Sidhwa's Fiction." Dhawan and Kapadia, *The Novels of Bapsi Sidhwa.*

Ross, Robert L. "The Search for Community in Bapsi Sidhwa Novels." Dhawan and Kapadia, *The Novels of Bapsi Sidhwa.*

——. "*Cracking India*: A Feminine View of Partition." Dhawan and Kapadia, *The Novels of Bapsi Sidhwa.*

——. "Bapsi Sidhwa's Commonwealth Witness: The Crossing of Religious and National Boundaries." A Paper presented at VII Triennial Conference of the Association for Commonwealth Language and Literature Studies, 16-23 June 1986, Singapore.

Singh, Avadhesh Kumar. "The Sense of Community in the Parsi Novels," *Literary Criterion*, Vol. 32, no. 3, 1996.

Singh, Jagdev. "*Ice-Candy Man*: A Parsi Perception on the Partition of India," *Literary Criterion*, Vol. 27, no. 3 (1992).

Singh, Khushwant, "*Ice-Candy Man*: Partition Story," *Tribune*, 13 Jan. 1990. Sunday Plus.

Sundaram, Sudha. "Partition in Historical Fiction." *Literary Criterion*, Vol. 28, no. 3, 1993.

Zaman, Niaz, "Images of Purdah in Bapsi Sidhwa's Novels," Jain and Amin, *Margins.*

III. Reviews

Graebar, Laurel. "The Seeds of Partition." Review of *Ice-Candy-Man. New York Times*, 6 Oct. 1991.

Gutman, Ruth, "Visiting Prof's Novel to be in Film (27 Feb. 1997) 4 par. Online, *The Mount Holyoke News*. Internet. 2 Apr. 1997. http://www.mtholyoke.edu/org/mhnews/S97/feb27/news/Nnovel.htm

Hariharan, Githa. "A Review of *Ice-Candy-Man*. http://members.aol.con/_ht_a/bsidhwa/cracks_India_Indian.html?mtbrand=ADL_US

Hashmi, Alamgir. "The Year That Was: Pakistan 1988." Review of *Ice-Candy Man. Kunapipi* 12.1 (1990).

Jain, Madhu. "Sensitive Servings: Deshpande and Sidhwa Fetch Notice." Review of *Ice-Candy Man. India Today* 15 Sep. 1989.

Lievin, Anatol. Review of *Ice-Candy Man. Literary Review* Mar. 1988.

Lukmani, Yasmeen. Review of *Ice-Candy Man. India Today*, 15 Sep. 1989.

Singh, Khushwant. "*Ice-Candy-Man*: Partition Story." Review of *Ice-Candy-Man. Tribune*, 13 Jan. 1990: 1. "Saturday Plus."

Tharoor, Shashi. "Life with Electric-Aunt and Slave Sister." Review of *Ice-Candy-Man. New York Times Book Review*, 6 Oct. 1991.

Wiggins, Marianne. "The Melting Stomach." Review of *Ice-Candy-Man. New Statesman*, 26 Feb. 1988.

Contributors

Subhash Chandra	S.B.S. College University of Delhi
Rashmi Gaur	Indian Institute of Technology *Roorkee*
Pashupati Jha	Indian Institute of Technology Roorkee
Novy Kapadia	S.G.T.B. Khalsa College University of Delhi
Nagendra Kumar	Indian Institute of Technology Roorkee
V.L.V.N. Narendra Kumar	Govt. Polytechnic for Women Ethamakkala
Reena Mitra	Christ Church College Kanpur
Pallavi	College of Engineering Roorkee
K Nirupa Rani	Andhra University Visakhapatnam
Rahul Sapra	S.G.T.B. Khalsa College University of Delhi
Jagdev Singh	Punjab Agricultural University Ludhiana
Vanashree Tripathy	Banaras Hindu University Varanasi
Niaz Zaman	Dhaka University Bangladesh